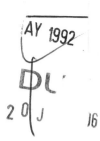

The Circus.

THE GEORGIAN BUILDINGS
OF BATH

from 1700 to 1830

by

WALTER ISON

KINGSMEAD PRESS
BATH

First published in 1948
Reprinted 1969
Revised edition 1980

Kingsmead Press
Kingsmead Square
Bath

SBN 0 906230 21 7

Text set in 11/12 pt VIP Plantin, printed by photolithography,
and bound in Great Britain at The Pitman Press, Bath

PREFACE

The first edition of this book (published by Faber and Faber in 1948) was researched and written just after the Second World War had ended. Archival sources were scarce and difficult of access, and no funds were available for research expenses. My wife's great generosity in devoting a legacy to aid me in my work more than justified the original dedication which also heads this new edition.

Most of the material for the first edition resulted from my prolonged search through Bath newspapers and other documents of the period, and from examination of records and topographical collections then in the Bath Municipal Reference Library, and I shall always be grateful to Miss Elsie Russ for the help and good advice she gave me then and later.

I consulted many books on Bath, but by far the most useful were John Wood's 'Essay towards a Description of Bath' and the late Mowbray A. Green's 'Eighteenth Century Architecture of Bath'. The latter was, at that time, the only considerable work bearing on my subject in a general way. By accepting certain statements in Green's book and some others, I perpetuated some of their mistakes, mostly due to certain houses in Bath having been wrongly identified as the former homes of the two John Woods and other Bath notables. I drew attention to this in 1954, hoping that the record would be straightened.

This second edition has been made possible by the enterprise of Brian Frost, who produced the excellent reprint of the first edition. Had there been time I would have liked to re-write the entire book. Instead, I have checked and considerably amended the original text, adding several appendices containing the results of my later researches into the lives and works of the two John Woods.

To conclude, I wish to thank my friends in Bath and Bristol who have helped me in the past and more recently. To name them all would take more space than my publisher can provide. I must also thank those officers of the Bath and Avon councils who responded so quickly to my requests for information and photostats of documents in their care.

W. I.

TO LEONORA

CONTENTS

DECORATIONS

ACKNOWLEDGEMENTS

Illustrations

Reproduced by courtesy of the Victoria Art Gallery, Corporation of the City of Bath
The Victoria and Albert Museum

Photographs

By courtesy of:
Aero Films
Bath Preservation Trust
Bath Spa Department
Brian Davies
Mrs E. L. Green-Armitage
Mrs Mowbray Green
National Buildings Record
R. F. Wills
St. Mary's Church, Bathwick

Figures on pages 116, 117, 120, 125, 132, 133, 134, 135 are reproduced from John Wood's 'Essay Towards a Description of Bath', published in 1749.

Figures on pages 58 (top right), 88, 92 are reproduced from Pierce Egan's 'Walks through Bath', published in 1819.

Figures on pages 38, 39, 47, 95, 96, 98, 99, and the vignettes are from drawings by Leonora Ison, while all other drawings are by the author.

INTRODUCTION

Bath is, beyond any question, the loveliest of English cities, this high place being held as much by the virtue of the architectural and material unity pervading the Georgian city as a whole, as by the excellence of individual buildings. The harmony which prevails is in a large measure due to the city's development having taken place within the compass of little more than one hundred years, and under unusually propitious circumstances.

These words began the Introduction to the 1948 edition of this book. Since then the face of Bath has been badly scarred by wholesale demolitions of minor buildings, including entire streets of small Georgian houses, built for artisans but often exhibiting on a small scale the excellencies of the patrician houses. It is conceded that many of these small houses had become sub-standard and in need of repair, if not complete modernisation, but in many cases their carcases could have been retained. Even their destruction might have had a minimal effect on the appearance of the city had they been replaced with buildings of a similar scale and unassertive character, but they have invariably given way to large structures of brutal expression, utterly alien to the basic elegance of Bath. Indeed, it is not unfair to say that not one post-war building, apart from some Georgian replacements, can be pointed out as an addition to Bath's sum of fine architecture.

It is amazing that this tragedy could have been enacted when 'preservation' and 'conservation' are the watchwords of architectural policy in historic towns. Even more disturbing is the undoubted fact that the final responsibility for this campaign of destruction must lie with the Council's own advisors, appointed, presumably, in good faith to preserve Bath from the fate which has overtaken other, less important, cities. As the 'acres of Georgian rubble' grew larger and larger, it could only be a matter of time before the protests of local preservationists grew so loud and persistent that the outrage became a national scandal. Long articles appeared in *The Times* (April 3rd, 1972) *The Architectural Review* (May 1973) and, most importantly, in Adam Fergusson's book of indictment, justly titled *The Sack of Bath* (1973). It is enough to peruse Mr. Fergusson's pages to see how much has been recklessly destroyed and what damage has been inflicted by those responsible for the new buildings. Most of the streets destroyed, or left for unofficial vandals to wreck, were included in Appendix I of my book's 1948 edition, and I have therefore amended this list.

With relief one turns to the beneficial changes made in the city. Cleaning and restoration have returned many fine buildings to much of their original splendour, notably in the Circus where only the plane trees remain to excite controversy. The restoration of the Assembly Rooms has been, in the main, a success, and their value as an amenity to the city has been proved. Hardly less important, and wholly successful, has been the general restoration of the Pump Room complex, where the architects preferred fidelity to Baldwin's original design rather than take the advice of the Council's official advisor who wanted the unsightly Victorian additions to be retained. The Council must be praised for restoring Norfolk Crescent and completing Nelson

Place. Some adventurous restorations have been carried out by St. John's Hospital's Trustees, and by the Bath Preservation Trust, whose splendidly restored and furnished house in the Royal Crescent is an added amenity to Bath.

It only remains for me to point out the changes in this new edition. As a result of continuing my researches, I have been able to correct the text as well as take note of changes made since 1948. I have also added five new appendices, all relating to the two John Woods. Appendix V covers in some detail their major building projects, and Appendix VI is in effect a concise biographical account. Many of the illustrations are new and have been reproduced from photographs specially taken to show the buildings in their cleaned and restored condition.

AN HISTORICAL SURVEY OF
THE GEORGIAN DEVELOPMENT OF BATH

The Principal Events and Personalities

During the eighteenth and early part of the nineteenth centuries Bath underwent a complete metamorphosis, a spontaneous and orderly process of rebuilding and extension, based on the classic ideal visualized by an architect of great talents and enterprise. It was no ordinary city of haphazard form, dictated by commercial or political requirements, that the Georgians created, but a pleasure resort, a fashionable metropolis designed as a setting for the brilliant social parade of their leisure. With splendid houses laid out in a sequence of squares, crescents and terraces, it became one of the most beautiful cities of its era, and the prototype for our best urban developments.

The magnitude of the achievement can best be judged by comparing the survey plans produced by Joseph Gilmore in 1694, and Charles Harcourt Masters in 1794. In Gilmore's plan we have the best evidence remaining of the medieval walled city, closely built in a valley north of a sharp bend in the Avon, with the sixteenth-century abbey its dominant feature. The few buildings outside the city walls were located in a small suburb which had grown up around the approach from London, and in the single street leading from the South Gate to the Old Bridge. Gilmore's representations show the principal buildings to have been stately and well-built, but the city as a whole exhibited all the medieval disregard for defined planning.

This insignificant city, with little to recommend it beyond the medicinal springs and a charming situation, was chosen by the arbiters of fashion to be their summer retreat, and following in their wake came all of those possessed of rank or fortune, ostensibly seeking health from the waters, and enjoyment of simple rustic pleasures. 'The Company was numerous enough to form a Country-Dance upon the Bowling-Green; they were amused with a Violin and Hautboy; and diverted with the romantic walks around the city.' But the contemporary *Bath Guide* discreetly omits all reference to the continuous gaming which provided the chief attraction, and drew sharp-witted adventurers of small fortune to the city.

One of the many who sought an easy livelihood in this way was Richard 'Beau' Nash, soon to become 'the King of Bath' and chief architect of its fortunes. The only crown worn by Nash was a white beaver hat, and his subjects were at the same time his patrons, but 'by the Force of Genius he erected the City of Bath into a Province of Pleasure, and became by universal Consent its Legislator, and Ruler'. When his fifty years' reign had ended, Bath was so transformed 'as to be able to vie with any city in Europe, in the politeness of its amusements, and the elegance of its accommodations'.

Bath reached the zenith of its prosperity round about 1790, and Harcourt Masters' survey shows the vast increase in the city's area, and the spacious formality of much of its planning. Even the original nucleus had been

1

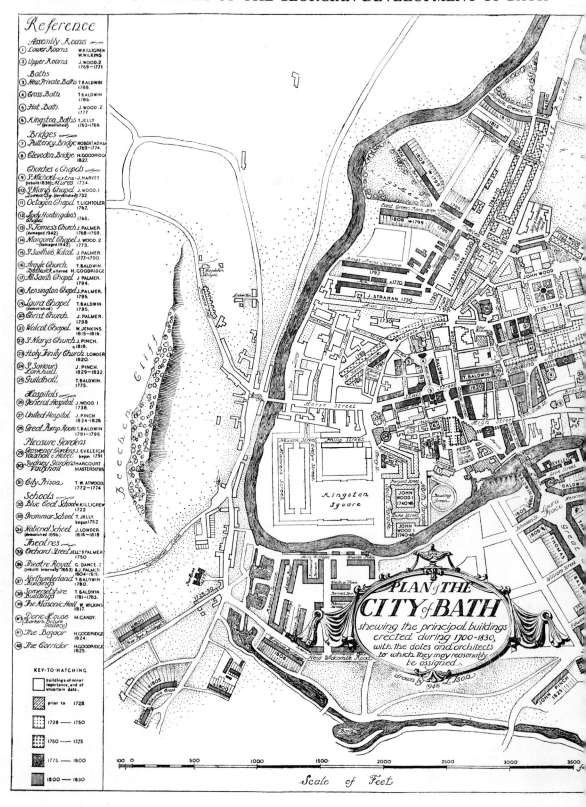

Reference

Assembly Rooms
1. Lower Rooms — W. KILLIGREW / W. WILKINS
2. Upper Rooms — J. WOOD. 2 / 1769–1771

Baths
3. New Private Baths — T. BALDWIN. / 1788.
4. Cross Bath — T. BALDWIN. / 1786.
5. Hot Bath — J. WOOD. 2 / 1777
6. Kingston Baths (demolished) — T. JELLY / 1763–1766

Bridges
7. Pulteney Bridge — ROBERT ADAM / 1769–1774.
8. Cleveton Bridge — H. GOODRIDGE / 1827.

Churches & Chapels
9. St Michael – extra (rebuilt 1836) — J. HARVEY / M. URES. 1734.
10. St Mary's Chapel (demolished) 1732 — J. WOOD. 1 / Queen Sq.
11. Octagon Chapel — T. LIGHTOLER / 1767.
12. Lady Huntingdon's Chapel. 1765.
13. St James's Church (damaged 1942) — J. PALMER. / 1768–1769.
14. Margaret Chapel (damaged 1942) — J. WOOD. 2 / 1773.
15. St Swithin's, Walcot — J. PALMER. / 1777–1790.
16. Argyle Church, Bathwick altered — T. BALDWIN. / H. GOODRIDGE.
17. All Saints Chapel — J. PALMER / 1794.
18. Kensington Chapel — J. PALMER. / 1795.
19. Laura Chapel (demolished) — T. BALDWIN. / 1795.
20. Christ Church — J. PALMER. / 1798
21. Walcot Chapel — W. JENKINS. / 1815–1816.
22. St Mary's Church — J. PINCH. / c.1818.
23. Holy Trinity Church — LOWDER / 1820.
24. St Saviour's, Larkhall — J. PINCH. / 1829–1832.
25. Guildhall — T. BALDWIN. / 1775.

Hospitals
26. General Hospital — J. WOOD 1 / 1738.
27. United Hospital — J. PINCH / 1824–1826
28. Great Pump Room — T. BALDWIN / 1791–1795

Pleasure Gardens
29. Grosvenor Gardens, Vauxhall & Hotel — E. V. ELEIGH / begun 1791
30. Sydney Gardens, Vauxhall — H. ARCOURT / MASTERS 1795

31. City Prison — T. W. ATWOOD / 1772–1774

Schools
32. Blue Coat School — W. KILLIGREW / 1722
33. Grammar School — T. JELLY / begun 1752.
34. National School (demolished 1896) — J. LOWDER. / 1816–1818

Theatres
35. Orchard Street — JELLY & PALMER / 1750
36. Theatre Royal (rebuilt internally 1863) — G. DANCE. 2 / & J. PALMER. / 1804–1805.
37. Northumberland Buildings — T. BALDWIN. / 1780.
38. Somerset Buildings — T. BALDWIN. / 1781–1783.
39. The Masonic Hall — W. WILKINS / 1817.
40. Doric House (Barkers Picture Gallery) — M. CANDY.
41. The Bazaar — H. GOODRIDGE / 1824.
42. The Corridor — H. GOODRIDGE / 1825.

KEY·TO·HATCHING
- buildings of minor importance, and of uncertain date.
- prior to 1728
- 1728 — 1750
- 1750 — 1775
- 1775 — 1800
- 1800 — 1830

PLAN of THE
CITY of BATH
shewing the principal buildings
erected during 1700–1830,
with the dates and architects
to which they may reasonably
be assigned.

drawn by ___son
1946

100 0   500   1000   1500   2000   2500   3000   3500
Scale of Feet

extensively replanned and rebuilt, so that the Abbey and some seventeenth-century mansions were the only substantial remains of the medieval city.

While the first extensions seem insignificant when compared to the spectacular later developments, they were strongly opposed by many influential citizens, who saw only the prospect of ruin in any additions to the city. In his *Essay towards a Description of Bath*, John Wood wrote with mocking contempt of an attitude which clearly had threatened the success of his first schemes, and he could find little to say in favour of the new buildings, which were mostly the work of artificers engaged in one or more of the building trades. Wood makes reference to three 'stone-cutters' named Harvey, one of whom built the first Pump Room in 1704, while another brought upon himself all of Wood's powers of vituperation by displacing him in rebuilding St. Michael's Church. Some interesting buildings, with a coarse and vigorous character, were built by William Killigrew, or Kelligrew, whom Wood dismisses as 'a Joiner, who laid his Apron aside about the year 1719', and although comment is not spared on the over-elaborate character of the St. John's Court houses built about 1720 by Thomas Greenway, this stone-mason and his sons subsequently acquired a great reputation for producing vases and architectural ornaments, for which they were frequently employed by Wood, both in Bath and Bristol.

There is ample evidence of the architectural transition then in progress, when orthodox Palladianism was beginning to supplant the individual use of local vernacular forms. Certain houses in the new streets formed at this time, of which Green Street (1716) can be considered typical, show stylistic anachronisms and appear to have been built without regard to neighbouring heights or frontage lines. Even those buildings which adhere more closely to the new principles of Palladianism are treated as individual units and not considered as parts of any comprehensive architectural scheme. It thus remained for John Wood to introduce into Bath, early in the second quarter of the century, the grand manner of uniform building.

An entry in the registers of St. James's Church, Bath, recording the baptism on August 26th, 1704, of John, son of George Wood, probably relates to the future architect, whose education as a citizen's child at Bath's Charity School proves his local birth. Added confirmation is the full knowledge of local history and legend displayed in Wood's *Description of Bath* although, regrettably, he tells nothing there of his family and upbringing. Perhaps, as a precociously gifted youth, Wood was noticed by a prominent and charitable member of Bath society, Lady Elizabeth Hastings, through whose influence he was employed, around 1720, by her Yorkshire neighbour, Lord Bingley, at Bramham Park near Leeds. While working there, Wood made a survey of the complex park layout, absorbing ideas which later bore fruit in his town planning. Even more valuable experience was gained while working in London for Lord Bingley and his friend, the Duke of Chandos, just when the Grosvenor and Harley estates were developing as fashionable suburbs, each having its chapel and market, and handsome streets leading into a grand square. That Wood's Palladian taste was formed by what he saw in London is evident from his first works in Bath, the lodging-houses built in 1727–30 for the Duke of Chandos, where the fronts were clearly influenced by those of Colen Campbell's terrace-houses in Old Burlington Street, built in 1718–23. Furthermore, Wood's Palladian 'palace front' in Queen Square was probably inspired by Edward Shepherd's earlier, but abortive, attempt to create a similar composition in Grosvenor Square, London.

During the autumn of 1706 the Corporation had applied to Parliament

'for a Power to amend the principal Roads leading to Bath; to pave, cleanse, and light the Streets, Lanes, &c. of the Town; and to regulate and licence a sufficient Number of Chairmen, that nothing might be wanting for the publick Utility of the City'.

Some few years later a scheme was promoted to make the Avon navigable to Bristol, and a Parliamentary Act to that end was obtained towards the end of 1710. The improvements act was supplemented by another granted in 1720, and in 1724 John Hobbs, a Bristol timber merchant, opened a subscription to provide funds for carrying out the navigation scheme, and so—to quote Wood's own account—

'when I found Work was likely to go on, I began to turn my Thoughts towards the Improvement of the City by Building; and for this Purpose I procured a Plan of the Town, which was sent me into Yorkshire, in the Summer of the Year 1725, where I, at my leisure Hours, formed one Design for the Ground, at the North West Corner of the City; and another for the Land, on the North East Side of the Town and River.

'After my Return to London, I imparted my first Design to Mr. Gay, an eminent Surgeon, in Hatton Garden, and Proprietor of the Land; The 31st of March following, I communicated my second Design to the Earl of Essex, to whom the Land, on which it was proposed to be executed, then belonged: And in each Design, I proposed to make a grand Place of Assembly, to be called the Royal Forum of Bath; another Place, no less magnificent, for the Exhibition of Sports, to be called the Grand Circus; and a third Place, of equal State with either of the former, for the Practice of medicinal Exercises, to be called the Imperial Gymnasium of the City, from a Work of that Kind, taking its Rise at first in Bath, during the Time of the Roman Emperors.'

This basic conception was to remain uppermost in Wood's approach to his later and more practical projects, finding ultimate expression in the forms and names given to some of the monumental features of his planning.

His designs remained under consideration until the autumn of 1725, and on November 18th of that year he fixed 'preliminary articles' with Gay, whose land was considered most suitable for development, both by reason of its altitude and immediate proximity to the existing city. Gay gave to Wood a 'letter of attorney' to enter into agreements with anyone willing to build houses to form Barton Street, the intended link between the old and new quarters.

Wood found much to criticize in the antiquated methods used by the Bath builders, and to obtain workmanship of the standard he deemed necessary for the proper execution of his designs he introduced new methods and skilled tradesmen, previously employed by him in London, Yorkshire and elsewhere, for his first undertakings in Bath. These were a court of houses for the Duke of Chandos, including St. John's Hospital, and the projected construction of a canal (more probably the formation of the New Quay) intended to improve navigation of the Avon from Bath to Bristol.

Having finished his engagements elsewhere, Wood finally settled in Bath on May 16th, 1727, during which year his son and successor was born. The first of several schemes for building a general hospital was made at this time, Wood taking his instructions from Humphrey Thayer, the treasurer to the charity, who also proposed building a row of houses and an assembly room on the site later known as The Terrace Walk.

The death of George I brought a severe setback to Wood's prospects, for fear of political repercussions caused Gay to withdraw his support of any plan to extend the city. Wood now propounded a scheme for replanning and rebuilding the existing city, but the Corporation dismissed the idea as being 'chimerical' although some of the more enlightened members favoured its adoption.

Faced by an impasse, Wood resolved to

become 'sole contractor' for building a great residential square, and his first step towards this end was to secure from Gay a 99 years' building lease of sufficient land on which to begin the east side of Queen Square. Additional land was leased at intervals as the work progressed, the first dating from November 28th, 1728, and the last from October 14th, 1734. Queen Square was completed in seven years and marked the first stage in the creation of the New of Upper Town of Bath, and although circumstances had forced some modifications to be made to the original design, the splendour and uniformity of the new buildings set up fresh standards for urban developments, and gained for Wood the admiration and support of many leading citizens.

To meet the varying requirements of his prospective tenants, Wood devised houses of different size and degree conforming to six definite standards which he classified as first-rate to sixth-rate buildings, in that ascending order of magnificence. His methods of financing construction were sound and simple. Having first designed the elevations he sub-leased sites for individual houses to builders or building-tradesmen, giving them full liberty to plan the interiors to suit their prospective tenants, but demanding strict adherence to this exterior design. So great was the demand for accommodation that the builders had little difficulty in obtaining agreements for long tenancies, which their bankers accepted as security against advances of money.

While Wood was engaged in building Queen Square, a considerable development took place in the King's Mead area to the west of the city, with the formation in 1727 of Kingsmead and Beauford Squares; Kingsmead, Monmouth, and Avon Streets; and the New Quay. The architect responsible for laying out these streets was John Strahan of Bristol, whose patron John Hobbs was a Bristol timber merchant and one of the principal leaseholders. The fact that Hobbs had already employed Strahan to carry out the Avon navigation scheme instead of Wood provided sufficient reason for the latter to write in his *Essay* a scathing criticism of Strahan's 'piratical' architecture, contrasting the builders' disregard of plans and instructions given them with the superior results achieved in Queen Square. The mediocrity of Strahan's layout fully justifies Wood's condemnation, but the small houses remaining in Beauford Square conform to such a high standard of accomplishment that Wood's strictures must be partly dismissed as the rancorous expression of a disappointment felt by one who had been superseded by an inferior rival.

Wood's next considerable undertaking was intended to realize the primary feature of his original conception—'The Grand Place of Assembly to be called the Royal Forum of Bath'. The Parades and their connecting streets were the only part of this immense project to be carried out, and the high-handed action of his sublessees forced Wood to modify his design and omit the giant Corinthian order which was intended to give the effect of importance desirable in buildings occupying so salient a position. Built upon a low-lying and marshy site, with the houses raised upon vaults and fronting on to broad terraces, intended for use as summer and winter promenades, this great structure foreshadows the later 'Adelphi' of the Adam brothers.

With the King's Circus, forming the second element of the Upper Town he had created, the elder Wood's actual contributions to the development of Bath came to an end. Here is one work on a grand scale where his intentions were fully realized, and in subtlety of design and richness of detail it is unsurpassed by any other of his works in Bath. Begun in 1754, the year of his death, the Circus was largely built under the superintendence of John Wood the younger.

Several houses and villas in the country around Bath were designed by Wood, the most famous being Ralph Allen's great mansion of Prior Park, which, by reason of its magnitude and proximity to the city, comes within the scope of this study. Begun in 1737 it is said to have been intended to demonstrate the qualities of local freestone, and was still unfinished when a quarrel with Allen caused the work to pass from Wood's control into less competent hands.

The elder Wood died on May 23rd, 1754, when at the height of his success. An obituary notice in the *Bath Chronicle* sums up his character and comments upon his achievements in Bath and Bristol—

'Last Thursday Morning, about Three o'clock, died after a long and tedious illness, in the fiftieth Year of his Age, John Wood Esq., one of His Majesty's Justices of the Peace for the County of Somerset, celebrated for his Designs, Plans and Skill in Architecture: more particularly in this, and a neighbouring City, the second great Mercantile Trading City of this Kingdom. All which is known to be the Effect of his great Genius: as well as undefatiguable Study and Application, in this very noble and useful Science: Amidst a world of Calumnies, Falsehoods and Discouragements, which he bravely surmounted: He not only raised himself in the Esteem of his Superiors: but in the Compass of a few Years, by an honest and commendable Industry, obtain'd an handsome Competence for himself and Family—In a word, he had no enemies but those who either envied Him Themselves, or went too far in crediting the defamatory Reproaches and Scandals of Others.'

His gifts and achievements give Wood pride of place among English provincial architects, and even his faults of character, the jealousy of rivals and the high-handed attitude adopted towards those who failed to agree with him, were in a large measure due to his hatred of mediocrity and an unswerving devotion to the highest principles of his art.

John Wood the younger, departing to some extent from his father's original intentions, lengthened the streets leading east and west from the Circus, and added the superb Royal Crescent to the monumental sequence. Begun in 1767 and taking about eight years to finish, this is at once the finest building in Bath and the greatest single achievement in the whole field of our urban architecture. Linking the Crescent with the Circus is Brock Street (*c.* 1767), which with Rivers Street (*c.* 1770) and Catharine Place (*c.* 1780) were the other extensions west of the Circus made by the younger Wood.

The virtues of his second masterpiece, the New Assembly Rooms (1769–71), are more to be observed in the logical brilliance of the plan and the sequence of exquisite interiors, rather than in the external elevations designed to conform with the contemporary houses in Alfred and Bennett Streets, which were built under Wood's direction and form with Russell Street the principal extensions east of the Circus.

The Hot Bath, built for the Corporation between the years 1773–77, was the younger Wood's last work of individual importance in Bath. This small building, with an ingenious plan expressed in elevations of a simple Doric character, demonstrates the wide range of his abilities in designing a small structure such as this is, and handling in so masterly a fashion the monumental conception of the Royal Crescent.

The restrained personality and unspectacular career of the younger Wood have caused some writers to regard him merely as the skilled executor of his father's ideas, whereas the finest achievements of the son surpass those of the father, both in breadth of conception and subtlety of realization. In fact, the work of the younger Wood represents the highest point of the Palladian achievement in Bath, for the dominance of that architectural tradition was already waning, and may be said to have ceased with Wood's death at the early age of 54, on June 18th, 1781, an event recorded by the *Bath Chronicle* in the following brief notice—

'(Saturday last) died at Batheaston, John Wood, Esq., many years one of His Majesty's Justices of the Peace for this County, and well known for his great skill in architecture.'

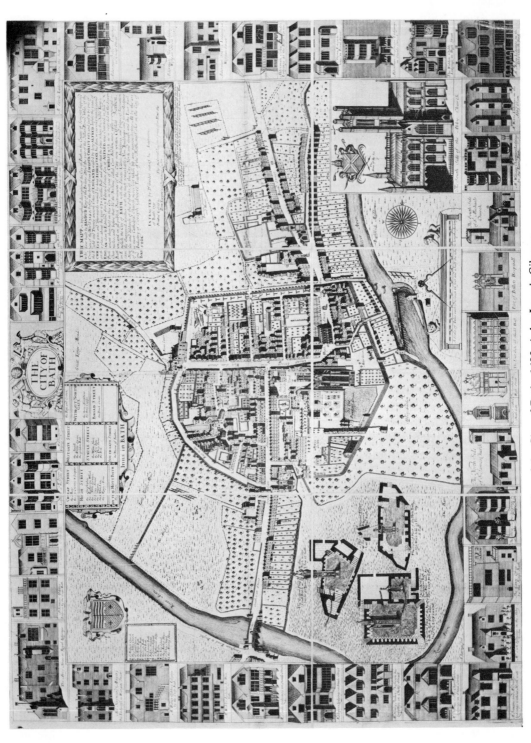

Plan of the City of Bath, 1692–4, by Joseph Gilmore.

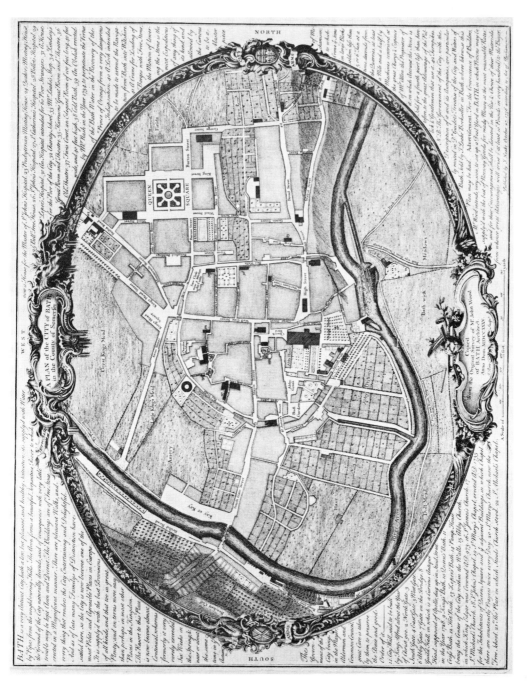

Plan of the City of Bath, 1735, by John Wood.

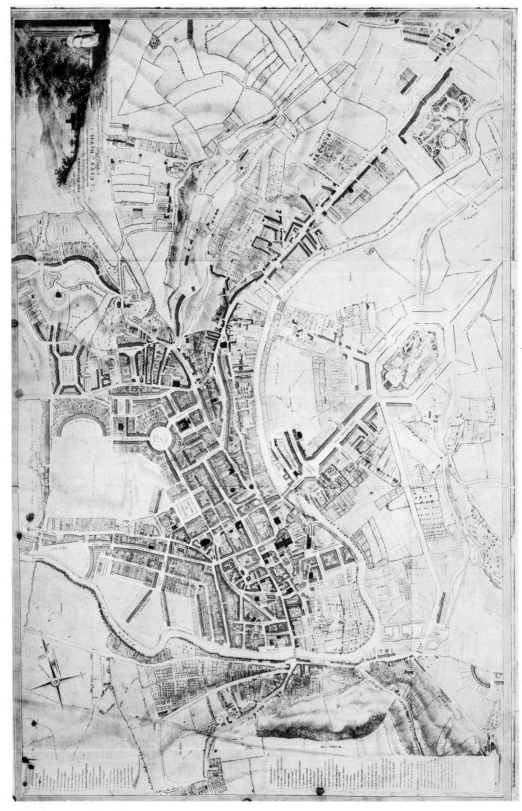

Plan of the City of Bath, c. 1810, by C. Harcourt Masters.

In 1760 began one of the most involved chapters in the architectural history of Bath. The old Guildhall, built from a draft reputedly given by Inigo Jones, had not only become inadequate for its purpose but its island site in the Market Place was an obstruction to traffic. After many debates the Corporation resolved at their meeting on May 19th, 1760 'that the Town Hall be newly built in a more commodious place, and a Committee formed'. The matter appears to have lapsed until March 4th, 1763, when the Committee was empowered to negotiate the purchase of certain houses in the Market Place, and on April 21st following, the Mayor, the City Chamberlain, and Messrs. Wiltshire, Coward, Lawrence, Street and Warr Atwood were appointed to consider proposals for the new building.

The first design was submitted by Thomas Lightoler, or Lightholder, then engaged in building the Octagon Chapel behind Milsom Street. Lightoler described himself as a carver, and was well known as an author of builders' pattern books, collaborating with Halfpenny and Morris besides publishing a curious collection of farm buildings of his own invention. On June 5th, 1766, the Committee decided that another plan besides Lightoler's should be produced, and in the following August, Lightoler, the younger Wood and Richard Jones, City Surveyor and former clerk of works to Ralph Allen, were invited 'to draw ground plans of the intended Market and Town Hall, on a less expensive scale than those already produced'. Lightoler's revised design was accepted at the meeting of October 6th, 1766, and in January 1767 the Corporation resolved to pay Wood the sum of 30 guineas for his second plan.

The following March saw the production of yet another plan, signed by the Mayor, Henry Wright, and adopted in place of the one already voted for. On November 16th, 1767, the Committee decided to 'contract with Lightoler for drawing the plans and section of the building and making a perfect model of same at a price of not more than £100, to be paid when plans are complete. The Committee

to have the power to call him to their assistance at a price of not more than 25 shillings per day.'

In all of these manoeuvres may be detected the hand of Thomas Warr Atwood, a member of the Common-Council serving on the Building Committee. Atwood was a wealthy plumber and glazier who used his family's considerable influence to obtain the appointment of architect to the city estates and waterworks. In this capacity he was able to control the Corporation's building policy and contract for much of the work entailed, thus laying himself open to charges of corruption which were doubtless fostered by rival builders, such as Thomas Jelly and William Sainsbury, who now saw themselves more or less excluded from sharing in the Corporation's building work.

In 1770 the Corporation approved of his design for the new prison in Bathwick, necessitated by the impending demolition of the old one to clear the approach to William Pulteney's projected bridge to Bathwick. Atwood also obtained leases of Corporation properties on which he built, as private speculations, the great crescent-like range of The Paragon, and Oxford Row on the east side of Lansdown Road. The elevations of all these buildings are excellently designed in conformity with the defined standards for Corporation property and differ but little from other buildings erected under similar circumstances by Jelly and others.

Although the site for the new Guildhall had been sufficiently cleared for William Chapman, the Mayor, to lay the foundation stone on February 11th, 1768, it was not until April 1773 that the City Chamberlain received instructions to obtain tenders from builders. Nothing further transpired until July 3rd, 1775, when the Corporation met to decide that

'Mr Atwood's plan for rebuilding the Town Hall be used accordingly. The Committee to advertise for proposals for building same according to the plan delivered by Mr. Atwood and signed by the

Mayor (Philip Ditcher). Mr. Atwood to be thanked for his attention, etc., in management of the business relating to the Public Improvements of this City.'

The matter had no sooner reached this settled stage when John Symons, a prominent surgeon and member of the Common-Council, put before the Committee a new plan for a Guildhall, market and shops, designed by John Palmer, a young architect and builder, which his senior associate Thomas Jelly offered to build for no further consideration than the grant of a 99 years' lease of the shops and houses planned as part of the layout. Despite its many advantages, Jelly and Palmer's proposal was rejected after a hasty consideration by the Corporation, who probably resented this attempt to interfere with their plans now that work had at last begun on Atwood's building.

This ill-considered decision was strongly criticized in a letter appearing in Keene's *Bath Journal* for August 21st, 1775, wherein the writer, signing himself 'Citizen', demanded publication of the Corporation's reasons for so lightly dismissing Palmer's plan when even Atwood was alleged to have admitted to its superior merits, and its adoption would save the city some £6,000. Atwood was accused of attempting to avoid further criticism by unduly expediting progress of the work, but the writer contended that even were his building finished it would still be an advantage to the city if builders were paid £300 to demolish it and rebuild according to Palmer's designs.

The appearance of this letter began a furious controversy and the correspondence columns of the public journals were filled with letters for and against the conflicting proposals. There were violent attacks on the Corporation and Atwood, ranging from citations of the latter's incompetence and mock serious laments on the inconvenience of the new Butter Market designed by 'Simkin Solder', and culminating with a vicious onslaught by 'Citizen' who pilloried Atwood as 'The Bath Vitruvius' and sarcastically listed as 'great public services' some of the public works alleged to have been promoted solely for personal gain. This letter ended by suggesting that there should be set up outside the slaughter house a lead statue of 'Vitruvius', with the following near-quotation from *The Beggar's Opera*:

> See the Bill *I* hold,
>   let the Chymists toil like Asses,
> My fire their fire surpasses,
>   and turns all my Lead to Gold.

While supporters wrote to refute these charges of incompetence and corruption, Atwood maintained an aloof silence and merely defended his attitude by contending that adoption of Palmer's scheme would reduce the area allotted to the public markets by 4,638 superficial feet. Palmer countered this assertion by declaring that Atwood had greatly over-estimated the area of the site, and both protagonists were induced by Symons to submit their cases to a decision by arbitration, for which purpose he brought in Thomas Paty of Bristol. Palmer attended the inquiry while Atwood was represented by his clerk and close associate, Thomas Baldwin. The findings of the arbitrator completely vindicated Palmer, for it was revealed that Atwood had included in his measurements the sites of three buildings which he had previously stated to be unobtainable, the omission of which reduced the difference between the market areas of the two schemes to a mere 735 superficial feet in Atwood's favour.

Publication of Paty's verdict brought no change in the Corporation's attitude, and Palmer's supporters continued their attacks on Atwood until his death under tragic circumstances silenced any further criticism and ended the dispute. No reference is made to the affair in the obituary notices, of which the following is taken from the *Bath Chronicle*:

'*Wednesday, November 15th, 1775.*

'This morning died Mr. Thomas Warr Atwood, a common-council man of this city, partner in the New Bank, and an eminent plumber. His death was occasioned by the violent contusions he received in the head, etc., by the falling in of the floor of an old house in the market place.'

Atwood's burial place in the churchyard of Weston, near Bath, is marked by a monument of great elegance, designed by Baldwin (see Title-page).

Thomas Baldwin was obviously the most acceptable successor to Atwood, and after the whole question of the Guildhall rebuilding had been reconsidered by the Corporation, they commissioned him to prepare fresh designs which were adopted towards the close of 1776. Baldwin was 25 years old when the Guildhall was erected, and his building is not only a very distinguished achievement but evidences the fact that he had already chosen to hitch his architectural wagon to the rising star of Robert Adam, rather than follow in the strictly Palladian steps of the Woods.

Baldwin began his career as a speculative builder round about 1780, when he erected Northumberland Buildings on some ground leased from Dr. Harington. During 1781–83 he built Somersetshire Buildings, the group of five houses dominating Milsom Street. Both ranges serve to demonstrate his easy mastery over the problem of composing effective street frontages.

An appointment as City Surveyor in 1776 was renewed yearly until the Corporation's meeting on October 3rd, 1785, when they elected Baldwin to fill the combined offices of Deputy Chamberlain and Surveyor, with a yearly salary of £210. At this same meeting the Committee for Improving the Baths and Pump Room decided to adopt Baldwin's proposal to add a colonnade to the Pump Room, provided the cost did not exceed the estimate of 130 guineas. Some few years previously, Baldwin had restored the King's Bath and built an elegant pavilion over the spring, and on July 3rd, 1787, he was appointed Inspector of the Baths in order that he might have a first-hand opportunity of studying the question of further improvements. The Committee met to consider his plans and estimates each evening from February 5th to March 11th, 1788, and the Minutes for this last date record that 'the Plans and Estimates (£47,163 16s. 5d.) of Mr. Baldwin for the General Improvement of the City are hereby approved. The City Members, with Mr. Baldwin and John Palmer, Esq., to wait upon William Pitt, Esq. (Rt. Hon.) with the said plans and estimates for his inspection, and if approved to procure a Bill in Parliament for carrying the same into execution.' 'The Bath Improvement Act', approved by Parliament in 1789, gave Baldwin his opportunity to create one of the most exquisite architectural ensembles in the city.

In addition to these official undertakings Baldwin was now engaged in planning the extensive development of Bathwick New Town, which a broadsheet published on March 31st, 1788, the occasion of laying the first stone of Laura Place, described as the natural sequel to Sir William Pulteney's building of Pulteney Bridge in 1770. The bridge had been designed by Pulteney's friend, Robert Adam, who also prepared two schemes for laying out Bathwick, but for reasons of local policy he was supplanted by Baldwin, who devised a new layout incorporating some features of Adam's designs. Baldwin leased a great deal of land for personal investment, and within a few years a considerable part of Argyle Buildings, Laura Place, Henrietta Street and Great Pulteney Street had been completed by him, in association with Eveleigh, Gwillim, Mais and others.

About this time Baldwin advertised the intended publication of his designs, and notices appearing in the Bath newspapers for the latter part of 1788 announce that:

'Speedily will be published
'Plans and Schemes for improving the Lower Town of Bath, with a plan, elevation and section of the New Town building on part of an Estate belonging to Miss Pulteney, commonly called Bathwick Fields.
'Likewise Plans, Elevations and Sections of the Guildhall, Markets, Cross Bath,

Pump Room, Private Baths and Pump Rooms now erecting on the East Side of Stall Street. With various other designs executed in Wales, Somerset, Wiltshire, etc. Also designs for Houses, Villas, and Lodges'
'by Thomas Baldwin, Architect, Bath.'

These advertisements continued to appear at intervals until July 1789, with the added information that the work would be issued in 14 parts, each containing 6 plates with letterpress. The price to subscribers was to be £4 10s. of which half was to be paid on delivery of the first part, promised for the second week of July 1789. So far as it is known the production did not materialize, although much work must have been done by way of preparation.

It seems probable that preoccupation with private business had led Baldwin to neglect his duties as Deputy Chamberlain, for when the official appointments came up for consideration in October 1791, his re-election solely as architect and surveyor, at a salary of £105 per annum, could only mean that his relations with the Corporation had become strained. Later in the month he was ordered by the new Chamberlain, Dr. Henry Harington, to deliver up all books, including the landed and water rentals, belonging to the Corporation. Baldwin's non-compliance with this order brought a further demand in November, accompanied by the threat that in event of his refusal a Bill in Chancery would be filed against him. Ordered to attend the Chamberlain's office on April 25th, 1792, to explain and settle his accounts with the Committee of the Corporation, Baldwin pleaded the lack of certain papers essential for closing and perfecting the accounts, and the meeting was postponed until May 21st following.

Meanwhile this mysterious notice appeared in Keene's *Bath Journal* for April 21st, 1792:

'As Mr. Thomas Baldwin has, and is on the point of publishing, Facts relative to the Corporation, and the Parish of St. Michael (an old 20 years old suit) The Freemen of this City may flatter them-

selves they will not be Forgot by him, in the statement he is forming, as the late publication evinces the old saying—Too many Cooks spoil the Broth.'

Unfortunately for our curiosity, no revelation of these facts can be found in any of the newspapers published during the ensuing months.

The Corporation's records show that Baldwin had failed to deliver up the books in his possession by June 1792, and on July 10th following it was resolved

'that Thomas Baldwin, Surveyor, be discharged from any future employment under the Corporation. A Bill to be filed in Chancery against him for full account of all monies received and paid by him as Deputy Chamberlain of the City, and not accounted for. And also for a delivery of all Books, Papers, etc., belonging to the City that are in his possession.'

Public expression of the general dissatisfaction felt at the slow progress being made with the improvements to the city, caused Baldwin to publish in the *Bath Journal* the following letter addressed to the Improvements Committee:

'Bath, October 1st, 1792.
'Gentlemen,
Many insidious insinuations having been thrown out respecting the slow progress of the Pump Room and Improvements in general, carrying on under my direction, and of the low state of your Finances—I think it necessary to inform you that I shall have printed, and will send to every Gentleman named in the Act for his consideration, A General Statement of Proceedings relative thereto, home to September 29th, 1792: which I flatter myself will clearly prove that had the Conveyance, so frequently applied for, been engrossed and sealed at the time it ought to have been, the Builders would long since have had their Title Deeds and that you could have raised

Money to discharge your Tradesmen's Bills, and for other necessary purposes.

I remain, Gentlemen,

Your most obedient and very humble servant,

Thomas Baldwin, Architect to the Committee for Improving the City.

As in the case of his previous threat to reveal facts concerning the Corporation, no further public statement appears to have been made and there is nothing officially recorded in the Corporation's Minutes.

During the fateful year of 1793, when panic had seized investors throughout the country, two of the leading Bath banks failed and in their collapse involved many of the speculating builders. The development of Bathwick had been largely financed by Messrs. Bayly, Sons, Gutch and Cross, trading as the Bath City Bank, and their failure in April brought financial ruin to Baldwin and Eveleigh, as well as a number of lesser contractors. Notices of the bankruptcy of Baldwin and his associates appeared in the *Bath Chronicle* for November 22nd, 1793, and his property assets, which included houses in Queen Street, Northumberland Buildings, Great Pulteney Street and Harington Place, were offered for sale during January 1794.

Although John Palmer was appointed to succeed him as City Architect and to finish the Great Pump Room, Baldwin continued to practise as an architect, as is evident from his advertisement in the *Bath Chronicle* for April 10th, 1794, inviting builders to tender for works in connection with the proposed Vauxhall and Ranelagh Gardens in Bathwick, subsequently carried out under the direction of Harcourt Masters. During the early part of the nineteenth century Union Street was built to Baldwin's designs, and he was employed to rebuild for Thomas Johnes his 'Gothic' mansion of Hafod in Cardiganshire, besides acting as consulting architect for some works of restoration at Bristol Cathedral.

After the sale of his house, No. 6 Great Pulteney Street, Baldwin removed to No. 3 Harington Place, a property settled on his wife for her life's interest, where he died on March 7th, 1820, aged 70. His passing was noticed with hardly more than a bare comment in the public journals, although Baldwin had effected more changes in the general appearance of Bath than anyone since the Woods. Baldwin's earlier buildings are among the finest in Bath, and although his Bathwick designs are mannered and poorly detailed, the sum total of his achievement entitles him to a high place among the minor architects of the eighteenth century.

A contemporary and associate of Baldwin, John Eveleigh is another Bath architect whose beginnings and training are wrapped in obscurity. He first appeared in Bath during the late seventeen-eighties when building activity was at its height, carrying out work with Baldwin and others in Bathwick. The business relationship which existed between Baldwin and Eveleigh varied according to circumstances, for while the latter contracted independently for many works as private speculations or commissions, he acted as Baldwin's assistant in others.

The following advertisement appeared in the *Bath Chronicle* at intervals during January 1790, and gives some idea of the multifarious scope of Eveleigh's business as an architect and builder:

'Eveleigh, Architect; with gratitude for favours received, acquaints the Nobility, Gentry and Builders, that he has for sale some of the most superb Chimney Pieces ever executed by any Artist, on various subjects, in Marble or Wood, with Copper ornaments,—esteemed by the first Nobility in the kingdom, cannot be minutely described, but may be seen at his Office, Spring Gardens, Bath.

'Also the Patent Water Closets, which may be fixed in any parlour, bed or dressing-room, without the least effluvia.

'Has some of the first workmen of the Copper Company to cover houses, dormers and gutters (cistern-heads, water and soil pipes, etc.) which being air as well as water-tight is a preservation against fire (the expence being little more than common slating). He has covered with copper his two large houses (adjoining Mrs. Macartney's Laura Place) which admits of two tiers of garrets and terrace, with Chinese fence; where will be fixed some of the above Chimney-Pieces, and two of the Water Closets in each house—Will be finished convenient and elegant, which will either be let or sold.

'N.B.—Designs for Mansions, Villas, Dwellings, etc., executed in the Gothick or modern taste. Buildings superintended, estates surveyed, rents collected, etc.'

A few of Eveleigh's ledgers and notebooks remain to form an interesting record of his clients, and show how large and varied a practice he carried on before bankruptcy ended his career in Bath. The entries in his ledgers show that his charges for architectural services were often ridiculously small, but it must be remembered that in his dependence on building and the sale of builders' merchandise for his profits, he often supplied designs as a means of ensuring employment in those directions.

Many of Bath's building speculators employed him to design their buildings and advise on the finishings, and entries in a ledger against John Morgan, a builder and carpenter, may be taken to afford proof, additional to the evidence of details in the building, that Eveleigh designed Camden Crescent, a work which has been attributed by turns to Chambers, his pupil Reveley, and the younger Wood. Eveleigh's other works in this quarter of Bath include a range of houses originally called Sion Row, built in Camden Road for the attorney John Jelly, and the layout and many of the houses of Beaufort Buildings, designed for Messrs. Gunning and Tanner.

His works in the Lansdown quarter included two private houses which exist no longer. For designing and supervising the building of Summer Hill Place, on Sion Hill, he charged twenty guineas to his client, the prominent physician Caleb Hillier Parry, while a fee of only three guineas was charged to the irascible Philip Thicknesse for the design of St. Catherine's Hermitage, behind Lansdown Place West. Eveleigh's most important work in this quarter is the central feature to Somerset Place, a highly original composition with points of detail common to his other works, and for which design he is reputed to have been paid only one guinea.

Round about 1786 he contracted to build Bailbrook Lodge, and lay out the surrounding gardens for Dr. Denham Skeet, an undertaking which involved him in an expenditure of over £12,000. In June 1791, he began building, with William Hewlett and others, the still more costly project of Grosvenor, and this great range of houses was still unfinished in 1793, when his finances were completely wrecked by the failure of the Bath City Bank. Eveleigh's interest in Grosvenor were offered for sale by auction on November 14th, 1793, and a few days later he was adjudged bankrupt and summoned to appear with Baldwin and others on November 25th–26th, at the Argyle Coffee House, for a disclosure of assets.

Eveleigh made no attempt to resume practice in Bath and we next hear of him in Plymouth, where in 1800 he contracted to build a new Guildhall on an obviously inadequate site. The resultant building, a failure in every way, was a flat and uninspired design in a wiry 'Gothick' manner, without a trace of the imaginative gusto which distinguishes his Bath buildings, where he used a curiously personal idiom, successfully fusing elements drawn from Baroque and Adam sources. Although they undoubtedly possess many features which might offend the purist, his designs for Grosvenor and Somerset Place have a vigorous and original quality which lifts them far above the general level achieved by pattern-book architects.

The most successful rival of Baldwin and Eveleigh was John Palmer, whose father, Thomas Palmer, was a prosperous glazier associated with Thomas Jelly, the master-builder. John Palmer began his career of architect and builder as a partner in Jelly's firm, some time about 1765, but there is little to record of his early years apart from the important part he played in the controversy arising over the Guildhall rebuilding. During 1768–69 Messrs. Jelly and Palmer rebuilt the body of St. James's Church, in which a hybrid 'Gothick' exterior was combined with a sober classic interior, and there can be little doubt that Palmer also designed St. Swithin's, Walcot, where the interior has a marked similarity to that of St. James's.

The old theatre in Orchard Street was reconstructed by Palmer in 1775, but his most active period began round about 1789, when he became associated with Charles Spackman, a wealthy coachbuilder who later became an auctioneer and valuer, and built the suave and elegant Lansdown Crescent with its flanking wings, and the curiously attractive All Saints' Chapel settled on the slopes below. In 1791 he designed St. James's Square and its four tributary streets for James Broom and William Hewlett, and shortly afterwards he was employed by John Jelly, the attorney, to build two terraces of houses and Kensington Chapel on the London Road, this last adding to his reputation for having designed more buildings for religious use than any other of his contemporaries.

On September 24th, 1792, the Corporation elected Palmer to serve as Supervisor of Bounds, an appointment shortly preceding his succession to Baldwin as City Architect. The first reference indicating that Palmer had taken over the work of completing the Pump Room is contained in the Corporation's Minutes for December 10th, 1793, it being recorded that

'the Committee appointed to manage the business of the Pump Room, produced a statement of Monies wanted by the Commissioners to carry on the Improvements of the City, the sum being £9,550 14s. 8d. and £2,600 to finish the Pump Room. Resolved it shall be referred to the Mayor (Dr. Henry Harington), Mr. Horton and Mr. Wiltshire, who are to meet and consult with the architect, Mr. Palmer, upon the same and report upon.'

There is no further official comment upon the matter until October 5th, 1795; when the Corporation decided to pay Palmer £600 towards finishing the Pump Room,

'£400 immediately and the residue later, he to send in the bills to the Chamberlain'.

The last work of importance upon which Palmer was engaged was the new Theatre Royal in Beauford Square, built during 1804–5, largely from designs by George Dance the younger, although some contemporary accounts make it clear that Palmer did not scruple to minimize the part played by his distinguished collaborator in producing this delightful building.

Palmer died at the age of 79, on July 19th, 1817, at his house No. 6 Charles Street, and a memorial tablet in St. Swithin's Church marks his burial there. As a character he seems to have been held in high regard by many distinguished citizens, and, so far as it is known, he was not subjected to the sudden reversal of fortune that almost ended the careers of his rivals. His buildings, while lacking the stamp of an original mind, are distinguished by sober good taste and excellent craftmanship, and Lansdown Crescent and Kensington Chapel worthily uphold the fine architectural tradition established in Bath.

Some reference has already been made to the publication in 1794 of Charles Harcourt Masters' survey of Bath, a work originally undertaken to enable him to construct an accurate model of the city to the scale of 30 feet to one inch. During 1789–90 this model was exhibited at his house, No. 21 Orchard Street, where it was to be viewed between the hours of 10 a.m. and 3 p.m. daily, for an admission charge of two shillings. Sheldon, a drawing master living at Westgate Buildings, immediately countered this attraction by showing a

The Royal Crescent and its surroundings, looking north.

Queen Square and its surroundings, looking east.

The Circus and its surroundings, looking east.

Great Pulteney Street and its surroundings, looking west.

rival model to the slightly larger scale of 24 feet to 1 in., but with the added realism of an Avon flowing with water. Masters' work received the gracious approbation of Royalty and was later exhibited in London, where it was again faced with Sheldon's competition. It would be interesting to know something of the ultimate fate of these models.

Masters' most important building was the Sydney Hotel, erected towards the close of 1796. In the fulfilment of Baldwin's intention, to provide an effective termination to the vista along Great Pulteney Street, the hotel was sited at the western end of the hexagonal pleasure garden within Sydney Place. The original design was an agreeable essay in the mild Graeco-Roman taste of the period, but its character was transformed when Sir Reginald Blomfield was employed to convert the building into a museum. Masters was much employed as a land surveyor and had extensive property dealings in Widcombe, where he designed Widcombe Crescent and Terrace, and in Lyncombe. One of the least ambitious of his works, Cottage Crescent (now Bloomfield Crescent), was made the subject of a particularly scathing analysis by Richard Warner in his *Walk through some of the Western Counties of England*. Towards the end of his career Masters practised under the name of Harcourt, at first on his own account and later in partnership with George P. Manners.

The general tendency to over-build, which had brought so many speculators to their ruin, was followed by a period of economic unrest caused by the Napoleonic Wars, and building was almost at a standstill by the end of the eighteenth century. Contemporary writers have described the desolate appearance given to some parts of Bath by ranges of buildings left in all stages of construction, but with the restoration of peace and more stable conditions during the second decade of the nineteenth century, not only were these completed but many new schemes were projected.

Some of the finest of these new buildings were designed by John Pinch, an architect whose achievement has been most unjustly neglected. Beginning as a builder with a yard in Spring Gardens, probably Eveleigh's old premises, and an office in Chatham Row, Walcot, Pinch went into bankruptcy soon after 1800 and his stock of materials was advertised for sale during February 1804. After this inauspicious beginning he went into practice as an architect and surveyor, with an ever increasing measure of success.

John Pinch designed several of the early nineteenth century buildings in Bathwick, the most beautiful being New Sydney Place, a terrace of houses built about 1807–8. Some fine groups of houses sited on the Lansdown slopes are also by him, including Cavendish Place (1808); the upper houses of Park Street; Cavendish Crescent (1817); and Sion Hill Place (1818). Although building of these ranges was begun round about the dates stated, completion was sometimes delayed for many years and some houses in Cavendish Crescent were still unfinished when offered for sale in April 1829. The house now terminating the west side of Park Street was intended to be No. 1 of Regent Place, a long range planned by Pinch to extend in a north-west direction and join up with the road below Somerset Place. The former United Hospital in Beau Street was built during 1824–26 from designs by Pinch, but the proportions of his fine classic front have been spoiled by the addition of a heavy attic story.

St. Mary's Church, Bathwick (1814–20), designed in the 'Florid Gothic' style, and planned to suit ritual arrangements then in use, was followed by the finer church of St. Saviour, Larkhall, probably designed by Pinch before his death in 1827 and carried out by his son and namesake during 1829–32. Adversely criticized by the later Gothic revivalists who were called in to make their unsympathetic alterations and additions, these beautiful churches are now appreciated for their outstanding merit of consistency with the prevailing character of the city.

After practising in Bath for some thirty years, John Pinch died at his house in Duke Street on March 11th, 1827, aged 57. His practice was continued by his son, an able architect whose sympathies, as exhibited in the building he added to the west side of Queen Square, were with the Greek revival rather than with the eighteenth-century traditions to which his father had shown himself a true heir. The domestic buildings of the elder Pinch are the logical outcome of Baldwin's work, to which an effect of extreme elegance has been added by generally attenuating the proportions of the fenestration, and using sharply-cut mouldings and minor detail of refined delicacy, particularly in the metalwork of fanlights, balconies and verandas.

The turn of the century marks an end to the extreme conservatism which hitherto had confined the designing of Bath's buildings to local architects and builders, and the beginning of a series of interesting contributions made by some of the great exponents of the Greek revival in London. The Masonic Hall in York Street, built in 1817, was designed by William Wilkins, as was also the massive Doric portico added in 1806 to the Kingston Assembly Rooms. Decimus Burton, called in to advise upon improvements to the baths, designed the Tepid Swimming Bath adjacent to Wood's Hot Bath, but subsequent rebuilding has destroyed his work. The lovely picture gallery of Doric House on Sion Hill was designed for Thomas Barker, the painter, by Joseph Michael Gandy, the assistant and disciple of Soane, while the layout of Victoria Park, with its Gothic farmhouse and an entrance screen in the Soanic manner, represents the first and best work of Edward Davis, a pupil of Soane and later appointed City Architect. Perhaps the most considerable of these 'London' works was Partis College, Lower Weston, completed in 1827 from the designs of Samuel and Philip Flood Page.

One of the most able disciples of the Greek revival was the local architect Henry Edmund Goodridge, son of James Goodridge, an eminent builder who had carried out much of the later work in Bathwick. The premises built for 'The Bazaar' in Quiet Street (1824), the High Street front of 'The Corridor' (1825) and Cleveland Place and Bridge are representative works of Goodridge included within the scope of this review. While his later designs show some curious essayings into eclecticism, these early buildings are entirely orthodox and form a worthy close to a study of the great period of architecture in Bath.

The popularity which had so suddenly raised Bath to pre-eminence among fashionable resorts, declined with an equal rapidity towards 1840, bringing a fall in property values and causing the abandonment or curtailment of many projected building schemes. Plans of the city published around 1825 show fine streets and squares originally proposed to be built on sites now covered with a squalid chaos of buildings erected by later generations, who neither understood nor followed the fine principles of development so nobly observed by the builders of Georgian Bath.

THE PLANNING OF THE GEORGIAN CITY

and the process of its evolution

The planning of Bath has been subjected to some adverse criticism on account of an apparent lack of continuity throughout its development. In many respects this fault is only observable on paper, or when looked at from the standpoint of academic purism, but in defence of the eighteenth-century builders it must be emphasized that many factors stood in the way of a completely homogeneous development. No settled limit to the city's extension was ever visualized, and the sense of anti-climax which is sometimes present is often due to this cause. Furthermore, the buildings outside of the city's boundaries were the enterprises of various builders and architects who worked without more reference to each other than was necessary to avoid the clash of interests.

The varied nature of the site, with its rapid changes of level and contour, would have prevented any plan with the academic qualities of Edinburgh New Town from being put into effect. But as a compensation we have a series of *coups d'oeil* of accidental and remarkable beauty which could not have occurred in a conventional layout on a more or less level site. From the romantic aspect of visual beauty Bath is incomparably more lovely than its theoretically more perfect rivals, and in the same way the unorthodoxy of some of its individual buildings gives them a liveliness and interest lacking in the more correct designs. It is a point of some interest that the only part of Bath which might reasonably be criticized as monotonous is the correctly laid-out New Town of Bathwick, built to an academic plan on an artificially levelled site.

In considering the development of the city's plan during its growth we will take for a starting point the first small extensions made to the north-east of the old walls. The few streets formed at this time were of modest dimensions and the developments generally so haphazard as scarcely to warrant the description of planning. With the coming of John Wood these timid extensions were thrown into insignificance by the grand scale of his formal layout from Queen Square to the King's Circus.

The younger Wood, departing to some extent from his father's original scheme, extended the streets leading east and west from the Circus by making Bennett Street the principal approach to the New Assembly Rooms and thence to Lansdown Road, and Brock Street the link with the Royal Crescent. The siting of the Assembly Rooms is poorly related to the Circus, but otherwise the whole layout is as well considered as site conditions would allow. Running parallel with Brock Street, Rivers Street was for some time the northernmost boundary of the built-up area, and is connected with Brock Street by Church Street, Catharine Place and Margaret's Buildings, and by Russell Street with Bennett Street and the Assembly Rooms.

After 1780 several new streets were built in the irregular triangle formed by Cottle's Lane, behind Rivers Street, and the curving Lansdown Road, but of these only the 'T' shaped combination of Portland Place and Burlington Street have any architectural or planning merit. The fine ranges of houses lining Lansdown Road were built to follow the natural course of that thoroughfare.

East of Queen Square development proceeded on regular lines with the laying out of George and Milsom Streets soon after 1761, and while the west side of London Road presents the miscellaneous assembly of Harlequin's Row, or Vineyards, the east side is distinguished by the uniform series of Bladud's, Paragon and Axford's Buildings. The great London Road itself is lined with more or less continuous building stretching far beyond the general confines of the city.

Beyond the Royal Crescent to the west there is only the great range of Marlborough Buildings fringing the fields and common lands, but to the south-west, beyond the Bristol Road, are the poorly planned developments of 1727, only partially redeemed by the fine layout of Green Park and Norfolk Crescent, originally projected at the close of the eighteenth century.

North of the Royal Crescent, but unrelated thereto, is St. James's Square with its four tributary streets, and further north are Cavendish Place and Crescent, laid out along the edge of the High Common. Sion Hill is dotted with charming villas while the northernmost of the Georgian terraces, Sion Hill Place, is sited in park-like seclusion.

Somerset Place and Lansdown Crescent, with its flanking wings, form a great serpentine line of houses winding across the Lansdown slopes, and were designedly built some way off from the denser area of the city in the valley below. Camden Crescent is part of a similarly conceived scheme and formerly stood in lofty isolation, overlooking the approach to the city from London.

The Parades were designed by Wood to form a complete unit jutting out from the west side of the old city and affording, from the raised north and south terraces, extensive prospects over the beautiful surrounding countryside. The buildings are not aligned with the Avon, which seems to have been consistently ignored, for no riverside terraces or buildings, except a proposed crescent in Bathwick, were ever projected.

The Bath Improvement Act of 1789 provided for the rebuilding of a considerable area within the old city, which was carried out to designs by Thomas Baldwin, who also laid out a second town on the Bathwick side of the Avon. From the narrow connecting link of the Pulteney Bridge the road widens first by way of Argyle Buildings, then by the irregular octagon of Laura Place, into the broad and straight Great Pulteney Street which, after bifurcating to form the hexagonal enclosure of Sydney Gardens, was planned to rejoin and continue on its straight course. The subsidiary streets designed to lead from Laura Place, northwards to a square of vast dimensions, and southwards to a great riverside crescent, and the streets radiating from the angles of Sydney Place, were only partially built.

THE PUBLIC BUILDINGS

ASSEMBLY HOUSES

The Lower Rooms (gutted by fire 1820, finally demolished 1933)

Bath's first assembly house was erected during 1708 by an unnamed builder for Thomas Harrison, who had been encouraged by Beau Nash to build the rooms as a profitable speculation. The original building was of modest size and simple character, and stood on the east side of the Terrace Walk overlooking Harrison's Walks, a formal garden bordering the river which was for many years a favoured resort of fashion. In 1720 Harrison employed William Killigrew to add a large ballroom, and the suite was again enlarged and remodelled in 1749–50, during Simpson's tenancy, when the basement was used for a playhouse.

The Lower Rooms are a conspicuous feature in Malton's views of the North Parade, appearing as a uniform building with the garden front composed of three equal bays, each containing two tall arched sash-windows, with wide intervening piers around which the entablature and surmounting pedestal parapet are returned. The principal features of the interior are described in *The New Bath Guide* for 1792, at which time the tenant was James Heaven:

'Mr. Heaven's Ball-room was built in the year 1750, is 90 feet in length, 36 in breadth, and 34 in height; with a very fine stucco ceiling. The view of the river, valley, and adjacent hills, makes it one of the pleasantest morning rooms in the kingdom. There is in it a portrait of the late Richard Nash, Esq.; and it is elegantly furnished with chandeliers, girandoles, etc.

'The Card-room is 60 feet long and 30 feet wide, with a coved ceiling, and has in it another portrait of Mr. Nash. There are also two Tea-rooms, 40 feet by 24 each.'

The opening of the Upper Rooms caused a gradual decline in the popularity of the Lower Rooms, and although the Duke of Kingston, to whom the property had reverted, spent a considerable sum in generally improving the accommodation, the building's career as an assembly house ceased with a destructive fire on the night of December 21st, 1820. The impressive 'Paestum' portico, added in 1806 from William Wilkins' designs, was retained when the premises were rebuilt to house the Royal Literary Institution. This building was demolished in 1933 and the wheel of time has now turned the full circle, for this site, which originally served for the town's 'jakes', then becoming so much the centre of social activity that Garrick was once moved to observe that 'here the Genius of Bath would always hover and preside', is again a place of public convenience.

Lindsey's, afterwards Wiltshire's Rooms (demolished when York Street was built)

In 1728 Humphrey Thayer (or Theyrs), a London apothecary who had made considerable property investments in Bath, employed the elder Wood to design a range of buildings fronting on to the west side of the Terrace Walk. This was to include an assembly house,

25

to be rented by Dame Lindsey, a retired singer who was something of a harpy, if Wood's account of her is to be trusted. The new assembly house was opened by Thayer with a public breakfast on April 6th, 1730, and a ball was given on the following day. The tenancy eventually passed into the hands of Walter Wiltshire, against whom Nash brought his ruinous action for fraud, but when the Upper Rooms were opened this suite was relegated for use as a warehouse. The building was demolished when York Street was formed early in the nineteenth century.

ing with the first-floor windows of the adjoining houses are three recessed panels, and the attic story windows are circular, with radiating sashbars. *The New Bath Guide* for 1764 contains the following description of the interior:

'Mr Wiltshire's Room is 86 feet in Length, 30 in Breadth, and 30 in Height; this has a Cove Ceiling, and is a very neat Room; it is likewise ornamented with a Portrait Picture and Bust of the late Richard Nash, Esq., besides many curious Landscapes.'

Harrison's & Lindsey's Assembly Rooms, from the Grand Parade.
(Water-colour by T. Malton. jr. c. 1777)

The elevation of Lindsey's Rooms can be studied in Malton's view of the North Parade, where it is seen to form part of a terrace of houses, distinguished only by the superior scale of its three windows, each dressed with an architrave, frieze and cornice. Correspond-

The New, or Upper Assembly Rooms

The continuous growth of the Upper Town as the fashionable residential quarter of Bath, led some of the leading residents to formulate proposals for building a suite of assembly rooms, with coffee rooms and a tavern, on the site just beyond the north-west corner of Queen Square. The necessary capital of £12,600 was to be raised by a tontine subscription, and the first meeting of those who had agreed to become shareholders was held in January 1765, at No. 6 Brock Street, then tenanted by John Wood the younger. Disagreement among the shareholders as to the advisability of combining a tavern with an assembly house led to the project being set aside, and in 1768 Wood began to build on the intended site the range of houses forming Queen's Parade.

Meanwhile Robert Adam had been invited, probably at the instance of William Pulteney, to submit a scheme for 'a commodious suite of Assembly Rooms to be erected on a site to the east of the Circus'. Adam produced a design of Augustan splendour, the drawings for which are preserved in the Soane Museum,* but his scheme proved too costly for adoption and the Committee decided to accept the less ambitious plans which Wood had prepared for the same site. A new tontine subscription list was opened during November 1768, when Wood announced his daily attendance at No. 6 Brock Street 'to explain the Plans to any Gentleman who will do him the honour of calling on him for that purpose'.

On May 24th, 1769, 'a band of music attended, and great ceremony was observed on the occasion' when the foundation-stone was laid by Wood, in the presence of the Mayor and members of the Corporation, and the shareholders; the party retiring after the ceremony to the Guildhall, where they were

*See Appendix III.

The New Assembly Rooms. Alfred Street front from west.
(*Water colour by T. Malton, jr. c. 1777*)

refreshed with a collation of cakes and wine provided at the expense of the city. The shareholders then appointed a committee of management, with a furnishing sub-committee, to decide on any questions which might arise during construction of the building. By such judicious management, and with the unremitting attention of John Wood and his clerk of works, William Kingston, to their task, the rooms were completed by the autumn of 1771, having cost some £20,000 to build and equip.

A 'Grand Ridotto' held on the night of September 30th, 1771, opened the long career of these splendid rooms, which were to see many turns of fortune and a brief return to their original glory before they were gutted by fire during the German raids of April 1942. Fortunately, the superb chandeliers had been removed to safety before this disaster occurred. Soon after the war Sir Albert Richardson was entrusted with the building's restoration but controversy over its future use delayed work for some ten years. Eventually an architecturally faithful restoration was decided on and the rooms were reopened in 1963. Oliver Messel supervised the colour schemes, that of the Ball Room being largely based on Wood's original specifications. Regrettably, Mr. Messel's designs for appropriate furnishings were not carried out.

The rooms are admirably laid out on a symmetrical plan (Fig. 1) with a central spine of vestibules and ancillary apartments, entered

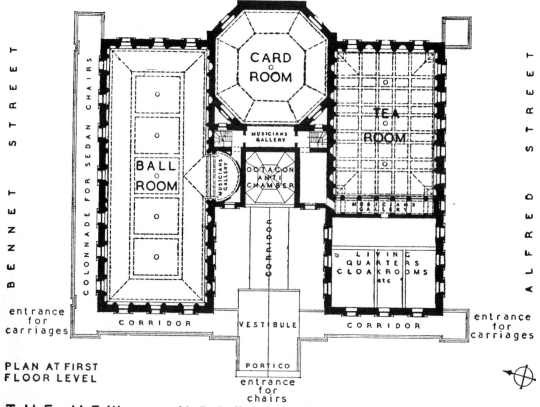

Fig. 1.

from the west portico and leading east to an octagonal hall. This gives access to the Octagon Card Room on the east, the Ball Room on the north, and the Tea Room on the south. These last two rooms are contained in the two parallel blocks of building which dominate the external composition from the west. There, the entrance portico of three bays, with Roman Doric columns and antae supporting the plain entablature and triangular pediment, is flanked by the 'sashed corridors' forming a projecting ground story to the two main blocks. Their upper stages are alike in containing three equally-spaced windows, dressed with blind balustrades, moulded architraves, and triangular pediments resting on consoles. These windows ornament the plain ashlar face which rises to the crowning entablature. Above its modillioned cornice is a pedestal-parapet with open balustrades between the wide end dies and the great central chimney-stack, its panelled face finished with an entablature and blocking-course.

The upper part of the Bennett Street front is similarly detailed, but here the projecting ground story is a Doric colonnade of thirteen bays, each framing an arched opening. Paired columns emphasise the doorway in the central bay, and at each end is a small pavilion containing an arched doorway. This ground-story projection originally consisted of small shops, but these were removed to form a corridor on the north side of the Ball Room. The seven first-floor windows lighting the Ball Room are arranged in groups of three flanking

The New Assembly Rooms. West front.

one, and there are two chimney-stacks, each centred over the pier between the second and third windows at either end of the front.

The finest elevation is that to Alfred Street, where only the single story entrance pavilions at either end of the front project beyond the Tea Room block. There are three tiers of nine equally spaced windows in the main building face, those to the ground-story being without architraves. The deep platband marking the first-floor level provides a plinth for the fine range of windows, richly dressed as 'tabernacles', and above them is a corresponding tier of square lights set within moulded architrave frames. The two chimney-stacks are centred over the piers between the third and fourth windows from either end of the front.

The following description of the interior is taken, with minor emendations of spelling and punctuation, from a contemporary edition of

arcade, at the ends of which, under trussed coverings and into two pavilions, the company alight from carriages and enter without incommoding the chairs. From the Hall, through an Octagon Antichamber in the centre of the building, which has four marble chimney-pieces, and under a cupola richly ornamented (from whence drops a chandelier), the company are led to the Grand Ball Room by an avenue on the left; to the Concert or Card Room in front; and to the Tea Room on the right.

'The Ball Room is 105 ft. 8 in. long, 42 ft. 8 in. wide, and 42 ft. 6 in. high, wainscoted to a height of 4 ft., over which the stucco rises 8 ft. 6 in. to a rich fretwork on which stands the sub-plinth of the order, which is Corinthian and consists of forty columns and pilasters

The New Assembly Rooms, The Octagon Antechamber.

The New Assembly Rooms. The Octagon Cardroom.

The New Bath Guide, and might have been written for that work by Wood:

'The entrance for chairs is on the west side, under a portico of the Doric order, from whence three doors open into the Hall, in the centre of which hangs a chandelier. At each side is a sashed

12 ft. high, with its entablature curiously enriched; above which is a plinth, ornamented with a rich Vitruvian scroll, from whence rises the cove 11 ft. 6 in. high, the angle bracket of which forms a quarter-circle. From the front line of the cove into the ceiling is a soffit, divided into compartments which are decorated with garlands, palm and laurel branches,

festoons, etc. The ceiling is divided into five compartments, the centres of which are embossed seeds through which, from the trussed beams in the roof, hang five chandeliers. The proper colour of the ornament is interspersed with Naples yellow. The room is lighted from the east, west and north, by thirteen windows, to which are blinds painted by a masterly hand (Edmund Garvey, R.A.) with a variety of figures, vases, etc., which rise over the openings of each window from behind a timberwork that supports the columns. Opposite the windows, on each side of the orchestra, are niches for various figures. The orchestra is 21 ft. wide, circular backed, and formed into a niche elevated to the level of the ceiling. There are seven marble chimney-pieces, decorated with festoons, flowers, leaves, etc., carved in wood.

'The Card Room is an octagon of 48 ft. diameter, has four marble chimney-pieces properly ornamented, is wainscotted, stuccoed and ceiled nearly in the same manner as the Ball Room, and in the stucco are ornamental frames for portrait paintings. This room has two doors besides that which fronts the entrance, one of which opens to the Hall, and the other to the Tea Room. In this room is a fine portrait of Captain Wade, late Master of Ceremonies, painted by Mr. Gainsborough.' (This painting, with other portraits of former M.C.s, was removed and sold during the early part of the present century.)

'The Tea Room is 60 ft. long, and 42 ft. wide. At the west end is a colonnade of the Ionic order, 7 ft. wide, consisting of six columns and ten pilasters 11 ft. 6 in. high, with its enriched entablature which continues round the room. These support the Corinthian order of equal number, and the orchestra, the front of which is bounded with a rich gilded iron railing that extends from column to column. From hence the Corinthian order continues round the room and consists of thirty columns and pilasters, with their capitals, festoons, etc., curiously carved in Bath stone. The entablature is of stucco, above which is a pedestal wrought in mosaic-work, from whence rises a cove, the line of which is relieved by a swelling soffit of laurel leaves interspersed with berries, which are continued to and from, across and along the ceiling, rolling under each other and forming by their intersection the most beautiful network, embellished with garlands, laurels, palm branches, festoons and wreaths of flowers. This room is wainscotted the same as the Ball Room, has three glass chandeliers, and four marble chimney-pieces properly decorated, and is lighted from the east and south sides by eight windows. Behind the Ionic colonnade, and under three stone arches carved with vine branches and grapes, is the bar, from whence over a side-table the waiters take the tea to the company. Leading from the Tea Room through an anti-chamber are the ladies' drawing rooms and water-closets, the gentlemen's being in another part of the building. The Card and Tea Rooms are of the same height as the Ball Room, and every room is superbly furnished.'

The most important addition made to the rooms subsequent to their completion in 1771, was the Card Room built during 1777, to the east of the great Octagon Room. This Card Room is a rectangular apartment measuring 70 ft. by 26 ft. 6 in., and has no particular architectural distinction, the walls being simply decorated, with a dado capped by a moulded chair-rail, above which the surface is divided into panels with narrow moulded surrounds. From the delicate cornice a segmental cove rises to the plain flat ceiling, the cove being broken on the north, south and east sides by windows set in oval frames of palm branches and wreathing.

The New Assembly Rooms. The Ballroom, looking west.

The New Assembly Rooms. The Tea Room, looking west.

THE BATHS AND GREAT PUMP ROOM

The baths formed around the hot mineral water springs, which are the *fons et origo* of Bath's existence, were all rebuilt during the era of the city's greatest prosperity, and are still substantially Georgian structures, although expediency and changing methods of treatment have necessitated their partial reconstruction. While the alterations made during this century have, on the whole, been sympathetic to the original character of the buildings, the Victorian city architects were quite ruthless, destroying much of interest and unnecessarily disfiguring that which they suffered to remain. It is, therefore, fortunate that the authorities at present in charge of the bathing establishment have adopted the enlightened policy of removing, as far as possible, the evidence of Victorian bad taste, and restoring the buildings to their original elegance.

The Kingston Baths (demolished)

During the demolition of the old Abbey House or Priory in 1755,

'there were discovered some cavities which led to the remains of several very noble Roman Baths and sudatories. . . . The spring which supplied these baths being cleared from the rubbish, etc., and the several antient sewers for carrying off the water from the baths repaired, his Grace the late Duke of Kingston built on the same spot several baths and sudatories, upon a new plan, approved by some of the most eminent physicians, as well for the elegance and neatness of the design, as the utility of the several apartments.'

These baths and sudatories, seven in all, were designed and built during 1763–66 by Thomas Jelly, but they were entirely demolished when the great Roman Bath was opened up and the Pump Room suite extended.

The Hot Bath (now The Old Royal Baths)

There can be little doubt that the strong influence exerted by such builders as Thomas Jelly and Warr Atwood over Corporation affairs caused both the Woods to be excluded from participating in many of the civic building undertakings, and although the younger Wood was invited to submit a competitive plan and estimate for rebuilding the Guildhall, the Hot Bath is the only civic building which he was directly commissioned to design. It was probably their desire to avoid any repetition of the acrimonious controversy which had arisen over the Guildhall rebuilding, which led the Corporation to pass the following resolution at their meeting of October 30th, 1775:

'It being the desire of the Mayor and Corporation as well as Mr. Wood, to render his plans as compleat as possible, and it being their opinion that further information respecting the building of the Hot Bath may be received. It is therefore determined to postpone the said building until the first Monday after St. Thomas's Day next, and this to be carried into execution. Notice to be given by Advertisement in both the Bath papers that a Committee will be held at the Guildhall every Monday fortnight previous thereto at 5 o'clock in the evening to receive the hints of any gentlemen that may tend to the improvement of Mr. Wood's plans, and that Mr. Wood be requested to attend at the appointed times. The first Meeting to be held 6 November next.'

The building must have been completed some time previously to June 1778, for the Minutes of the Corporation's meeting held on 29th of that month record their decision to pay Wood '100 guineas for his services, trouble, and attending as architect and otherwise in and about the forming, building, and making the new Baths'. During the following November,

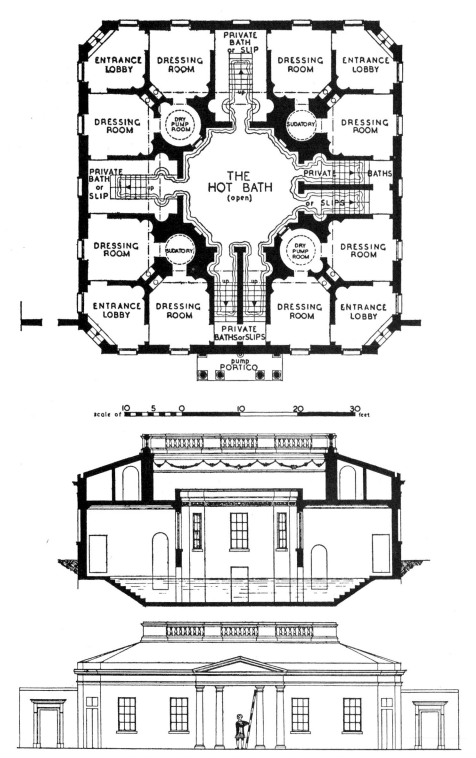

Fig. 2. The Hot Bath, (a) Plan, (b) Section, (c) Elevation.

The Hot Bath. Exterior from north-west.
(*Engraved drawing by T. H. Shepherd, 1829*)

The Cross Bath. Exterior from east.
(*Engraved drawing by T. H. Shepherd, 1829*)

Wood published a description of his design, accompanied by engravings of the plans, a section and an elevation, and on these the following notes have been based (Fig. 2a, b, c). Later alterations have spoiled the balance and clarity of Wood's original planning, although the chief architectural features have generally been sympathetically restored by the late Alfred Taylor.

Wood planned an ingenious arrangement of dressing-rooms and small private plunge-baths, symmetrically disposed around the octagonal central bath, the whole being contained within a building measuring only 56 feet square, with the four corners splayed off to form entrances to the dressing-rooms. A mineral-water pump, intended for the free use of non-subscribers to the baths, was sheltered by the portico projecting from the west front. The exterior is quite simply treated, the plain ashlar walls being pierced at regular intervals with rectangular windows without architraves, and finished with an entablature and dwarf parapet. The chief interest is provided by the portico in the middle of the west front, comprising one wide and two narrow bays formed by Roman Doric columns with plain shafts, supporting the entablature and its surmounting triangular pediment. The building has suffered in appearance by removal of the low-pitched roof which formerly rose from the dwarf parapet to the base of the balustrade surmounting the walls enclosing the open bath. The elevations of this latter are more richly treated, the walls to the inner octagon being finished with a plinth of Vitruvian scrolling below a pedestal parapet. The surrounding walls to the gallery are adorned with a deep continued frieze, finely carved with drapery swags depending from rings and decorated with knots of fruits and flowers, surmounted by the crowning pedestal, with open balustrades between wide dies, which forms an effective finish to the exterior. Apart from additions made to the north and south sides, the chief external alterations have consisted of cutting a doorway in the wall behind the portico and lengthening the windows.

The Cross Bath

The Cross Bath derived its name from a cross erected in its centre, which was rebuilt in an elaborate form during 1688 by the Earl of Melfort, Secretary of State to James II, to commemorate the satisfaction of Mary of Modena with the results attendant on her bathing at this spring. The bath retained its medieval form and appearance until round about 1784, when the cross was removed, the spring secured, and a small pump room added from designs by Thomas Baldwin, who rebuilt the bath a few years later to form an effective terminal feature to Bath Street. (Figs. 3 & 5.)

Fig. 3. The Cross Bath. East Front, before alteration.

The baroque forms of the plan are curiously reminiscent of Borromini, and are expressed in elevations which are still beautiful in spite of alteration and neglect. Some idea of the original appearance of this building, before windows and doors were blocked up and an open screen added to the parapet, is conveyed by T. H. Shepherd's drawing, engraved and published in 1829, although this was made after the bath had been altered by Palmer in 1798.

The central feature of the east front is of serpentine plan and contains the principal doorway, dressed with Baldwin's typical detail, with a rectangular window set in the plain wall face on either side. At each end of this feature is a small pavilion containing a plain rectangular doorway set between engaged three-quarter columns, having plain shafts and Corinthian capitals supporting a projecting entablature with a dentilled cornice, which is returned and continued across the exposed elevations of the building. Above the serpentine centre is an attic pedestal, its die being adorned with an oval panel placed between two of rectangular form. From the centre rises a chimney-stack, its face decorated with a shallow arched recess containing a low-relief vase, and finished with an entablature. Festooned vases were originally placed at each end of the attic coping. The north front is distinguished by a fine semi-circular portico of four Corinthian columns, while the quadrant wall to the south-east is correspondingly adorned with engaged three-quarter columns.

The drawing of the interior in its original state has been reconstructed from various sources. The curved side walls were decorated

Fig. 4. The Cross Bath. Interior, before alteration.

with large vases in low-relief set in shallow arched recesses, and a figure of Bladud, after the painting by William Hoare, stood in a niche at the south end (Fig. 4). Parts of this decoration survived the vandalism of C. E.

Davis, who converted this lovely building into a cheap swimming bath during the 1880s.

The Pavilion over the King's Bath Spring (demolished)

The Pavilion which Baldwin designed to protect the King's Bath spring, and afford shelter for bathers, was erected round about 1788 to replace a dilapidated structure of somewhat similar form. Baldwin's short-lived building, it was demolished early in the nineteenth century, is shown in two drawings made in 1789 by S. H. Grimm. The main structure was cruciform in plan, with a doorway in each end face and a Doric portico in each angle. The cruciform structure was surmounted by a low flat-roofed attic, from the centre of which a stepped pyramid rose to a pedestal with a vase and pineapple finial, other vases being placed above the porticoes.

The Pump Room Colonnade, New Baths, and Great Pump Room

In 1705 the Corporation, advised by Dr. Oliver and other leading physicians, decided to build a Pump Room for the convenience of those who came to drink the waters, and raised funds to purchase some houses from one John Amour to provide a suitable site on the north side of the King's Bath. This first Pump Room, built in 1706 by John Harvey, is shown in contemporary engravings to have been a simple one-story building rather like an orangery, and is thus described by Wood:

'This Room is entirely built with Free Stone, and the Floor is paved with the same Material: It is four and thirty Feet and a half in length from East to West; six and twenty Feet in Breadth from North to South; and eighteen Feet in Heighth. The North Front is composed of four large Apertures, each of which is six Feet six Inches broad, and fourteen Feet six Inches high, with Columns between them of the Corinthian Order; and

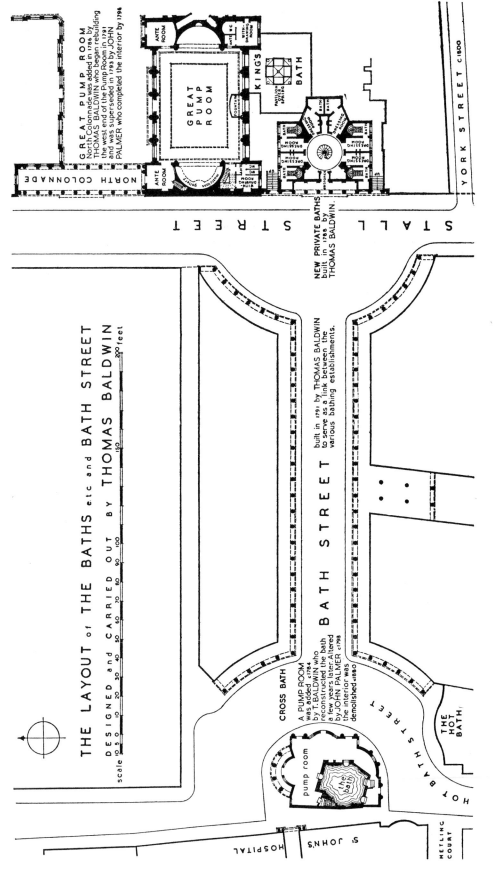

THE LAYOUT of THE BATHS etc and BATH STREET

DESIGNED and CARRIED OUT BY THOMAS BALDWIN

scale 10 5 0 10 20 30 40 50 60 70 80 90 100 150 200 feet

GREAT PUMP ROOM
North Colonnade was added in 1786 by THOMAS BALDWIN who began rebuilding the west end of the Pump Room in 1791 and was superseded in 1793 by JOHN PALMER who completed the interior by 1796

NORTH COLONNADE

ANTE ROOM

GREAT PUMP ROOM

BATH DRAWING ROOM

WC

ANTE ROOM

DRAWING ROOM

SQUARE

KING'S BATH

PAVILION OVER SPRING

BATH

DRESSING ROOM

DRESSING ROOM

DRESSING ROOM

DRESSING ROOM

BATH

BATH

BATH

BATH

ENTRANCE

NEW PRIVATE BATHS built in 1788 by THOMAS BALDWIN.

STALL STREET

YORK STREET c1800

STREET STREET STREET

BATH STREET
built in 1791 by THOMAS BALDWIN to serve as a link between the various bathing establishments.

CROSS BATH
A PUMP ROOM was added c1784 by T. BALDWIN who reconstructed the bath a few years later. Altered by JOHN PALMER c1798 the interior was demolished c1880

pump room

the bath

HOT BATH STREET

THE HOT BATH

METLING COURT

HOSPITAL

ST JOHN'S

Fig. 5.

The King's Bath and Pump Room in 1789
(*Drawing by S. H. Grimm*)

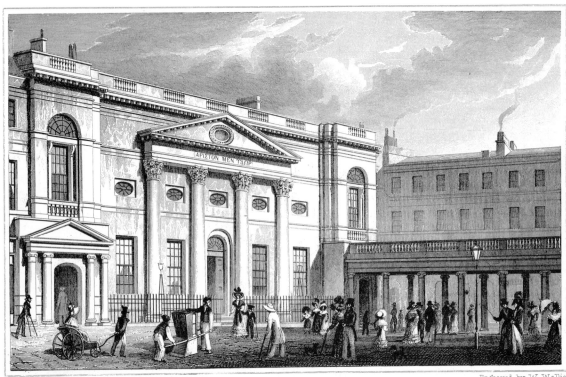

Drawn by Tho. H. Shepherd.

Engraved by W. Wallis

The Great Pump Room. North front to Abbey Church Yard.
(*Engraved drawing by T. H. Shepherd, 1829*)

the South Front is composed of the like Apertures, with Pilasters between them of the Dorick Order.

'These large Apertures are filled up with Sashes and Sash Doors; and a Gallery projects out of the Wall at the West End of the Room, sufficient to hold a small Band of Musick for the Entertainment of the Water Drinkers every Morning during the seasons.

'This Structure was designed by the abovementioned John Harvey, the second of that Name; and, considering the Time when built, is one of the best Pieces of Architecture the City could boast of, even for ten or fifteen Years after the Room was erected: The large Apertures were, however, ill concerted; because they render the Room too hot in Summer, and too cold in Winter; and this Intemperature, increased by a stone Floor, as well as a North Entrance, affecting the Invalids, infallible Experience immediately drew Doctor Oliver's Censure of Inconvenience against the Building.

'The Pump, to supply the Drinkers with Water, is placed against the middle Pier on the South Side of the Room; and it is cased with Marble: The Conduit yields the Water at two Cocks; and it stands with a Ballustrade, at such a Distance as is necessary for the Waiters to receive the Water in Glasses, and hand it to the Company as they can advance to the Rails: For the Croud is now become so great in the Height of the Season, that it is a Doubt whether four or five Cocks more would supply the Drinkers with the Water, with that Regularity that is prescribed for them.'

Despite's Wood's criticisms and Dr. Oliver's censure, the original building served its purpose until 1751, when it was considerably extended. In 1784 Thomas Baldwin was employed to build an annexe containing some water-closets, and two years later he added the

lovely colonnade on the north side, this design forming the underlying motif for most of his later work in the vicinity.

The principal elevation of the colonnade faces Stall Street, and is divided into nine equal bays by ten columns, with plain shafts and Ionic capitals. The delicately profiled entablature breaks slightly forward over the three middle bays, to receive the triangular pediment, with its tympanum decoration of beautifully carved female-headed sphinxes on either side of an oval wreath enclosing a profile head of Hygeia, with an Æsculapian serpent drinking from a kylix. This pediment breaks the general lines of the parapet, which has a section of blind balustrading over each second bay (Fig. 6).

This same design was adapted to form the elevation of the New Private Baths built from Baldwin's plans during 1788–89. The foundation-stone, laid by the Mayor, Leonard Coward, on May 10th, 1788, bore the following inscription:

HYGEIÆ
ÆSCULAPII FILIÆ
THERMULÆ VOTIVÆ
A.D. 1788
SUB
LEONARDO COWARD
PRÆTORE URBANO
PUBLICO SUMPTU CURATÆ
T. BALDWIN, *extruxit*.

For some reason the Æsculapian descent of the Goddess of Health was greatly ridiculed by the wits of the time.

The middle five bays of this colonnade form an entrance portico to the baths. In each adjoining bay is an arched niche above a rusticated base, and each end bay contains an arched doorway. Baldwin planned the interior with a skilful arrangement of dressing rooms and baths round a top-lit rotunda, in its centre being a spiral stair leading down to the 'slips' serving the King's and Queen's baths (Fig. 5). Successive alterations have obscured the clarity of these arrangements and obliterated much of Baldwin's charming decorative detail. Fortunately, the incongruous three-storied

The Great Pump Room and New Private Baths. Exterior from north-west.
(*Engraved drawing by T. Spornberg, c1800*)

pavilion at the south end and the ridiculous false attic above the colonnade, added by C. E. Davis in 1886, have now been demolished and a new end pavilion has been built to accord with Baldwin's original design.

Between the twin colonnades rises the west front of the Great Pump Room, a fine design by Baldwin which has sometimes been attributed to other hands. Confusion has arisen from the Corporation's employment of successive architects to superintend the rebuilding of the Pump Room complex. An attribution to Willey Reveley, who gave plans for the Baths and Pump Room in 1793, is surely negatived by the fact that Baldwin was building this west front in 1791. John Palmer can also be ruled out by the fact that he was not brought in to complete Baldwin's building until 1793.

Baldwin designed the west front as a decorative screen wall having a ground story of rusticated and vermiculated masonry, ornamented with four large paterae placed to centre with the paired columns of the upper stage. A panelled bandcourse, level with the balustraded parapets of the twin colonnades, finishes the rustic base. The lofty upper wall face is recessed behind an engaged order of giant plain-shafted Corinthian columns, spaced in pairs to form three wide bays interposed between four narrow bays. In each wide bay is an aedicule, in effect an arched niche of segmental plan flanked by narrow panelled pilasters rising from a balustraded pedestal to finish with consoles supporting a frieze, carved with a festooned bucranium, and a triangular pediment. The moulded sills and cornices of

The Great Pump Room. General view of exterior from north-west.

these aedicules are echoed in the narrow bays. Above the entablature of the giant order is a pedestal-parapet having blind balustrades above the wide bays (Fig. 6).

tall arched opening with a balustraded base, containing a window framed by pilasters, and a large fan-light filling the lunette. The crowning entablature is in continuation of that to the

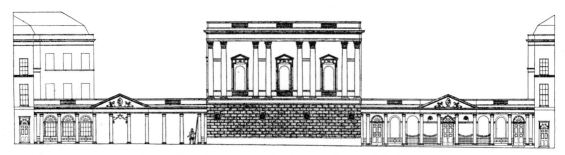

Fig. 6. The Great Pump Room. West front and flanking colonnades.

The north front, facing the Abbey Church Yard, is an inferior design and lacks the breadth and cohesion of the west front. It consists of a wide main block flanked by narrow pavilions of bold projection. The ground-story of the main block contains five openings, consisting of an arched entrance with two tall rectangular windows on either side. Above an architrave stringcourse is a clerestory of five oval lights set within oblong openings. The three middle openings of both tiers are brought within an engaged portico of four columns, with plain shafts and Corinthian capitals, which has the appearance of being an afterthought and was originally intended to form a projecting feature. The columns carry a full entablature, of which the architrave only is continued across the rest of the front. The frieze has a sunk panel containing the following inscription in raised and gilded letters 'ΑΡΙΣΤΟΝ ΜΕΝ Τ'ΔΩΡ' (a Pindaric quotation in praise of water). The modillioned cornice is returned to form a triangular pediment, its tympanum decorated with a wreath of oak leaves and acorns surrounding an oval concave panel. A fine doorway decorated with paired Ionic columns supporting a triangular pediment, forms the ground-story of the east pavilion, and is designed to correspond with the colonnade abutting against the west pavilion. The upper part of each pavilion consists of a

west front, but its architrave and frieze are broken by the apex of the pediment surmounting the portico.

The Pump Room interior is reputed to have been completed by Palmer, and lacks the decorative richness of Baldwin's magnificent banqueting hall in the Guildhall. Of rectangular form, excluding the segmental recesses at each end, it measures 60 feet in length, 46 feet in width, and 34 feet in height. The dominating feature of the decoration is the giant order of engaged half-columns, and quarter-columns in the angles, with moulded bases, fluted shafts, and Corinthian capitals, dividing the side walls into five equal bays, and each end wall into similar bays flanking a wide segmental recess. The north wall contains in its middle bay the arched entrance with its glazed doors, and a window in each of the two bays on either side. This treatment is varied slightly on the opposite wall where each second bay contains a fire-place with a panel above. The glazed alcove in the middle bay is a modern addition, being designed to accommodate the mineral-water fountain and leave the main floor unobstructed. Between the columns and below the oval clerestory windows runs a band of guilloche moulding, broken to form springings for the moulded archivolts framing the elliptical semi-domes ceiling the recesses. The musicians' gallery, of serpentine form with a

The Great Pump Room, interior looking east.

simple wrought iron railing, is contained in the west end recess, while that at the opposite end has a central niche containing a life-size statue of Beau Nash. Each bay on either side of these alcoves contains a pedimented doorcase. From the fine entablature which surrounds the room rises a plain segmental cove, a continuous band of moulding effecting its junction with the plain flat ceiling.

Now that the exterior has been cleaned and restored, and the interior redecorated in a cream colour with gilt enrichments, nothing remains of a disastrous refurbishing carried out in 1880 by C. H. Davis. Even his alcove for the pump has been rebuilt in a chaste Doric style. Below Nash's statue, by Prince Hoare or Joseph Plura, stands a superb long-case clock by Tompion. The room is well furnished with appropriate paintings, chairs and rout-seats in the style of Chippendale and Hepple-

white, and a handsome crystal chandelier hangs from the ceiling.

The old Tepid Swimming Bath (demolished 1923)

Some time during 1829 the city chamber invited Decimus Burton to submit plans and suggestions for improving the baths, which were in due course received and approved. For some reason the works, which entailed recon-structing the Hot Bath and adding thereto a tepid swimming bath, were carried out during 1830 by George P. Manners, then the city architect, although Burton is generally cre-dited with the impeccably Classic design of the Tepid Bath. The bath was contained in a lofty hall, measuring 61 ft. in length and 22 ft. in width, both ends being semi-circular. Eight large dressing rooms, with fire-places, were ranged along one side of the bath hall, each with a door giving on to a small landing from which steps descended into the water, there being no surround to the pool. Plain ashlar walls, lined with tiles to within a few feet above water level, rose to an architrave stringcourse, its continuity broken only by an arched window at either end. Above this stringcourse was an attic, with clerestory windows on the long side walls and panels on the curved ends, spaced between Doric pilasters which carried the main entablature surrounding the flat ceiling. This was of plain plaster, broken by three circular lantern lights on low drums. The pool had a uniform depth of 4 ft. 6 in. and contained 666 hogsheads of mineral water. The old Tepid Bath was demolished during 1922 to make way for the new swimming bath.

BRIDGES

The Old Bridge

The Old Bridge, also referred to as St. Lawrence's Bridge, was built in 1362 to carry the road from Bath to Wells. Gilmore's map gives some idea of the original appearance of this medieval bridge of five arches, with the minute chapel of St. Lawrence in the middle of its east side and the defence towers at the southern end. During 1754 the Bath Corporation rebuilt the bridge on the existing piers, to a design for which Richard Jones claimed the credit. The engraving by Watts shows the bridge in its Georgian dress, with five segmental arches decorated by archivolt mouldings and resting on elongated octagonal piers, the roadway rising from each end to meet in a sharp break over the middle arch. The parapets were carried on bold consoles, and consisted of sections of open balustrading between dies placed over the piers and the centre of each arch. The bridge assumed its present nondescript appearance during the last century, when the road was widened and footways were cantilevered out from each side.

Pulteney Bridge

In or about the year 1768 William Johnstone Pulteney obtained a private Act of Parliament permitting him, subject to the consent of the Bath Corporation, to construct a bridge connecting Bath with the Bathwick estate, which had been brought to him by his marriage to Frances Pulteney. The Corporation's Minutes contain the following references to their negotiations with Pulteney:

'*February 6th*, 1768
'A Committee appointed to confer with Mr. Pulteney on his proposal for building a Bridge to Bathwick.'

'*January 2nd*, 1769
'William Pulteney to have liberty to build a Bridge from Bath to Bathwick, at or near the present Ferry. The Corporation to allow him a way to High Street. He to purchase the necessary buildings.'

Pulteney employed his friend Robert Adam to design the bridge, this being the first of several commissions connected with the development of Bathwick, and the only one to be realized. The bridge was under construction from 1769 to 1774, and its builder, one Reed, was financially ruined by his undertaking. The western midstream pier must have been insufficiently piled, for signs of subsidence were already apparent by 1779, and in 1804 it was found necessary to rebuild that section of the bridge.

It seems quite permissible to regard Adam's design as a skilful adaptation of Andrea Palladio's project for the Ponte di Rialto, Venice, illustrated in Il Terzo Libro dell'Architettura (Fig. 7). Although the main fabric of Adam's bridge has survived with little change, the shop ranges lining the roadway have undergone many alterations, especially on the north side. Despite a most praiseworthy attempt to restore the south side, the original appearance of Pulteney Bridge can best be studied in the very accurate delineations made by Malton and Watts. The description that follows has therefore been based on these views, and on

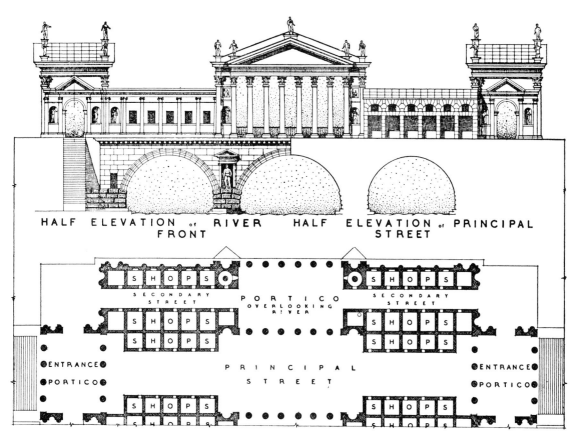

HALF ELEVATION of RIVER FRONT

HALF ELEVATION of PRINCIPAL STREET

SHOPS

SECONDARY STREET

PORTICO OVERLOOKING RIVER

SECONDARY STREET

SHOPS

SHOPS

SHOPS

SHOPS

SHOPS

ENTRANCE

PORTICO

PRINCIPAL STREET

ENTRANCE

PORTICO

SHOPS

SHOPS

Fig. 7. Andrea Palladio's design for the Rialto Bridge, Venice.

Adam's original drawings in Sir John Soane's Museum (Fig. 8 and Appendix III).

The river is spanned by three arches of segmental form, which rest against massive abutments at either bank and on two triangular-headed piers in mid-stream. Archivolt mouldings decorate the arch voussoirs; the plain spandrels are pierced by circular windows centred over each pier; and the bridge structure is finished with a boldly moulded stringcourse underlying the pedestal of the super-imposed buildings. This delicately moulded pedestal is broken forward below the pavilion-like features in the centre and over the mid-stream piers, while its topmost member provides a continuous sill to the windows. Centred over the middle arch of the bridge, and dominating the composition, is a great venetian window framed by wide piers, each containing a narrow window, and an unmoulded arch which surrounds the fan-shaped lunette and breaks into the open bed of the crowning triangular pediment. The three lights of the venetian window are set between slender Doric half-columns and antae, carrying an entablature which is continued from either side of the arched middle light, round each building face, and returned into the corresponding venetian window of the road frontage. The frieze decoration of fluting is applied only to these central features. The balancing wings contain seven rectangular windows of uniform size and spacing, but over each midstream pier a pavilion feature is created by framing the window with Doric pilasters and breaking the entablature slightly forward to carry the low attic story, which has a pyramidal roof and is linked by an open

The Old Bridge.
(*Engraved drawing by W. Watts, 1794*)

Pulteney Bridge, The south side.

Pulteney Bridge, The south side.
(Water-colour drawing by T. Malton, jr. c.1777)

Pulteney Bridge. The roadway from Bridge Street.
(Water-colour drawing by T. Malton, jr. c.1777)

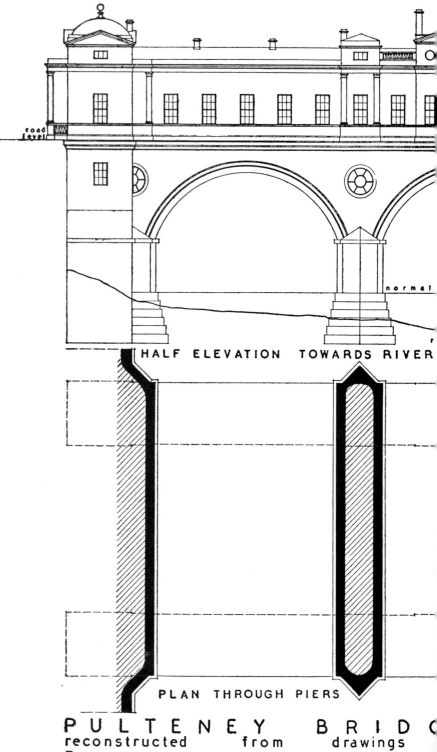

road
level

HALF ELEVATION TOWARDS RIVER

normal

PLAN THROUGH PIERS

PULTENEY BRID
reconstructed from drawings
Robert Adam Thomas Malton & William W

Fig. 8a.

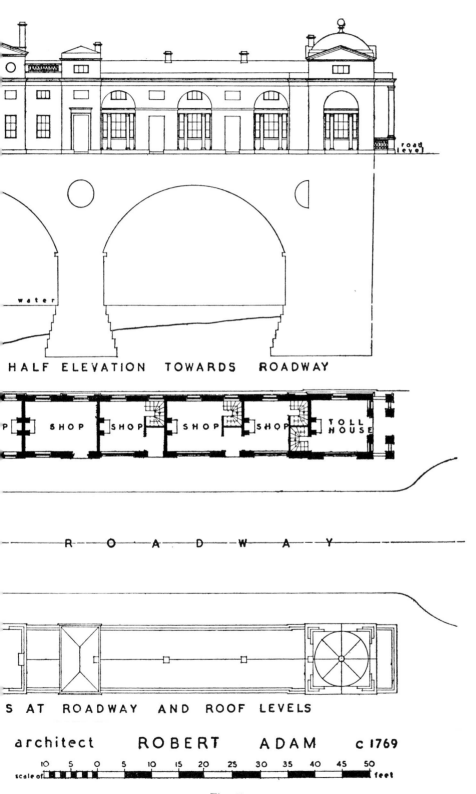

HALF ELEVATION TOWARDS ROADWAY

water

SHOP   SHOP   SHOP   SHOP   TOLL HOUSE

R — O — A — D — W — A — Y

S AT ROADWAY AND ROOF LEVELS

architect   ROBERT   ADAM   c 1769

10   5   0   5   10   15   20   25   30   35   40   45   50

scale of   feet

Fig. 8b.

Cleveland Bridge, with Camden Crescent.
(*Engraved drawing by T. H. Shepherd, 1829*)

balustrade with the pedimented central feature. At the further end of each wing the wall face is decorated with a single pilaster, serving as a respond to those of the pier pavilions and to the columns of the porticoes fronting each terminal pavilion. These last rise from the abutment piers and are square in plan, with a triangular pediment surmounting each face of the low attic story, which is roofed by a saucer-dome finished with a ball-finial.

The roadway elevations are somewhat similar in composition to the river frontages. The venetian window again forms a dominant central feature, but the flanking wings are more elaborately treated. Each contains three arched openings which form shopfronts, the doors being set in the wide intervening piers. The plain impost is returned into the arch reveals, and its lines are continued below the solid lunettes by the cornice of a simple entablature, which is supported by slender Doric pilasters subdividing each shopfront into one wide and two narrow bays. Each terminal pavilion has a similar arched shopfront in its roadway front, while the end elevations are decorated with porticoes of Doric columns, arranged in pairs to form one wide and two narrow intercolumniations, the latter being closed with balustrades between the column bases.

Cleveland Bridge

Cleveland Bridge was constructed by a private company at a cost of some £10,000, and officially opened on September 28th, 1827, when it was called the New Bridge. The embanked approach from the Bathwick side was formed at the expense of the Duke of Cleveland, then lord of the manor, after whom the bridge was eventually named.

In designing this fine structure, Henry Edmund Goodridge successfully combined the beauty of antique detail with an honest and expressive use of modern materials. The roadway, some 37 ft. wide, crosses the river in one span of just over 100 ft., being carried on a series of parallel arches of ironwork, segmental in form and with latticed spandrels, which rest against the massive abutment piers at either bank. On either side of each entrance to the bridge, and rising sheer from the abutment piers, are small Doric temples, originally designed to serve for toll-houses, with four-column porticos surmounted by triangular pediments. Cleveland Place was designed by Goodridge to provide a worthy approach to the bridge, but unfortunately his ideas were never fully carried out to completion.

THE CHURCHES AND CHAPELS

Apart from some noteworthy exceptions, the churches and chapels erected in Bath during the Georgian era show no considerable architectural merit, although collectively they present an interesting facet of contemporary taste, reflecting an attitude towards religious observance which regarded church-going as an integral part of the social round, but saw no reason to perpetuate the chilly discomfort of medieval buildings.

The Parish Church of St. Michael-extra-Muros (rebuilt 1836)

The available facilities for religious observances were soon rendered inadequate by the rapid increase in the size and population of Bath, and, to meet the needs of his own tenants, John Wood offered to rebuild the ruinous old church of St. Michael, partly at his own expense, on condition that a number of pews were allotted for the use of residents in and around Queen Square. The parishioners refused to grant this concession, and in 1734 placed the rebuilding of the church in the far less capable hands of John Harvey, a stone-cutter and probably the son of that Harvey

who had built the first Pump Room. Wood directed his considerable power of execration against Harvey's church, which was certainly detailed with capricious disregard for the proprieties of Palladianism (Fig. 9), but it is apparent that the plan was skilfully contrived to fit a cramped and awkward site, and the exterior was an attractive composition. The

Fig. 9. John Harvey's Church of St. Michael-extra-Muros.

interior measured approximately 65 ft. east to west, and 37 ft. north to south. Three wide arches, carried on square piers with Doric capitals and entablatures, separated the correctly orientated nave from the single wide aisle on its south side. This segmental-ended aisle was entered through the doorway behind the portico, which formed the central feature of the south front. Harvey's building was demolished shortly before 1836 to make way for the present church, designed by G. P. Manners, which contains some interesting memorial tablets and the two painted panels of the reredos, attributed to William Hoare and one Robinson, from the old building.

St. Mary's Chapel, Queen Square (demolished c. 1875)

Wood's failure to effect an arrangement with the Parish of St. Michael led him to promote the building of a chapel in Chapel Row, set back from the south-west corner of Queen Square. St. Mary's Chapel, begun in 1732 and opened for service on December 25th, 1734, was the first of Bath's many proprietary chapels, having been built at a cost of £2,000, subscribed by Wood and eleven other shareholders. Wood's building was a fine Classic temple, probably modelled on St. Paul's Church, Covent Garden, the chief external feature being a Roman Doric portico, distyle in antis. The central doorway was a sham, access to the chapel being through a door in each side wall of the portico. Measuring 67 ft. by 48 ft. and 36 ft. in height, the interior was planned as an apse-ended basilica having galleried aisles on its south, north and west sides. Roman Ionic columns of stone supported the galleries and an entablature surrounding the central ceiling, which was elaborately enriched with stucco decorations of Baroque character. Some Ionic capitals and a base left on the site were melancholy relics of this fine building, regrettably demolished some time about 1875 under the pretext of road widening (Fig. 10).

See also Appendix V (pages 226 & 227)

The Octagon Chapel, Milsom Street

The most famous and successful of Bath's proprietary chapels was the Octagon, built with funds raised by a subscription promoted by the Rev. Dr. Dechair and William Street the banker, and opened for service on October 4th, 1767. Thomas Lightoler was employed to prepare the plans, which were engraved by William Linley, the clerk of works, and published some time during 1786.

The chapel is contained within a rectangular building behind the houses on the east side of Milsom Street, and was originally approached

Fig. 10. St. Mary's Chapel, Queen Square.

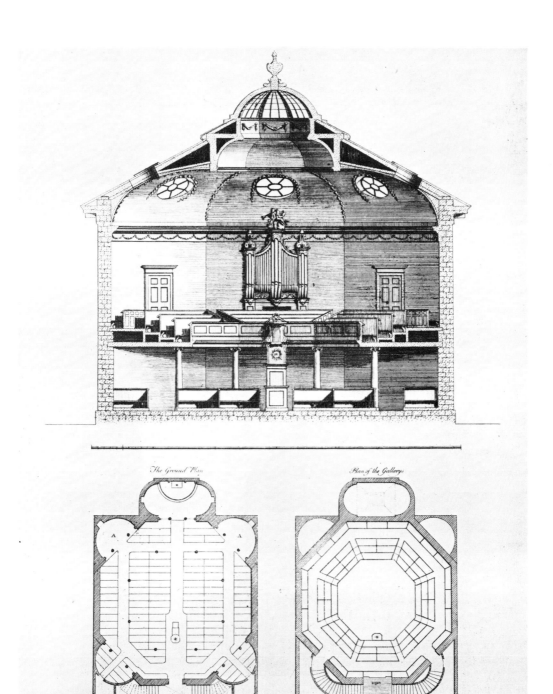

The Octagon Chapel. Plans and section.
(*engraving after a drawing by T. Lightoler*)

by way of a covered passage. In the forepart of the rectangle is a square lobby, ceiled with a shallow vault in plaster, leading to a narrow vestibule from which stairs on either side ascend to the gallery, and doors lead to the chapel. The chapel derived its name from the plan form, which is an octagon of some 50 ft. diameter, the triangular spaces remaining within the square being filled by semi-circular alcoves, of which those on either side of the sanctuary are equipped with fire-places. Beyond the west side projects the sanctuary, square in plan with an apse on either side, in which the communion table was placed. The encircling gallery, which originally rose in four steppings, is supported by eight stone columns of the Ionic order. The organ, on which Herschel performed, was placed in a chamber above the vestibule, with its case projecting from the west wall into the gallery.

The building is well finished internally, with excellent joinery including some fine mahogany doors. The walls encircling the gallery are decorated with deep festoons and pendants of husks and are terminated by a richly modelled entablature. At a height of some 29 ft. from the ground-floor rises a shallow octagonal dome, each face containing a circular window with radiating glazing bars, set in a frame of scrolling. The small inner dome rises to a shallow drum, decorated with festoons in panels, forming the base to the central lantern-light. The original decorations in compo and plasterwork, particularly those in the sanctuary and on the domed ceiling, reflect Lightoler's skill as a carver and modeller. The sanctuary contained an altar-piece, representing 'The Pool of Bethesda', painted by William Hoare, R.A., who received for this service the sum of £100 and the use for his lifetime of a seat in the chapel.

The alterations made to adapt the building for showrooms did not affect the structural form, and much of the original decoration was retained. Some Adamesque decoration added by Messrs. Mallett has not impaired the charm of the interior, which has been restored for use as an exhibition room.

Lady Huntingdon's Chapel. Vineyards (now Trinity Presbyterian Church)

The famous Chapel in the Vineyards, opened for service on October 6th, 1765, was built and originally maintained by Selina, Lady Huntingdon, and formed the centre from whence she directed her efforts to carry into the heart of the aristocratic and fashionable world, the spirit of Wesley's and Whitefield's revival. In Horace Walpole's characteristic account of his visit to Wesley's 'opera', the original state of the building is well described.

'The Chapel is very neat, with true Gothic windows (yet I am not converted), but I was glad to see that luxury is creeping in upon them before persecution: they have very neat mahogany for branches and brackets of the same in taste. At the upper end is a broad *haut-pas* of four steps advancing in the middle: at each of the broadest parts are two of my eagles, with red cushions for the parson and clerk. Behind them rise three more steps, in the middle of which is a third eagle for pulpit. Scarlet armchairs for all three. On either hand a balcony for elect ladies. The rest of the congregation sit on forms.'

The chapel is a simple rectangular building, measuring internally 59 ft. 8 in. by 39 ft. 9 in., with a height of 26 ft. 2 in. from the floor to the flat ceiling, which is surrounded by a segmental cove. There are four of Walpole's 'true Gothic' windows in the west wall and five in each side wall, and three eagles still serve their original purposes. The semi-circular apse in the middle of the east wall was designed to contain the communion-table, with the organ loft above. The gallery, which now surrounds three sides of the interior, was added in 1783 by a committee of subscribers appointed to administer the affairs of the chapel.

The most interesting external feature is the minister's lodging in front of the chapel, a charming little building with a two-story bay

Lady Huntingdon's Chapel. The minister's house.

Lady Huntingdon's Chapel. Interior, looking west.

front, with flattened ogee-arched windows and a battlemented parapet.

The Parish Church of St. James (demolished)

The body of St. James's Church was rebuilt during 1768–69, the cost of the work being defrayed partly by voluntary subscriptions, but mainly by loans raised on security of parish rates and pew rents. The architect employed was John Palmer, then in partnership with the builder Thomas Jelly, whose firm probably carried out the work. The Gothic tower had been rebuilt in 1716 and its retention led Palmer to introduce Georgian Gothic detail into the exterior of his essentially Classic building. The west end and tower were rebuilt in 1848 by George P. Manners, who also removed some of Palmer's more obviously 'Gothick' detail, and gave to the building a generally Italianate appearance. The interior was completely gutted during the German air raids and, despite the concerted efforts of preservationists to save the fine Classical tower, the building was completely demolished in 1957.

The north and south elevations were identical, both having three tiers of windows, three being contained in a wide middle bay and one in each narrow end bay. The three divisions were created by narrow buttresses having weathered offsets. The small windows lighting the crypt were without architraves, while those lighting the main floor and gallery had, respectively, segmental and round arches and were framed by heavily moulded architraves. A narrow stringcourse defined the gallery level, and the crowning cornice of Classical profile was surmounted by a parapet perforated by narrow trefoil-headed openings. The buttresses were surmounted by pinnacles (Fig. 11).

An east end projection contained the apse and two gallery staircases. The east elevation was divided into two equal parts by wide piers, each decorated with three tiers of two recessed trefoil-ended panels. In each division was a round-headed doorway set in a pointed-arched surround, with a round-headed window

Fig. 11. Exterior of St. James's Church, before the alterations of 1848

(from Egan's 'Walks through Bath' 1819).

above. The parapet above the cavetto-cornice was plain except for two flattened ogee-profiled projections forming bases for vases, centred above the doors and windows (Fig. 12). A porch of related design originally stood at the north-west corner of the church, against the old Gothic tower.

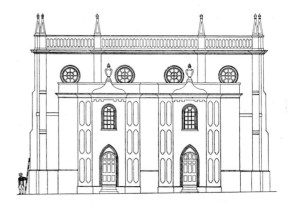

Fig. 12. St. James's Church. East elevation.

St. James's Church. Exterior from south-east.

St. Swithin's Church. Exterior from north-west.

As originally built the interior measured 61 ft. in length, excluding the eastern apse, by 58 ft. in width, and was divided into a wide nave and aisles, with galleries over the latter and across the west end of the nave. On each side of the nave were two widely spaced stone columns, with high pedestals, plain shafts and Roman Ionic capitals, which served to support the main structural members of the galleries and roof. The roof beams carried by these columns were decorated with panelled soffits, and on the nave side with a deep entablature from which a plain segmental cove rose to a flat ceiling, with an elliptical lantern-light in its centre. The architrave only was used to surround the flat ceiling compartments above the aisle galleries. The altar was set in an apse divided into three bays by paired pilasters with corner columns, and an entablature of the Roman Doric order. The middle bay contained Benjamin Barker's painting of 'The Supper at Emmaus', and the apse was ceiled

with a plaster semi-dome of graduated coffering. The Doric entablature of the apse was repeated below the panelled gallery fronts between the columns. The church contained a notable organ built by Seede of Bristol in 1782, upon which an inaugural recital was given by William Herschel.

Margaret Chapel, Brock Street (demolished)

Margaret Chapel, so named out of compliment to Mrs. Margaret Garrard, Lady of the Manor and patroness of the living of Walcot, served as a proprietary chapel for the use of residents in the neighbourhood of the Royal Crescent and the Circus. The chapel stood between some small houses on the west side of Margaret's Buildings, and was built round about 1773 for Cornelius Norton, who had subleased some of the surrounding property from the younger Wood. Norton paid Wood the sum of £100 to design and supervise the erection of the chapel, and William Linley was employed as clerk of works, he having acted in that capacity during the building of the Octagon Chapel. After Margaret Chapel had ceased to be used for a place of worship, it became in succession a skating rink, a swimming bath, finally a badminton hall before its interior was completely destroyed by German bombs.

Wood's building was unworthy of him, being an unusually poverty-stricken essay in the Gothic style as understood by the middle Georgians. The principal elevation to Margaret's Buildings was poorly composed and detailed in the manner of Batty Langley, while the Brock Street entrance, forming the centre of a terrace of houses, is distinguished by a fine and impeccably Classic three-light window, with a framing of Ionic columns and pilasters supporting an entablature which is broken forward over the middle light and surmounted by a triangular pediment.

The galleried interior, measuring 73 ft. by 60 ft., excluding the altar recess, was ceiled over without the aid of intermediate columns. Contemporary accounts describe it as being 'light, spacious and elegant', and list as its chief features an altar-piece depicting 'The Offerings of the Magi' by the Bath painter Williams, 'an exceedingly fine-toned organ, and two of Buzaglo's stoves'.

The Parish Church of St. Swithin, Walcot

The work of rebuilding St. Swithin's Church, to meet the needs of an increased population, was undertaken in 1777 and the western portion of four bays was opened for service during March 1780. Two further bays to the east were added during 1788, and the tower and spire were finished by 1790. There can be little doubt that the parishioners' decision to build a church on similar lines to that of St. James's Parish, led them to employ John Palmer as their architect.

The exterior is adorned with a giant order of Ionic pilasters with plain shafts, which rise from a deep plinth and divide the side elevations into six equal bays. The two tiers of windows, low segmental-headed lights to the ground-floor and tall arched lights to the gallery, are framed by heavily moulded architraves. A plain stringcourse marks the gallery level, and the fronts are finished with an entablature and plain parapet. Low wings, containing vestries and staircases, flank the base of the tower, which forms the centre of the west front. Its lowest stage contains an arched doorway, framed by engaged Doric columns carrying a triangular pedimented entablature, above which is an inscription-panel and a clock-dial set in a moulded surround. The main entablature provides the finish to this stage of the tower, on the front of which it is broken forward on consoles to carry a triangular pediment. The upper stage is set on a deep plinth and contains a louvred arched opening in each face, placed between engaged half-columns, with plain shafts and Corinthian capitals, which, with the responding pilasters at each corner, carry the entablature and plain parapet. Above this is a circular lantern, treated on a reduced scale, with eight open arches between engaged Corinthian columns supporting an entablature and plain parapet. From this rises the plain octagonal stone spire, which is finished with a ball and vane.

The interior measures approximately 68 ft. by 52 ft., and is similar to that of St. James's Church, except that here three widely spaced columns stand on each side of the nave, and the gallery is independent of them. The altar stands in a shallow bay, corbelled out over the lower road, and the side walls are adorned with many interesting memorial tablets, including one to the architect John Palmer.

Argyle Chapel, Bathwick

Argyle Chapel, built for a Nonconformist congregation which had originated with a group of secessionists from Lady Huntingdon's Connection, was opened for service on October 4th, 1789, by the Rev. William Jay. Thomas Baldwin was paid the sum of £4 for designing the chapel, which is represented on

St. Swithin's Church, Walcot. Interior, looking east.

All Saint's Chapel, Lansdown. Exterior from north-west.
(*Engraved drawing by W. Watts, 1794*)

a contemporary 'building token' as having a simple and elegant front, of two stories with a slightly projecting central feature surmounted by a flat triangular pediment, set back within a railed forecourt between the adjoining buildings.

The need for increased accommodation led the proprietors in 1821 to employ H. E. Goodridge to extend the building at both ends and build a new front. This was a fine example of Goodridge's Greek Revival manner, with a three-bay Ionic portico surmounted by a pedimented attic, but its character was completely changed when the attic was removed and the present upper story, of arched windows framed by columns and an entablature of the Roman Corinthian order, was added by Messrs. Hickes and Isaac.

All Saints' Chapel, Lansdown (largely demolished)

All Saints' Chapel, opened for service on October 25th, 1794, was built for the use of residents in the neighbourhood of Lansdown Crescent, by a committee of subscribers headed by Charles Spackman. The architect was John Palmer who produced a building of singular charm, greatly enhanced by its beautiful situation on a small eminence just below Lansdown Place West.

The chapel was built above a semi-basement story cutting into the sloping site, and on the east side was a large house originally built as a residence for Spackman, but later occupied by the architect John Lowder. The main building formed a rectangle, measuring internally 64 ft. by 46 ft., with the corners splayed off to contain the four fire-places. A single story extension on the north side contained the vestibule, with a vestry on one side and the gallery staircase on the other. The exterior was a picturesque composition, with 'Gothick' windows ranged between buttresses rising into sharp pinnacles above the open balustrading of narrow arches, and a small belfry tower surmounted the middle bay of the north front.

The original effect of the interior must have been wholly delightful, although somewhat theatrical. The deep gallery completely surrounded a central oval space, around which rose eight equally spaced piers, with plain cylindrical bases, corresponding in height to the pews, and engaged shafts crowned with capitals from which radiated the elaborate plaster fan-vaulting surrounding the oval ceiling panel from whence depended a great chandelier of glittering crystals. The twelve windows ranged round the wall behind the gallery had lunettes of painted glass, each representing the head of an Apostle surrounded by a rayed nimbus, while the window over the high altar was glazed with a transparency painting of 'The Last Supper'. All of this glass, designed and painted by Thomas Barker, disappeared along with the chandelier during the course of some 'improvements' which were made to the chapel during 1878.

The building had ceased to be used for its original purpose and was serving as a furniture store when fires caused by German bombs destroyed the interior, leaving a dramatic ruin to form the striking termination of steeply rising Park Street.

Kensington Chapel, London Road (disused)

Kensington Chapel, built by subscription and opened for service during January 1795, forms the central feature of a terrace of houses designed by John Palmer for John Jelly, the attorney and clerk to the parish of Walcot.

The London Road front is one of Palmer's ablest designs in the Classic manner. The masonry of the ground-story is rusticated and relieved by three widely spaced rectangular windows, with their keystones dying into the plain platband. The plain wall face above forms a setting for three lofty arched windows, corresponding in position and width with those below, grouped within a fine architectural framing of composite pilasters arranged in pairs on either side of each window, set upon a deep continued sill supported by consoles beneath the pilasters, and carrying an entablature which is returned and stopped against the marginal surrounds of the windows, to provide a springing for the moulded archivolts. The front is finished with a plain frieze and cornice, surmounted by a flattened triangular pediment. Access to the chapel was provided by side entrances under the flat segmental arched porches recessed into the flanking houses, which are architecturally treated to accord with the chapel (Fig. 13).

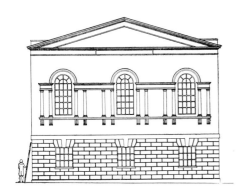

Fig. 13. Kensington Chapel. Front elevation.

The interior, measuring 62 ft. by 42 ft. 6 in., excluding the altar recess, was surrounded on three sides by a gallery and equipped with three fire-places. It has been stripped of furnishings and decorations and is now used as a warehouse. It is a matter for regret that the present occupants have found it necessary to disfigure Palmer's fine design with a large lettered sign.

Laura Chapel, Bathwick (demolished)

Laura Chapel, opened for service on November 19th, 1795, was built by Thomas Baldwin on a site behind some houses on the east side of Henrietta Street. The cost of the building was met by a tontine subscription and the ownership of the property passed to the Rev. Dr. Randolph. The chapel, which was oval in form and seated a congregation of 1,000, is described in a contemporary account as 'a very elegant and commodious building, rendered warm and comfortable in the winter season by fires in its recesses'. Early in this century the roof collapsed, leaving a ruin which was later demolished, and only the passages through the houses remain to remind one of its former existence.

Christ Church, Montpelier Row

Christ Church, consecrated on November 7th, 1798, was built as the result of strenuous efforts made by the Rev. Charles Daubeny, Archdeacon of Sarum, to provide a free place of worship for the poor of Bath. The site in Montpelier Row was given by Lord Rivers to the trustees, each of whom subscribed a minimum sum of £50 towards the building cost. The gound-floor was wholly given over to provide 800 places for the poor, and the gallery seats were let to obtain sufficient income to cover the annual expenditure.

The building was designed by John Palmer in the neat, rather mechanical style which, at that time, passed for Gothic. The principal elevation to Montpelier Row is divided by buttresses into five equal bays, with two tiers of windows lighting the aisle, and is finished with a battlemented parapet, continued between the bases of the pinnacles which surmount the buttresses. The original quatrefoil windows below the gallery level were replaced with larger lights when the eastern apse was added in 1886, but the arched openings of the upper range remain as originally designed. The square tower in the centre of the west side is similarly detailed, and flanked by low buildings containing the lobbies and gallery staircases. Internally, the wide nave is divided into five bays by piers with engaged shafts, which serve to support the projecting galleries over the aisles, and the deep continuous architrave which forms the springing for the canted wooden ceiling over the nave.

Walcot Chapel, London Road

The foundation stone of Walcot Methodist Chapel was laid on March 31st, 1815, and the

building, which was opened for service on
May 30th, 1816, was considered at the time of
its completion to be 'the most elegant structure
of its kind in this city'. The architect was a Mr.
W. Jenkins of London, who employed a local
builder named Cave to carry out the work.

There is a small garden forecourt with fine
gate piers in front of the façade, which is an
arresting composition in spite of certain
oddities in detail. It is divided into two stories
of five bays, the middle three being set slightly
forward. The ground-floor windows are set in
a rusticated arcade, from the centre of which
projects the porch, formed by two pairs of
Doric columns carrying a deep entablature
with triglyphed frieze. Above the first-floor
platband is a second tier of arched windows set
within plain recessed margins, between fluted
pilasters of a debased Corinthian order without
bases, two on either side of the middle window
and one at each frontage break. The architrave

Walcot Chapel. Exterior, from west.

Walcot Chapel. Interior, looking east.

and frieze of the main entablature are interrupted over the middle bay by a large tablet carved with the legend Deo Sacrum. Concave ramped parapets decorated with fan ornament flank a panelled screen wall above the three middle bays, which is surmounted by a triangular pediment containing a tablet inscribed 'Walcot Chapel 1815'.

The interior measures 71 ft. by 52 ft. and is surrounded on three sides by a horshoe gallery with a panelled front over an entablature supported by slender Doric columns. Behind the rostrum, which curves forward from the east wall, is a room for Communion Service, above which is the organ and choristers gallery. The wide three-centred arched opening is framed by pilasters, with fluted shafts and composite capitals, and an entablature with a richly scrolled frieze and panelled soffit to the cornice, the latter member only being continued round the main ceiling.

The Parish Church of St. Mary, Bathwick

The ruinous state of old Bathwick Church, and the need to provide accommodation for an increasing number of parishioners, led to the forming of a committee soon after 1810 to consider proposals for building a new church. A site at the foot of Bathwick Hill was given by the Earl of Darlington, and plans for a building thereon were drawn up by John Pinch, but although the foundation stone was laid on September 1st, 1814, it was not until some time during 1816 that builders were invited to tender for the work, the final date for submitting estimates being fixed at January 1st, 1817. The contract was placed with Walter Harris, and the church, with its east end temporarily finished with an apse, was consecrated on February 4th, 1820, after having cost more than £14,000, the money being partly raised by subscriptions, but mainly by loans on

St. Mary's Church, Bathwick. Exterior from south-west.

St. Mary's Church, Bathwick. Interior, looking east.

security of parish rates, a procedure for which it was necessary to procure two Acts of Parliament. Although Pinch had originally designed a chancel, fresh plans were made round about 1870 by J. Elkington Gill, but these were also abandoned when the present chancel, designed by G. E. Street, was added in 1873. Neither Street's chancel nor the later vestries are in sympathy with the original building, which has never received its rightful measure of praise, although it shares with the similar church at Larkhall the distinction of being by far the finest of Bath's Georgian churches.

John Pinch followed the conventional layout of late Georgian churches, and used a symmetrical plan with a wide nave of five bays flanked by lofty, galleried aisles. At the west end of the nave is a square tower, its ground-story originally serving for a vestry but now forming the baptistery, and an entrance porch on either side, with a gallery staircase and door into the aisle. The original seating arrangements were most peculiar and unsatisfactory, the congregation sitting in pews with their backs to the sanctuary and facing a monumental structure of wood consisting of three elevated reading desks, in front of the western gallery.

It is in the general composition and strong detailing of the exterior that this church is so far superior to its immediate predecessors. The bay divisions of the nave and aisles are marked by semi-octagonal buttresses, continued above the roof lines into crocketed octagonal pinnacles with tall panelled bases, those to the nave clerestory being detailed on a scale proportionate with their smaller diameter and height. The equilateral-arched windows of the aisles are divided by stone mullions and tracery into two tiers of three lights, while the clerestory windows have four-centred arches and one tier of three lights. Between the pinnacle bases, and above the continuous dripmoulds which mark the roof levels, are battlemented parapets, perforated with arches alternating with quatrefoils. The square tower, equal in width to the nave, is 100 ft. high, and at the corners are massive octagonal buttresses rising into pinnacles which add a further 15 ft.

to the total height. Encircling dripmoulds marked the horizontal division of the tower into three well-defined stages. Each exposed face of the two lower stages contains a large equilateral-arched window sub-divided into two tiers of four lights, with panelled surrounds and decorated spandrels, while the top stage containing the belfry has coupled two-light windows with louvred openings above a high panelled base. The crowning pinnacles and battlements are larger scale versions of those over the nave and aisles. The side porches present two elevations identically treated, with a door and surmounting window combined in a panelled surround.

The interior is in complete contrast to the richness and general orthodoxy of the exterior, being austere and rather eclectic in style, with a curious quality of studied elegance which, in spite of alterations, is very effective. The division of the nave into five bays, those at either end being slightly less wide than the middle three, is effected by piers of engaged shafts which serve to support the side galleries and to carry the deep wooden lintels which, with stone segmental relieving arches, support the clerestory wall. Attached triple shafts on the clerestory wall form the springing for a plaster vault of four-centred section, with moulded ribs and elaborately modelled bosses. The aisles are ceiled by plaster vaults of an almost flat section, and the gallery fronts are vertically panelled in wood. The plaster has apparently been removed from the random masonry of the gallery and clerestory walls, but the effect is pleasant.

Holy Trinity Church, James Street (demolished)

Some years after the building of Christ Church, in the Parish of Walcot, a fund was raised for the purpose of providing a similar free church for the poor living in the Kingsmead district. After efforts to find a more suitable site had failed, the building committee decided to build in James Street, on a plot of ground hemmed in on three sides by buildings. Clearance of the site began during May

1819 and the building was consecrated on December 10th, 1822.

The architect and builder of the church was John Lowder, a member of the wealthy family of Bath bankers. Lowder, who had achieved a certain measure of local fame by designing and building the extraordinary circular National School, first prepared plans for a 'Grecian' church. At the instance of members of the building committtee he substituted the 'Gothic' design which was carried out at a vastly increased expenditure of over £16,000. Although Lowder is reputed to have forgone all personal profit in the matter, the ensuing inquiries and troubles are said to have hastened his death.

Lowder's plan was certainly original, although its oddity arose partly from the difficult site conditions. The wide nave, in this case correctly orientated, was asymmetrically treated, with galleries on its northern side, and a low aisle with a high clerestory over on the south side. The front towards James Street was not without charm. Gabled buttresses divided the low aisle wall into six bays, the first and fourth from the west projecting to form shallow porches where the doors were recessed in moulded and splayed arches. Vertical panelling decorated all the other bays. The nave was lit by a lofty clerestory of five three-light windows, their varied heads of curvilinear tracery being framed by arches dressed with crocketted ogee dripmoulds rising to the perforated parapet. The west end bay contained the gallery staircase and projected to line with the aisle wall. This bay contained a window similar to those of the clerestory and finished with a flattened gable, flanked by tall pinnacles rising from buttresses. At the east end was a slender octagonal tower and spire, each gabletted face of the tower containing a tall lancet opening.

St. Saviour's Church, Larkhall

St. Saviour's Church was built as the result of efforts made by Archdeacon Moysey, who in 1824 issued an appeal for subscriptions

St. Saviour's Church, Larkhall. Exterior from south-east.
(*Lithograph by R. W. Billings*)

St. Saviour's Church, Larkhall. Interior, looking west.

towards a fund for building a 'Plain Free Church, for which a very beautiful, though simple and plain Plan in the Doric Order' had been obtained. The site, given by Miss Tanner, formed part of some land which her father had originally proposed to lay out as a residential square behind Beaufort Buildings. The foundation stone was not laid until April 2nd, 1829, and the church was consecrated on April 29th, 1832.

It is difficult to establish whether the architect was the elder John Pinch, who died in 1827 but might easily have made the design before then, or his son and namesake who carried on the practice in Bath. St. Saviour's bears a striking resemblance to St. Mary's, Bathwick, in its plan and general conception, but the exterior is treated in a lighter and more graceful manner, with a more restricted use of decorative detail, the style used being late decorated Gothic. The lofty aisles are divided into six bays by receding buttresses, with weathered offsets and crowning pinnacles, five of the bays containing large windows of decorated tracery, while the sixth and westernmost bay forms a porch, containing the gallery staircase, against the tower. The upper part of the nave consists simply of plain walling, finished with a perforated parapet similar to that of the aisles. The western tower, like its prototype at St. Mary's, is divided into three stages, the lowest forming the main entrance to the church, and has octagonal corner buttresses rising into pinnacles which terminate in finials at the height of 120 ft. above the ground.

The interior is divided into a wide nave with galleried aisles, as at St. Mary's, but the architectural treatment is altogether finer. Tall piers with engaged shafts on the four cardinal faces, and moulded splays continuing into wide, equilateral arches, carry a wall face without clerestory windows, but with elaborate semi-octagonal corbels, over the piers and level with the crowns of the arches, from which spring the ribs of a plaster vault of four-centred section. The aisle ceilings are simply divided into square flat panels, and the galleries are fronted with elaborate wood panelling.

The chancel was added in 1882 by C. E. Davis, then City Architect, whose flamboyant individualism led him to make some unfortunate changes in the character of the detail, and the elaborate Revivalist reredos was designed by J. D. Sedding.

THE FREEMASONS' HALL

(now the Friends' Meeting House)

'The Foundation Stone of this Masonic Hall, was laid with the usual ceremonies, August 4th, A.D. 1817, in the 57th year of the reign of his present Majesty, George the Third, and the year of Masonry 5817, in presence of the Masters and Wardens of the Bath Lodges. His Royal Highness, Augustus Frederick Duke of Sussex, being most Worshipful Grand Master of the United Grand Lodge of England, and Arthur Chichester, Esq., R. W. Provincial Grand Master for the County of Somerset. Brother Wilkins, Architect. Walter Harris, Builder.'

A brass plate bearing the inscription quoted above was placed, with a box of contemporary coins, in a cavity of the foundation-stone of the Freemasons' Hall in York Street, which was completed and dedicated with magnificent ceremony on September 23rd, 1819. Now the rites and mysteries of Freemasonry are celebrated elsewhere, and the building is the Meeting House of the Society of Friends.

The exterior is typical of its architect, William Wilkins, and is a scholarly composition of Grecian elements, except for the curious lapse of using rusticated arches to contain the side entrances. The wall of the great room is frankly treated as a decorative screen, with a central portico projecting from flanking wings. This portico is divided into three equal bays by two columns, with plain plinths and moulded bases, fluted shafts and Ionic capitals, between return walls finished with antae. The plinth and base moulding continues in the wings.

which terminate in corner pilasters. In the wall behind the portico is a blind doorway, and the single window decorating either wing was originally also blind, but has since been opened up. The whole front is crowned by a full entablature, surmounted by a triangular pediment over the portico. Three figures representing Faith, Hope and Charity, symbolizing the ideals of Freemasonry, originally stood on the acroteria of the pediment, and the architrave of the blind doorway bore the inscription: FREEMASONS' HALL A.L. 5817. (Illustration on page 79).

The principal feature of the interior is the Great Room, measuring 50 ft. by 30 ft., and originally lit solely by the two circular lantern-lights on high glazed drums in the main ceiling, from which elegant glass chandeliers were suspended. Seating was ranged round three sides of the room, at the east end being a semi-circular platform for the orchestra, with an organ gallery over.

THE GUILDHALL

The extraordinary series of events, and the personalities involved in the controversy arising over the Guildhall rebuilding, have already been recounted (pages 11–13). At the time of Warr Atwood's accidental death

'nothing more than the south-east wall and about 9 ft. of the west front and screen to the Green Market was then built, about 15 ft. in height, and in which condition it remained until 1775, when the first design (Atwood's) was reconsidered, and deemed insufficient for the business that may be transacted, as the greater part of the ground-story was intended for a Market House. Fresh designs were then ordered to be made by Thomas Baldwin, architect, which, being approved of, were carried into execution; in consequence of which that part of the hall and screen wall already mentioned,

was pulled down to make room for the structure as it now appears.'

Baldwin's building reaches a high level of accomplishment, the planning is efficient and straightforward, and the exteriors and interiors are well proportioned and beautifully detailed. The principal front to High Street has a central feature of three bays set slightly forward from narrow flanking wings. The ground-story is raised upon a plain plinth, and while each wing contains a single rectangular window set in rusticated walling, the masonry of the three arched openings to the central feature is rusticated and vermiculated, with moulded imposts and plain keystones to the arches. The central feature is continued above the platband by an engaged order of four equally spaced three-quarter columns, with full pedestals, plain shafts and elaborate Ionic capitals, which embrace the two upper stories and support an entablature, its frieze adorned with fluting and paterae, surmounted by a triangular pediment with a tympanum decoration of the City Arms flanked by festoons and pendants of husks.

Each bay of the central feature contains a first- and second-floor window, the first a tall light dressed with balustrade, architrave, frieze and cornice, and the last a square light within an architrave frame. In each flanking wing is a single window, dressed with an architrave and a triangular pediment supported on consoles, which is set within a slightly recessed arch, its moulded archivolt rising from an impost band decorated with Vitruvian scrolling. The main entablature is continued across each wing, where a panel, containing a relief of a vase between festoons of husks, breaks the architrave and frieze. The wings are finished with a pedestal parapet which has sections of blind balustrading corresponding in width to the arched recesses below, and is returned and stopped against the central pediment. Stone vases, of similar form but varied decoration, are placed above the breaks in the parapet, and the apex of the

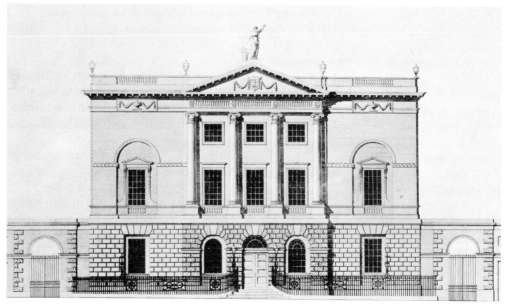

The Guildhall. West front.
(*Engraved drawing by T. Baldwin*)

The Guildhall and markets.
(*Engraved drawing by W. Watts, 1794*)

pediment is crowned by a figure of Justice, for once not blindfolded, holding scales and pointing to a book of law lying open on a pedestal.

The Adamitic saucer-dome which now crowns Baldwin's design was added by Brydon, who designed the extensions on each side of the original building. These extensions necessitated demolishing the low screens masking the markets, which were terminated by pavilions, that to the north forming a watch-house, and that to the south a lock-up.

The side elevations have been overbuilt and the beautiful elevation to the east is now partially obscured by a clutter of undistinguished buildings. This east front is a composition of considerable originality, the building face being sub-divided to form a central feature, three windows wide, slightly recessed between pavilions, each two windows wide. The ground-story windows are rectangular, and are set without architraves in a rusticated wall face which finishes with the plain plat-band at first-floor level. The tall rectangular windows to the first-floor are underlined by a pedestal course with blind balustrades below each light. The central feature contains three windows, of which the middle one is false, and all have architraves and are grouped within a

The Guildhall. West front.

framing of plain-shafted composite pilasters, supporting a frieze decorated with paterae and fluting, surmounted by a cornice accented by a triangular pediment placed above the false window. The two windows in each pavilion are set without architraves in a plain wall face, with a moulded stringcourse continuing the lines of the cornice to the central feature. The attic windows, forming the clerestory of the banqueting hall, consist of oval lights set in rectangular openings placed to correspond with the windows below. A panel, carved with a festoon looped below a patera, takes the place of the middle light, those on each side are framed by architraves, while those in the wings have plain settings. The main entablature is continued round the building, but is broken forward over each pavilion and surmounted by a triangular pediment. The pedestal parapet is decorated with blind balustrades corresponding to the windows below, and dies into the pediments. Vases again surmount the angle breaks, and a chimney, disguised as a classical altar, rises from the centre of the parapet (Fig. 14).

12 ft. high, furnished with every necessity for cookery; a bakehouse 20 ft. square, with two ovens, a tin plate warming cupboard, boilers, etc., and a large scullery, hall, housekeeper's room, a cold larder, pastry room, wine and beer cellar, and coal cellar. The ground-story consists of a vestibule 17 ft. long, 22 ft. wide, and 16 ft high, a justiciary room 39 ft. long, 32 ft. wide, with a drawing room for the mayor 21 by 22 ft.; town clerk's office, deputy town clerk's office, and common clerk's office, with a drawing room for the jury, record room and lobby, near the grand staircase, for the mayor's officers to wait in. The whole finished with stucco walls, enriched, and plain cornices, etc., suitable to the purposes they are appropriated to. From the vestibule on the right hand, you are led to the grand staircase, of which the walls and ceiling are richly embellished with plaster ornament, the steps Dutch Oak, enriched brackets, mahogany railing, and fancied ironwork, which leads to the principal story (Fig. 15). On the west side of the ban-

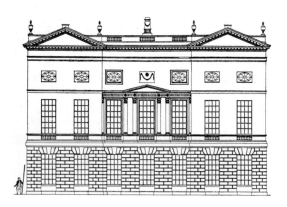

Fig. 14. The Guildhall. East elevation.

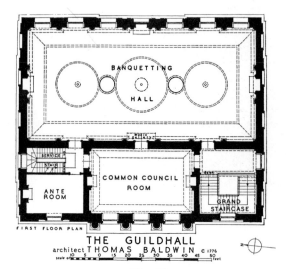

Fig. 15.

A contemporary account described the original arrangements of the interior:

'The basement consists of a noble kitchen, 39 ft. long, 31 ft. wide, and

queting room is a drawing room 37 ft. long, 22 ft. wide and 16 ft. high (occasionally used as a Council Room), this room has a cove ceiling, stucco walls, cornice, door and chimneys enriched. There is a private withdrawing room and water-closets for the ladies, and at the other end of the building, and on the same floor, water-closets for the gentlemen. The attic story consists of bedrooms, etc., for the hallkeeper; surveyor's office, storerooms, etc.'

The banqueting hall, which is approximately 80 ft. long, 40 ft. wide, and 31 ft. high, is beyond any question the finest interior in Bath, and a masterpiece of late eighteenth-century decoration. Each side wall is divided into seven bays of equal width, by engaged half-columns, with quarter-columns in the angles, having pedestals, fluted shafts, and Corinthian capitals of an original design. The second, fourth and sixth bays are treated as

shallow arched recesses, with moulded archivolts springing from an entablature which has its frieze enriched with festoons of husks ranged between rams' heads, vases and anthemion ornaments. This entablature is returned into the arched recesses and continued across with a frieze decoration of fluting and paterae. Each bay of the east side wall contains a window except that in the centre, where there is a fire-place, richly ornamented and surmounted by a panel filled with delicate plaster arabesques surrounding the City Arms. The arch lunette is filled with a radiating design of acanthus and honeysuckle ornaments. In the spandrels between the arches are clerestory windows of oval form, resting within festoons of husks looped over paterae. The west wall is without windows and the central arch is deeply recessed to contain a gallery for musicians, with a doorway below.

The Guildhall. Main staircase.

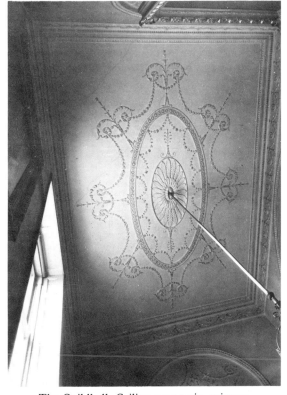

The Guildhall. Ceiling over main staircase.

The Guildhall. Banqueting Room.

The two remaining arched recesses also contain doorways, all with fine mahogany double-doors set within an orthodox architectural frame of architrave, frieze and cornice. The intervening bays are simply decorated with large panels, providing fields for pictures, and the clerestory windows opposite are echoed by their counterparts in modelled plasterwork. Each end wall is divided into three bays, that in the middle being treated as an arched recess, containing a fire-place with a plain panel over, and a lunette decoration identical with that on the east wall. The walls are finished with a continuous frieze of Vitruvian scrolling, surmounted by an enriched cornice from which rises the quadrant cove, decorated with diminishing honeysuckle ornament in the angles, and panels of fluting corresponding in width and position to the arched recesses. The main ceiling is flat, and decorated with three great circular panels, that in the middle being the largest, framed in a guilloche moulding which connects them with two intermediate grilles, contained in circular panels of a much smaller diameter. The large panels are filled with elaborate designs in plasterwork, arranged to radiate from central bosses of acanthus leaves. From these latter depend the three magnificent four-tier chandeliers of crystal, which surpass even those of the Assembly Rooms in the delicate intricacy of their design.

The Guildhall. Banqueting Hall.
Fireplace on east wall.

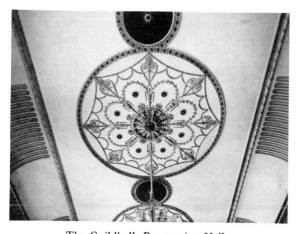

The Guildhall. Banqueting Hall.
Central panel of ceiling.

HOSPITALS AND CHARITIES

The General Hospital (renamed The Royal Mineral Water Hospital)

Although Nash, Allen, Oliver and Wood are the names most commonly associated in the public mind with the founding of The Charity of the General Hospital or Infirmary, the idea originated in 1716 with the Lady Elizabeth Hastings and Henry Hoare, who tried to enlist public support for a scheme to provide hospital accommodation for the deserving poor who came to Bath for their health's sake. In 1723 Sir Joseph Jekyl opened a subscription for the same cause, which met with sufficient support to justify the subscribers appointing some of their number to form a committee to administer the charity. This first committee included such well-known public figures as Richard Nash, Archdeacon Hunt, Henry Hoare, the Doctors Bave, Beeston, Bettenson and Cheyne, and the surgeon Jeremiah Pierce. Humphrey Thayer was chosen to act as secretary, and, early in 1727, brought John Wood into the scheme, Thayer promising that he and several others would each subscribe £100 towards the building fund, as soon as a site could be agreed upon and plans drawn up. Wood's first choice of a site at the north corner of the Ambury was influenced by its open aspect and nearness to the Hot Bath, from which spring it was proposed to feed the bath to be incorporated in the hospital building. Wood prepared alternative designs for building to a rectangular and circular plan, and although the landlord, Robert Gay, was at first opposed to the idea, Wood obtained not only his consent to the proposal, but a promise to give sufficient of his land to accommodate the selected design, which was for a circular building 70 ft. in diameter, with the bath in the centre. Matters were almost settled when Sir Joseph Jekyl insisted that the building should be planned and sited to permit future extensions to be made when funds permitted, in consequence of which Gay withdrew his offer and the scheme was permitted to lapse.

There followed an interim period of nearly

ten years, during which plans for various sites were submitted and rejected, before Wood made designs for a building on the Borough Walls site occupied by the old theatre, which had fallen into disuse when public playhouses were suppressed. Several of the original trustees of the charity had died by this time, and their places taken by others, of whom the most famous was Dr. William Oliver, who, making the cause his own, offered to give some of his land for the building, an offer at first accepted but rejected later in favour of the theatre site.

During January 1738 the trustees again appealed to the public for assistance, and a plan and elevation of the proposed building was published and circulated to promote the success of this and a further appeal, which resulted in some £2,000 being subscribed. On May 13th, 1738, demolition of the old theatre was begun and on July 6th following, the first stone was laid at the north-east corner of the new hospital, by William Pulteney, afterwards Earl of Bath. On this stone, which is no longer visible, was cut the following inscription:

> THIS STONE
> IS THE FIRST WHICH WAS
> LAID
> IN THE FOUNDATION OF THE
> GENERAL HOSPITAL
> JULY THE SIXTH A.D. 1738
> GOD
> PROSPER THE CHARITABLE UNDERTAKING

Wood fills some thirty pages of his *Essay* with a detailed account of the efforts made by himself, with others having the cause at heart, to accomplish the building of this hospital. His final remarks and a description of his designs are quoted below, with minor amendments of spelling and punctuation.

'The printed Plan of the Hospital was, for the sake of ornament, and to gain a point in the purchase of the land, made different to that which was intended for execution, but when the last bargain was completed for a stable belonging to Mr. William Boyes, at the south-west corner of the land purchased of Mrs. Carne, I produced the real plan to the trustees, who approving of it on the 25th of August, 1738, ordered it to be carried into execution instead of that which was printed. And thus, after more than eleven years spent in fruitless attempts, the work was put upon such a footing as to be carried on without the least impediment . . .

'The hospital, as it was finally fixed, upon August 25th, 1738, became a magnificent pile of building, of the Ionic order, consisting of a ground, principal, and chamber-story, and extending 99 ft. in front to the north, 84 ft. to the west, and 97 ft. to the east. The east and west sides are parallel, but they are not at right-angles with the north front, which contains five windows on each side of the door, and the central part of it makes a tetrastyle frontispiece, of almost whole columns, elevated upon a large plinth, and finished with a pediment, whose tympanum was proposed to be adorned with a bas-relief representing the Good Samaritan.

'The west front of this structure contains nine windows in its whole length, and this being divided into three parts, the middle part advances forward, and was intended to have been finished with a pediment, in the tympanum of which there was to have been a bas-relief representing the Pool of Bethesda. A principal and half-story appears between the plinth and crowning in this and the north front, and the quick descent of the ground, from north to south, increases the basement of the building so much to the west, that the plinth appears as a face to a three-quarter-story.

'The entrance into the building being in the north front, we first come into a vestibule, which has on the left side a room for the apothecary, another for the doctors; and on the right side there is the matron's parlour and bed chamber, with a room for the surgeons. To the south of this room, and in the west front of the building, there is a committee room, a secretary's office, and a room for the steward; parallel to which is the first ward for men, with a passage between that ward and the front rooms. In the east front of the hospital there is a spacious room adapted for a ward for women, and almost facing the vestibule the chief staircase is placed, a passage lying between it and the back part of the rooms in the north front, and extending from the women's ward to the west front wall of the building.

'The chamber-story of the hospital is divided into five wards, and the ground-(basement) story is appropriated for offices and lodgings for some of the servants of the house. The seven wards are capable of holding one hundred and eight beds, exclusive of those for the nurses, and the building may be enlarged to the south to receive any reasonable number of patients, since the land is in possession of such persons as have expressed an inclination to sell it to the governors of the charity.'

One of the most practical benefactors to the charity was Ralph Allen, who not only gave considerable sums of money, but supplied free from charge the whole of the 'wrought free stones, paving stones, wall stones, and lime', that were used in erecting the hospital.

By 1790 the accommodation of the building had become inadequate, and, after a proposal to remove to new premises had been rejected, the governors considered adopting the plans of

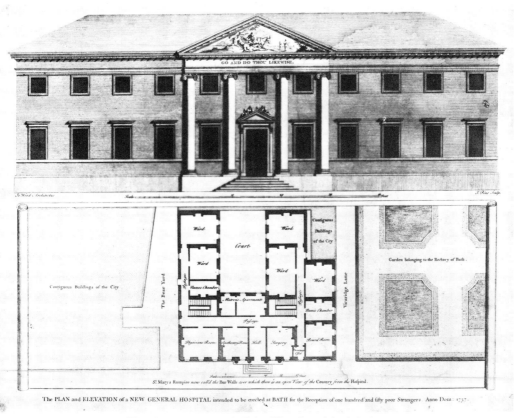

The General Hospital. John Wood's original design.

Baldwin for enlarging and improving the existing hospital. No further action was taken until round about 1793, when John Palmer was employed to add the heavy attic story which has proved so detrimental to the appearance of Wood's original design. The Royal Arms in the tympanum of the pediment was added towards the end of the last century, for although the sculptor Matthyssens prepared cartoons and a model for the bas-relief intended by Wood, his design was not executed. The tympanum of the pediment to the hospital extension, built during 1850–60 from designs by Manners and Gill, contains a relief of 'The Good Samaritan' carved by Ezard and obviously influenced by Matthyssens' studies.

The United Hospital (now the Technical School)

During the early part of 1823 it was resolved to effect a union between the Bath city infirmary and the casualty hospital, and the joint committee of those institutions employed John Pinch to prepare three different designs for the new hospital on as many different sites, the building to cost £5,000 exclusive of the ground. A site in Beau Street was eventually chosen, opposite to the Hot Bath and adjacent to the infirmary which was then housed in a large mansion built during the early eighteenth century for Dr. Bave. It was decided to proceed immediately with the new building, of which the foundation-stone was laid on August 6th, 1824, and the hospital opened for the reception of patients on June 24th, 1826.

The main front to Beau Street is bold in scale and severe in expression, exhibiting little of the gracious delicacy of Pinch's domestic work. It is, nevertheless, a fine composition, originally consisting of three lofty stories raised upon a basement plinth and vertically divided to form a central feature of three bays standing slightly forward from flanking wings, having four windows to each story. All the windows to the ground-floor are segmental-headed, those of the wings being set in a wall of masonry with the horizontal and voussoir joints rusticated, while the piers and arches framing the central doorway and flanking windows form a triple-arcaded base for the portico above the first-floor platband. This three-bay portico provides the chief focal interest, its two giant columns, with plain shafts and Ionic capitals, and corresponding antae carrying the panelled lintel which underlines the entablature and triangular pediment, of which the tympanum contains a carving of the City Arms and supporters. The two tiers of windows in the upper part of the wings are without architraves, but a pedestal course underlines those to the first-floor, and the plain sill continues below the upper range. The main entablature is returned and continued across the wings. Considerable additions, including the disproportionately heavy attic-story, were made to the building round about 1860, by Manners and Gill.

Partis College

Partis College was built and endowed by the widow of Fletcher Partis, in fulfilment of his intention to found a charity providing lodging and partial maintenance for thirty gentlewomen of reduced circumstances, to each of whom is allotted a four-roomed dwelling. Samuel and Philip Flood Page, of London, designed the buildings, which are sited at Newbridge Hill, some two miles west of the city centre. Partis College was completed in 1827, the chapel having been consecrated during the previous year.

The buildings are ranged round three sides of a quadrangular open space and form three detached blocks, of which the elevations are excellently detailed compositions in the current Greek Revival taste. The principal range faces the roadway and has for its central feature a chapel, fronted with a fine hexastyle portico of Ionic columns, with plain shafts, supporting an entablature and triangular pediment. On each side is a two-storied wing containing lodgings, with a simple elevational treatment consisting of regularly spaced door and window openings, set in a plain wall face

The former Freemasons' Hall, now the Friends Meeting House.

Partis College. Exterior from south-east.

which is finished with an entablature and dwarf parapet. The end lodgings are treated to form terminal pavilions, each building face being subdivided into three equal bays by plain-shafted Doric pilasters, and the pedestal parapet being increased in height over the middle bay. The smaller ranges of lodgings, at right-angles to the roadway, are flanked by similar terminal pavilions and treated in the same manner as the wings of the main building.

PLEASURE GARDENS AND HOTELS

Alfresco entertainments were a prominent feature of the social round during the seasons at Bath, the amusements offered following in the tradition of Vauxhall and Ranelagh Gardens, and consisting of public breakfasts, teas and dinners, musical entertainments and pyrotechnical displays, of which latter the most famous were those devised by the ingenious Signor Invetto at Sydney Gardens during the early nineteenth century.

At first the company resorted to Harrison's Walks and the Bowling Greens, but round about 1735 the scene of these activities was transferred to Bathwick, where Spring Gardens, and at a later date Bathwick Villa, continued to flourish until they, in their turn, were superseded by the magnificent rival establishments of Grosvenor and Sydney Gardens, both opened during the final decade of the eighteenth century. Bathwick Villa, originally a private residence, was a charming 'Gothick' structure, possibly built by the same hand as the Vineyards Chapel, which it closely resembled. The villa was demolished after serving a variety of purposes and its surrounding gardens were partly built over, while the Spring Gardens became a builder's yard, tenanted in turn by Eveleigh and Pinch.

Grosvenor

The great range of houses stretching along the London Road and forming Grosvenor Place is the only completed part of the immense building scheme designed by John Eveleigh, and undertaken by him in conjunction with William Hewlett and other speculating builders. Eveleigh's ledgers contain several references to this project including two items quoted below, which are in respect of fees charged to Hewlett and Townsend, with whom the speculation probably originated.

1791. To Messrs. Hewlett and Townsend:
Surveying and drawing a Plan of two fields belonging to Mr. Collibee and Mr. Hooper, London Road £3 3
Drawing Designs for Buildings, etc., in the above fields, and Elevations for Grosvenor Place, Grosvenor Street and Cumberland Street, Levelling, Setting Out, drawing Elevations and Outlays for different builders, and many attendances £31 10

'The first Stone of Grosvenor House, Vauxhall, was laid on June 24th, 1791, by John Eveleigh, Architect, being the Centre of 143 intended Houses, and at the entrance of Vauxhall Gardens, which will be build by Subscription, laid out with taste and elegance for the reception of Nobility, Gentry and the Public in general.'

This was the legend inscribed on a lead plate, placed under the foundation-stone of the hotel, which was laid at a ceremony accompanied by cannon firing and concluded with 'a liberal treat of beer' being given to the workmen and bystanders. The contemporary account states that

'the plan exhibits nearly a square, formed by a line of handsome houses towards the road, and the Avon, leaving a space of about 20 acres within, where there is to be a room of size and accommodation to entertain upwards of 2,000 people, and pleasure gardens are to be planted next autumn (regardless of expense and opposition) with the utmost exertion of taste and fancy—A full one-third of the above ground for these Houses is already taken'.

The scheme was centred around the hotel and pleasure gardens, for which a most elaborate layout was devised, including a 'saloon with organ, mechanism and orchestras, hot and cold greenhouses, conservatories, kitchen gardens, vineries, aviary, temple with chimes, labyrinth with merlin swings and cave, grotto, alcoves, etc.' During May 1792 Eveleigh advertised that the forward state of the gardens enabled him to invite intending subscribers to send him their addresses so that a committee of management could be formed. Subscriptions were to be £100 per share, entitling the subscriber to two tickets of admission to the gardens for each year. By the following September pleasure boats were plying between Eveleigh's wharf in Bathwick and the gardens, where parties were accommodated with teas.

Failure to obtain the necessary public support of the scheme upon which he had already spent over £7,000, forced Eveleigh to offer his share in the unfinished buildings for sale in November 1793. His interests were purchased for £5,500 by the mortgagees of the property, who put forward fresh proposals in May 1794, inviting subscriptions of £50 per share, to raise the £5,000 required to complete the hotel and gardens. The prevailing uncertainty of the times must have limited any efforts to finish the buildings, for *The New Bath Guide* for 1801 states that 'In Grosvenor Gardens is now erecting a spacious Hotel with a delightful garden, of near 14 acres, laid out with great taste for summer and winter amusements. . . . It is so far completed that Company may be accommodated with breakfasts, afternoon teas, and dinners, at proper notice. Subscribers for walking in the gardens pay 7*s*. 6*d*. the season, for bowling 3*s*. 9*d*., and for angling 3*s*. 0*d*. Pleasure boats attend.'

The eventual failure and closure of the gardens was due to the unfortunate choice of a low-lying site, subjected to mists and floods and in no way comparable with the superior and more easily accessible situation of the competing Sydney Gardens. The hotel and many of the houses remained in the unfinished state commented upon by Egan in his *Walks through Bath*, published in 1819. Eventually altered and completed to house the Grosvenor College, the former hotel has now been converted into flats and its remarkable front restored.

Grosvenor is one of the most exciting buildings in Bath, and the unquestioned masterpiece of John Eveleigh. Interest is naturally focused on the central hotel building, exuberantly decorated with rich detail and thrown into prominence by the sweep and simplicity of the flanking ranges of houses.

The hotel was originally designed with a carriage way into the gardens beyond, through a wide segmental-arched opening forming the centre of the ground-story, and treated to accord with the two windows on either side. These are set within plain margins recessed between rusticated and vermiculated piers, with moulded imposts from which spring arches of rusticated masonry with keystones carved into icicle-work masks. Above the first-floor platband the front is divided into six equal bays, by seven engaged columns of a giant order centred over the piers and keystone of the centre arch. These columns are raised upon pedestals and are composed of richly moulded bases, plain shafts of oval section decked at three intervals with bands of ribboned garlands, of which the lowest remains uncarved, and Ionic capitals with undercut floral garlands dependent between the volutes. Rectangular windows of equal size light the first and second floors, and are set without architrave surrounds in the bays between the columns. Below the first-floor windows there are blind balustrades continuing the lines of the column pedestals, while the upper range is underlined by a moulded sill continued between the columns. In each bay the wall face between the two tiers of windows is relieved by an oval panel, only three of which have been

Grosvenor Place. General view.

Grosvenor Place. Front of hotel, or tavern.

Grosvenor Place. Group of houses in the west wing.

carved with the emblematic subjects originally intended. Only the columns are crowned by the full entablature, with an oval patera carved on each section of the frieze, but the rich modillioned cornice is broken back and returned across the bays. The surmounting parapet consists of open balustrades between projecting pedestals centred over the columns.

The houses flanking the hotel are set well back from the London Road, with a private carriage way behind long and narrow strips of garden. Most of the houses conform to a standard type with three stories, basement and roof attic. The uniformly treated fronts have three superimposed tiers of three openings, equal in spacing, width and height, all without architraves but with projecting voussoirs to the flat arches of the ground and first-floor openings. The moulded continuous sills underlining the first- and second-floor windows, and the crowning entablature and plain parapet, group the houses into wings between intermediate pavilions. Each pavilion is composed of a similar house, slightly set forward and with a rusticated ground-story, on either side of a wide and tall house with five lofty windows to each of the upper floors, and the entablature and parapet raised by means of concave quadrant ramps at the party-wall lines. Each wing of houses is planned to sweep forward in a wide cyma curve to meet up with the hotel block. The projecting porches to several of the houses and to the hotel are additions made when the buildings were completed, and are detailed in the Greek Revival taste of the time.

The gardens are now used for horticultural purposes, but a fragment of building remains in the form of an arch, decorated with Doric columns, possibly forming part of a rotunda.

Sydney Gardens, Vauxhall and Ranelagh

Although Thomas Baldwin first promoted the scheme to build an hotel and lay out extensive pleasure gardens in the hexagonal enclosure of Sydney Place, and even advertised for builders to tender for the work during 1794, the project was actually carried out by Charles Harcourt Masters, who may possibly have based his designs on those of Baldwin. The gardens were first opened to the public during May 1795, but the foundation-stone of the hotel, or tavern, was not laid until November 15th, 1796. The building was altered and an attic-story added in 1836 by John Pinch the younger, who also prepared plans for building villas around the perimeter of the gardens. During the heyday of the gardens an attendance of some four thousand visitors was no uncommon occurrence, but when the public taste for alfresco entertainments declined, the gardens were taken over by the Bath Band and Floral Fête Committee, until the property was acquired in 1910 by the City Corporation. For a number of years the hotel was occupied by the Sydney College, but afterwards became untenanted and was in a semi-derelict condition when the trustees of the Holburne Museum purchased it in 1915. The late Sir Reginald Blomfield was employed to adapt the building for its new purpose, and managed to infuse a Gallic flavour which has quite altered the original character of Masters' work.

Fig. 16. Thomas Baldwin's design for the Sydney Hotel, dated February 3rd, 1794, and signed by a committee of subscribers, including C. Harcourt Masters.

Sydney House, as the hotel was named, was originally designed as a three-storied building, detailed with the somewhat attenuated classical taste of its period. The principal front facing Great Pulteney Street is dominated by its central feature, consisting of a portico projecting from the main building and based on a ground-story loggia. This latter consists of three equal arches with rusticated piers and voussoirs, and a similar arch in each return face. The keystones of the arches project slightly and die into the architrave of the surmounting entablature, which has a frieze carving of vases over the keystones, flanked by a double festoon between triglyphs over the piers. The ground-story to the flanking wings was originally continued beyond the building to form screen walls on either side, finished

Fig. 17. Sydney Hotel. Front elevation.

with the same enriched entablature and broken by tall rectangular windows. The portico, which embraces the two upper stories, is divided into three equal bays by Corinthian columns with plain shafts, the main building face being decorated with corresponding antae, and the entablature is surmounted by a triangular pediment with a plain tympanum. There are five rectangular windows lighting the first-floor, three being contained within the portico, and while all are dressed with thin pilaster-strips and consoles supporting decorated entablatures, the single window to each wing is finished with a triangular pediment. There was originally a tier of five square windows lighting the second floor, which were set within architraves rising from moulded sills with console supports. The main entablature is continued across the wings, but with the lower members of the architrave omitted. The building was originally finished with a pedestal parapet having sections of balustrading to correspond with the wing windows (Fig. 17). The delicate railings between the columns of

the portico were probably added when the building was altered by Pinch.

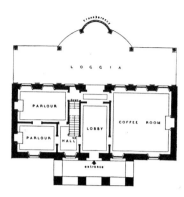

Fig. 18. Sydney Hotel. Ground-story plan.

The garden front has been completely altered, but its original appearance can be seen in the aquatint drawing by Nattes. From the ground-story of the main building projected a deep loggia, divided into three wide bays by Doric columns, the segmental middle bay being subdivided into three smaller bays, with a panel for transparencies occupying the centre. Above this loggia was a conservatory with large sash-windows, and an open orchestra occupied the segmental bay. Hemicycles of small alcoves, for private parties, extended from either side of the main building.

The original layout of the gardens is described in *The New Bath Guide* for 1801, where it is stated that:

'Sydney Gardens, Vauxhall, contains about 16 acres, interspersed with a great number of small, delightful groves, pleasant vistoes, and charming lawns, intersected by serpentine walks, which at every turn meet with sweet, shady bowers, furnished with handsome seats, some composed by nature, others by art. It is decorated with waterfalls, stone and thatched pavilions, alcoves; the Kennet and Avon Canal running through, with two elegant cast-iron bridges thrown over it, after the manner of the Chinese; a

Sydney Hotel, or Tavern. Garden Front.
(Aquatint drawing by J. C. Nattes, 1806)

sham castle planted with several pieces of cannon, bowling greens, swings, a labyrinth formed by enclosed pathways, the principal one of which, after many intricate windings, leads to a fine Merlin swing, and a grotto of antique appearance. On this way four thatched umbrellas are placed at equal distances from each other, which are intended to serve as a shelter from sudden rains and storms.'

Some features of this layout can be traced in the present arrangements, but the original charm has been largely obscured by the Victorian growth of laurels and other over-hardy evergreens. A charming rotunda with Ionic columns and serpentine screen walls, is an original feature still remaining at the east end of the gardens.

THE PRISON
(now converted into flats)

The Corporation's minutes for June 25th, 1765, record the grant of the site of the old city prison, housed within the tower of St. Mary's Church, 'to William Pulteney, on condition that he procures for the City a piece of ground 80 ft. by 60 ft. by the river and within 300 yds. from the east end of his intended bridge, for the purpose of building a New

Prison'. Besides granting the site, Pulteney commissioned Robert Adam to prepare a design for the prison, but local prejudice and intrigue led the Corporation to adopt the design made by Thomas Warr Atwood, for a building on a more modest scale than that proposed by Adam.

Although Atwood's plans were approved on September 24th, 1770, it was not until May 7th, 1772, that the foundation-stone was laid by the Mayor, John Horton. The building was probably finished by the end of 1773, for the records show that Atwood was to attend the Corporation on January 27th, 1774, to pass the accounts for the new prison and waterworks.

Contemporary descriptions of Atwood's building state its dimensions to be 60 by 80 ft., whereas it measures only 60 by 30 ft., the larger dimensions being those of Adam's intended building.

The building has three stories with a basement and roof attic, but the formation of Grove Street, intended for warehouses and made almost level with the river bank, has brought the original basement above street level, greatly detracting from the effectiveness of the design. The front is a scholarly essay in the Palladian manner, using the motifs commonly applied to domestic buildings erected at that time in the city. A central feature, three

The Prison. Grove Street.

windows wide, is slightly recessed between narrow pavilions with a single window to each tier. The rusticated ground story has a blind arch framing a rectangular window in each wing, and an arch of smaller radius in the middle of the front formed the original entrance. Above the platband is a pedestal course to the first-floor windows, which are dressed with moulded architraves, friezes and cornices, triangular pediments supported on consoles serving to accent the centre and end lights. The five windows to the second floor are set within moulded architraves, and the modillioned main cornice is surmounted by an open balustraded parapet, with solid dies at regular intervals.

SCHOOLS

The Blue Coat School (rebuilt 1860)

The Charity, or Blue Coat, School of Bath was founded in 1711 by Robert Nelson, an enlightened citizen, who raised a subscription with the object of providing free clothing and instruction for 50 boys and 50 girls. A site in the Saw Close being given with a generous subscription by the Corporation, William Killigrew was employed to design the schoolhouse, of which the foundation-stone, inscribed 'God's Providence is our Inheritance', was laid by Henry Hoare on October 12th, 1722.

Wood described Killigrew's building as measuring 60 ft. 3 in. in length, 22 ft. 3 in. in breadth at the east end, and 28 ft. 6 in. at the west end, and various engravings show it to have consisted of two lofty stories, raised upon a basement and crowned with a high attic. The principal elevation was a typical example of Killigrew's work, having many points in common with his other buildings. The two tiers of windows were arranged to form groups of two on either side of a group of three, the middle window of each tier being combined into an architectural feature composed of superimposed orders crowned by a segmental pediment. Between the window groups, and

Fig. 19. The Blue Coat School (demolished 1860)

(from Egan's 'Walks through Bath' 1819).

on a level with the aprons of the second-floor tier, were shallow niches designed for the reception of statuary. The attic-story was finished with three pediment-like gables, that in the centre being broken into by a bell turret, its ogee cap surmounted by a dragon vane (Fig. 19). This very interesting example of pre-Wood architecture was demolished in 1860 to make way for the present building designed by Manners and Gill.

The Grammar School

At the time of Wood's settlement in Bath the Free Grammar School of King Edward the Sixth was housed in the body of the secularized church of St. Mary, by the North Gate, the tower forming the city prison. This unsuitable arrangment led the Corporation to appoint a committee to consider proposals for a new building, and Wood was instructed to

The Grammar School. Front to Broad Street.

The Theatre Royal. Grand front to Beauford Square.

prepare the designs which he submitted in September 1742. He suggested building on the open area known as the Town Acre, but the Corporation having other plans for developing this particular site, Wood's proposals were rejected.

In 1744 the Corporation purchased the site of 'The Black Swan' inn on the east side of Broad Street, and the official minutes for March 5th record the decision that 'Thomas Jelly's plan be used for building the free school provided he bring an estimate for the expense'. Jelly was a capable designer and builder who was probably responsible for other Bath buildings of this time which have been loosely ascribed to John Wood. The foundation-stone for the new school was laid on May 29th, 1752, by Francis Hales, the Mayor, at a ceremony attended by members of the Corporation and the principal trade guilds. The builders were Jelly, Sainsbury, Brown and Smith, and the master mason, John Ford, who carried out a great deal of work for the Woods.

The principal front to Broad Street is an excellent Palladian composition, two stories high on a basement plinth, with a central feature three windows wide, broken slightly forward from narrow wings, each one window wide. The central doorway has engaged three-quarter Ionic columns and pilasters supporting an entablature and triangular pediment. Both tiers of windows are dressed with eared architraves, the inner members now cut away, and those to the ground-floor are surmounted by pulvinated friezes and segmental pediments. The modillioned main cornice is surmounted by an open balustrade over the wings, which breaks against the triangular pediment crowning the central feature. Busts of worthies are placed above the dies and on the apex of the pediment, which has in its tympanum the City Arms, carved with baroque vigour by 'Mr. Plura, the statuary' who received a total payment of 41 guineas for this work and the five busts. The piers to the shallow forecourt are nearly contemporary, but the connecting stone balustrading is modern and replaced an original iron railing.

The Bath and District National School (demolished)

The foundation-stone of the National School was laid with all due ceremony on October 16th, 1816, and the building opened for use on September 9th, 1816. The site was formerly occupied by the gardens of Weymouth House, designed by Killigrew, part of which was demolished and the remaining fragment incorporated into the new building. The school accommodated 1,000 pupils and was one of the first establishments to be conducted according to the educational theories advanced by Dr. Andrew Bell. The wedge-shaped classrooms conformed to a circular plan, the two-story elevation being treated in a simple Classic manner. The architect was John Lowder, a wealthy amateur who accepted no fees for his services, either in this or in his later work of building Holy Trinity Church. This curious school building was entirely demolished round about 1896, when the present Weymouth House Schools were built on the site.

THEATRES

During the Georgian era in Bath, several buildings were designed, or adapted to serve as theatres, of which the two most famous still survive to a substantial degree. Of these, the Orchard Street Theatre is historically more famous, but is far surpassed in architectural importance by its successor, the Theatre Royal in Beauford Square.

The Orchard Street Theatre (now the Freemasons' Hall)

The building of a new theatre in Bath was first projected in 1747 by John Hippisley, an actor, whose elaborately worded appeal for public support is fully quoted in Wood's Essay. This scheme was strongly opposed by the proprietors of 'Mr. Simpson's Theatre' described by Wood as 'a cellar under part of the Ballroom of Simpson's Assembly House which had been opened to succeed the original playhouse in Borough Walls, built in 1705 and demolished round about 1737 to provide the site for the General Hospital. Wood was actively interested in Hippisley's scheme and made plans for a theatre 'proposed to have been sixty Feet Long, and forty Feet Broad in the clear: it was to Front Westward to Orchard Street: and the Front was to have consisted of a Rustick Basement, supporting the Dorick Order: The Expence of Building it was computed at about one thousand Pounds.'

Hippisley's death gave only a temporary setback to the scheme, for the idea was afterwards taken up by John Palmer, a wealthy brewer and chandler, whose proposals, when issued to intending subscribers during March 1749, met with such success that work on the building was begun soon afterwards. Although the site chosen was that selected by Wood he was not employed to design the building, which was probably the work of Thomas Jelly, whose partner William Sainsbury is named as the occupant of a site identical with this one, in an old deed relating to some adjacent property in the Royal Forum. The theatre was a building of few architectural pretensions, for its exterior differs in no way from many of the houses built at the time, except for the width of its pedimented doorcase, and it may be presumed that the interior was at first of a corresponding simplicity.

The rapid development of Wood's Upper Town, and the general migration of fashionable society to that quarter, brought proposals for building a larger and more conveniently situated theatre. Palmer decided to counter these proposals by enlarging and generally improving his building, plans and estimates for the work being submitted by Jelly's partner, John Palmer the architect. These were rejected through the influence of one Mr. Arthur, the theatre manager, who had the auditorium remodelled according to this own ideas, with 'Gothick' decorations and a domed ceiling adorned with an 'alto-relievo of Apollo and the Muses'. In spite of the general approbation which greeted these decorations when the theatre reopened, they were soon wearied of and, what was worse, the dome was found to interfere with the sighting and the acoustics. It was, therefore, necessary to reconstruct the auditorium once more in 1775, when Palmer was entrusted with the work. The auditorium was increased in size and capacity, Arthur's offending dome was removed and replaced by an efficently ventilated ceiling, and a new proscenium was installed, decorated with columns of the Doric and Ionic orders. Palmer's improvements appear to have been entirely satisfactory, for there is no record of any further changes being made to the building up to the time of its closure in 1805.

The Orchard Street Theatre, like all playhouses, had its vicissitudes, but during its most successful period, which lasted from 1790 until the closing performance on July 13th, 1805, it was visited by almost all players of note in the British theatre of that time, and only the great London theatres surpassed it in fame and importance. It subsequently became a Roman Catholic Chapel in 1809, and later the Freemasons' Hall. Damaged by blast during the German air raids, it has been saved from impending demolition and restored.

The Theatre Royal, Beauford Square (rebuilt internally after the fire of 1862)

The scheme for building a new theatre to replace the inadequate house in Orchard Street was originally formulated during 1802, but no public announcement was made until August 1804, when the promoters opened a subscription, on the tontine principle, to cover the building cost. Shares were rapidly taken up, with several members of the Royal Family heading the list of subscribers, and in the following month work was begun in clearing the site, which consisted of some gardens and outbuildings belonging to houses in St. John's Court and forming the south side of Beauford Square. The foundation-stone was laid in December, and the new theatre opened on October 12th, 1805. The interior was completely destroyed by fire on April 18th, 1862, but the fine elevation towards Beauford Square, with the other walls and staircases which had remained structurally sound, were incorporated into the present theatre, designed by C. J. Phipps and opened in 1863.

Fig. 20. The Theatre Royal, Grand Front in Beauford Square

(from Egan's 'Walks through Bath' 1819).

The Theatre Royal was built under the superintendence of John Palmer, but the credit for designing the main front towards Beauford Square, and the original interiors, must rest with George Dance the younger (see Appendix 3). The most adequate description of the building is contained in Volume 13 of *The Beauties of England and Wales*, and quoted below:

'There are three entrances, in as many directions, the grand front being in Beaufort Square. The audience part is somewhat less than was that of the late Covent Garden Theatre, but the space behind the curtain is much larger. The length, within the main walls, is one hundred and twenty feet; the breadth sixty feet; and the height seventy. The exterior buildings, containing dressing-rooms, scene-room, wardrobe, and every other convenience for the artists, servants, etc.; the anti-rooms, and saloons to the boxes; rooms to the numerous private boxes; taverns, etc., are very extensive.

There are three tiers of boxes, excessively lofty, and affording a depth of nine rows towards the centre. Cast iron bronzed pillars are placed at a distance of two feet from the front, by which the first row of each circle appears as a balcony, independent of the main structure, and an inconceivable lightness is communicated to the *tout ensemble*. The private boxes are inclosed with gilt lattices: the entrance to them is by a private house, part of the property connected with the theatre, and they are accommodated with a suite of retiring rooms. The decorations are very splendid, particularly the ceiling, which is divided into five compartments, each of which is adorned by one of those exquisite paintings by Cassali, formerly belonging to Font Hill, Wilts. The wreaths of flowers, etc., which connect these paintings are executed with great skill and taste. The walls are covered with stamped cloth, stuffed, of a crimson colour, and are papered above to the top of the boxes, with paper of the same colour: an Egyptian pattern, fringed with a gold stripe. The seats and edges of the boxes are also covered with cloth. The front is painted of the same colour, with four broad stripes of gold, and the centre ornamented with tasteful scrolls of gold.'

The allegorical paintings of Andrea Casali, which formed an important feature of the decoration, were on octagonal canvas panels, which Dance incorporated into a design of elaborate delicacy, using plaster ornament of the same character as that in the ceiling of the eating-room at Pitzhanger Manor. The paintings, given by Paul Methuen of Corsham, were removed in 1839. Four were sold in 1845 to Colonel Blathwayt who set them in new ceilings at Dyrham, and the fifth is now in Ven House, Milborne Port, Somerset.

The 'Grand Front' in Beauford Square, although grimy, neglected and with its crowning ornaments rapidly decaying, is a very precious survival of Dance's work, full of original thought and detailed with Gallic fastidiousness. The sheaf of drawings relating to this building, which are preserved in the Dance Cabinet at the Soane Museum, show the evolution of the design. As originally built, the ground-story consisted of a range of doors and windows, unified by their being set within a regularly spaced arcade of nine segmental arches, the slightly recessed wings at either end being formed by single arches between wide piers. The windowless main wall of the theatre is set well back, but the forward part of the building is carried up for a further two stories over the five arches in the middle of the ground-story, with the stringcourse mouldings and parapet of the latter forming a pedestal to the first-floor windows. The first- and second-floor windows, of equal width and spacing but graduated in height, are set without architraves in a wall face which wide panelled pilasters divide into five bays. The entablature consists of a delicately moulded architrave; a deep frieze carved with a dramatic mask centred over each pilaster and a ribboned garland above each bay; and a cornice of bold profile. The architrave and cornice are returned and continued across the main wall on either side. Above the dwarf parapet of the central feature, and centred on low plinths over the first two pilasters at either end, are stone lyres, now very much decayed, while the middle bay is crowned by a magnificently vigorous sculptural representation of the Royal Arms (Fig. 20).

THE DOMESTIC BUILDINGS

Introductory Note

The analytical notes contained in this section describe the more important groups of domestic buildings in Bath, together with certain houses of more than ordinary interest; the notes and accompanying illustrations being arranged in chronological sequence and grouped into five periods, each covering twenty-five years, except for that dealing with the first thirty years of the nineteenth century. These detailed descriptions are, of necessity, confined in most instances to the exteriors of buildings, but a general note on planning and construction is given by way of a preface. A comparative selection of annotated illustrations of exterior and interior details, together with a general note on the interior decoration, closes this study.

Most houses can be allotted to one of two distinct categories; those designed to the special requirements of individuals, and those built to conform to an accepted standard of accommodation and intended for sale or lease. Many of the large houses in Queen Square, The Circus, and the Royal Crescent belong to the first category, and show plans and interior decorations of varied interest. The majority of Bath's houses fall within the second group and usually conform to the standard type of terrace house, differing only in dimensions and number of rooms, and in the quality of their internal finishings. Individually, perhaps, they are not of great interest, but collectively their exteriors often combine to form architectural compositions of considerable beauty, expressive of the best qualities to be found in urban design of the Georgian era.

PLANNING

The plan of a typical early eighteenth-century Bath house shows a simple and obvious arrangement of rooms, usually placed at the head and on one or both sides of the staircase landings. The rooms are often small in area and disproportionately lofty, and in some examples the building has only sufficient depth to admit one room between the front and rear walls.

This basic arrangement was improved and the rooms given some architectural sequence by the elder Wood, whose early house planning is exemplified in the arrangements of Nos. 24 and 25 Queen Square (Fig. 21). While No. 25 shows the simple terrace house plan which was to remain more or less standard throughout the Georgian era, No. 24 has a more complicated arrangement of rooms. This large double-fronted house occupies a plot some 45 feet wide, and forms the central feature on the north side of the square. The vestibule, placed in the centre of the front, gives access to a suite of two rooms on each side, and is connected by an arched opening with an inner hall from which the spacious staircase ascends, by way of deep apsidal-ended half-landings, to the first- and second-floors. At the head of the first-floor landing is a small ante-room and on

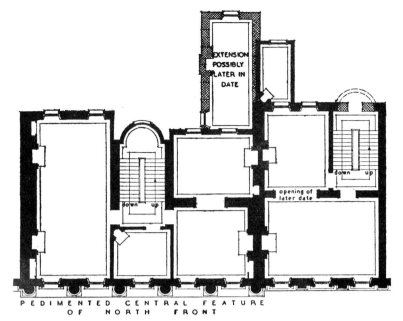

PEDIMENTED CENTRAL FEATURE
OF NORTH FRONT

FIRST FLOOR PLAN

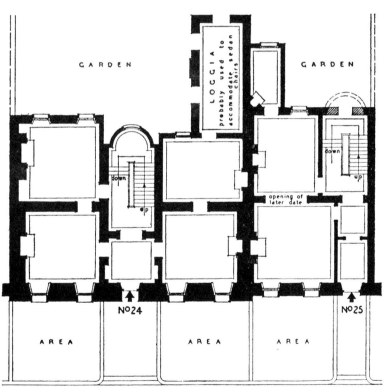

GROUND FLOOR PLAN

HOUSES ON THE NORTH SIDE OF
QUEEN SQUARE
architect·JOHN WOOD THE ELDER·built 1730

Fig. 21.

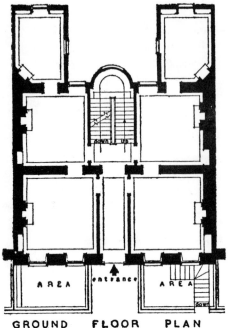

GROUND FLOOR PLAN
HOUSE in the centre of THE
designed by JOHN

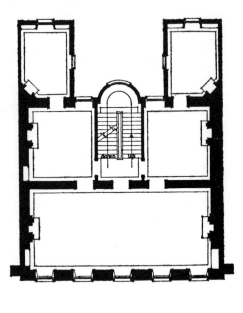

FIRST FLOOR PLAN
GRAND PARADE
WOOD I. c1740

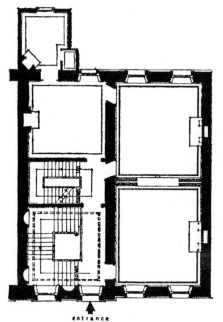

FIRST FLOOR PLAN
Nᵒ 15 QUEEN SQUARE
designed by JOHN WOOD I 1730

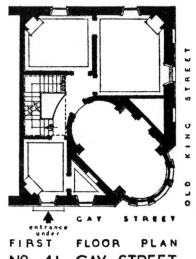

FIRST FLOOR PLAN
Nᵒ 41 GAY STREET
designed by J WOOD I 1740

scale of 10 5 0 5 10 15 20 25 30 35 40 45 50 feet

Fig. 22.

each side is a suite of two rooms. The light construction of the partition separating the rooms on the left would seem to indicate that these originally formed one long drawing-room. The main staircase finishes at the second-floor, which is given over to bedrooms and dressing-rooms, and a side staircase gives access to the attics. Kitchens and staff accommodation are contained in the basement, and extensions at the rear of the main building provide stabling and a portico for sedan-chairs. The two small rooms at the far end of the garden are presumed to have served as 'necessary houses'.

Changes in conditions of living and purpose have caused minor alterations to be made which have been detrimental to the internal appearance of this house, but the essential fact that this and similar houses were planned to provide suites of lodgings with some additional large rooms for entertaining, is often overlooked by those who criticize Wood's planning as immature and unpractical. In the centre of the North Parade, built some ten years later than Queen Square, is a large house of similar plan which has remained singularly free from alterations (Fig. 22). The original arrangments appear to be well adapted to its present use as a private hotel, under conditions which nearly approximate to those for which the house was built.

No. 15 Queen Square is a well-planned house designed by the elder Wood for 'Mr. Greville' (Fig. 22). The principal rooms on the ground- and first-floors are served by a splendid staircase contained in a two-story hall on the front of the building, while a secondary staircase gives access to all floors. An effective and convenient arrangement of rooms is shown in the plan of No. 41 Gay Street (Fig. 22). This is a house of moderate size, built at the corner of Gay and Old King Streets, with the principal room on each floor placed diagonally to command a view across Queen Square. These beautifully proportioned rooms are planned as a square, lengthened by the addition of two semi-circular apses, one containing the three-light window, and the other a centrally-placed doorway. The voids formed by this arrangement provide space for flues, cupboards and closets, and the top-lit staircase with straight flights and curved landings, gives direct access to every important room.

The plans of Nos. 7 to 9 and 17 to 19 The Circus, and No. 24 Royal Crescent, are sufficient illustration of the diversity in arrangement which may be found in the houses masked by these fronts of unbroken uniformity. The party and front walls are graduated in thickness in order to obtain interiors of perfect regularity within the curved setting-out, a point of finesse often neglected by later builders. Staircases are placed to suit the best arrangement of rooms, rising to the front in some houses and to the back in others, while in some instances they are contained in a well at the side-centre, top lit (Figs. 23, 24 & 25).

Most of the Brock Street houses belong to the standard terrace type, but there is an interesting example of dove-tailing in the plans of Nos. 6 and 7, giving No. 6 a wide frontage overlooking The Gravel Walk, and No. 7 a double-front to Brock Street (Fig. 25). Another case of this dove-tailing occurs in the planning of Nos. 1 and 2 Catharine Place, also designed by the younger Wood.

The standard type of terrace house, to which the majority of the Bath examples belong, usually has a street frontage varying from 20 to 25 feet in width, and a building depth of 35 to 50 feet, with a garden or yard at the rear according to the site conditions. Accommodation is arranged in a basement containing the domestic offices and kitchen; ground- and first-floors each with a large and a small reception-room; and bedrooms on the second- and third-floors, this last usually an attic story. The staircase well is placed at one side of the smaller room, rising either towards the front or rear of the house in order to allow the principal drawing-room, occupying the full width of the building plot, to be placed overlooking the best available prospect. Nos. 11 to 15 Alfred Street, ascribed to the younger Wood, belong to the more usual type of house, with a large room in front, and the staircase

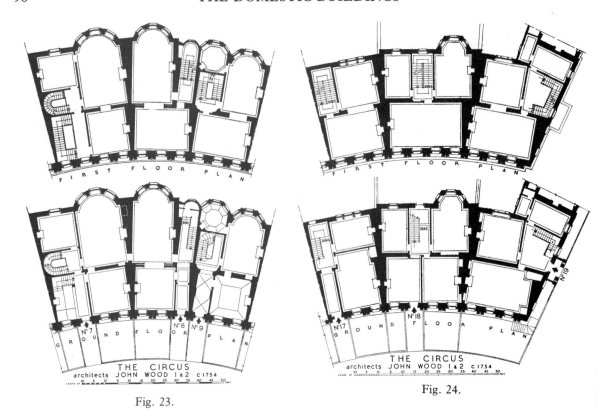

Fig. 23.

Fig. 24.

and secondary room at the back, this last being sometimes increased in area by addition of a bay (Fig. 25). No. 7 Alfred Street, having a return front to Bartlett Street, has the unusual arrangement of front and back rooms almost equal in size and placed on either side of a central staircase (Fig. 25).

The north part of Marlborough Buildings (Fig. 26), the south side of Brock Street, Queen's Parade, The Paragon, Belmont Row and the early nineteenth-century Widcombe Crescent are typical examples of terrace houses planned with the larger rooms placed at the back, overlooking a beautiful view. Sites were sometimes chosen for the views they offered, in spite of the fact that building of houses thereon entailed costly preparation in constructing vaults and retaining walls. The Paragon is a representative example, being sited on a narrow strip of land sloping between two roads having a difference of some 40 feet in their levels, and while the main front towards

London Road presents a normal appearance, at the rear is a great substructure of vaults supporting the hanging gardens entered from the basements of the houses.

Late eighteenth-century planning is illustrated by two houses in Lansdown Crescent, built during 1789–93 from designs by John Palmer (Fig. 26). Nos. 1 and 20, the very large houses at either end of the crescent, have side entrances leading into a spacious hall containing the main staircase, which serves only the principal rooms on the ground- and first-floors, while a secondary staircase gives access to all floors. Nos. 2 to 19 conform to the standard terrace plan, with rooms of such considerable dimensions that the unequal angles resulting from the curved setting out are scarcely noticed. The final example is from Sion Hill Place, built during 1818 to 1821 from designs by John Pinch (Fig. 26). These houses vary in size, those at either end being very large, and No. 5, the central house of which

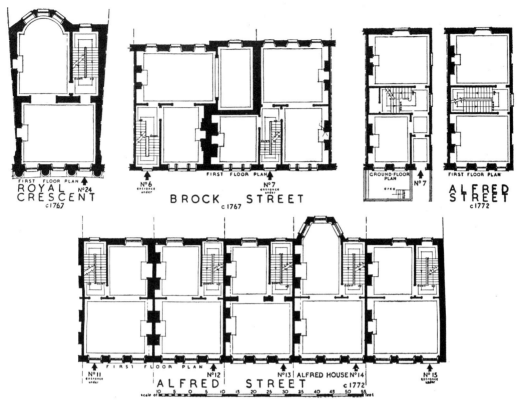

Fig. 25.

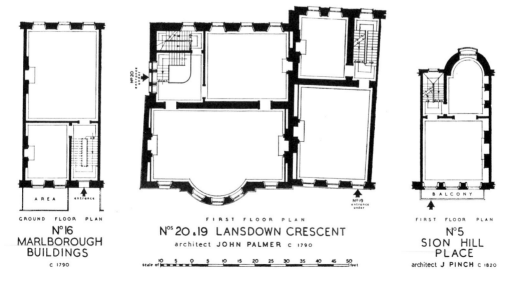

Fig. 26.

the plan is given, having a greater width than those intervening, but all their plans show how the simple terrace type persisted, with little variation, until well into the nineteenth century. Most of these later terrace houses have one feature which is a great improvement, in the substitution of a well-lit top-story for the former attic hidden in the roof behind solid or balustraded parapets.

CONSTRUCTION

The Georgian houses of Bath were generally well constructed, in accordance with the best standards of contemporary building practice, and the passage of years has proved the invalidity of so much of the criticism levelled against them during their erection. Their considerable architectural merit derives in a large measure from the structural and decorative use made of the beautiful local freestone with which they are built. The street frontages are almost invariably faced with finely worked ashlar bonded into a rubble core, and the party and other structural walls are finished in random masonry with ashlar dressings to external door and window openings.

John Wood the elder, who claimed to have introduced advanced methods of building practice into Bath, was highly critical of the manner in which the stonemason's trade around the city was divided into two distinct branches of operation. The practice then was for stones to be worked and wrought to a finished state by freemasons at the quarries, and then transported by primitive means over rough roads to the building site, there to be set up by rough-masons employed to build the rubble walling. The inevitable result of all this mishandling was that the arrises and mouldings were badly damaged before the stones were finally set into position. Another defect was the failure of the masons to realize the importance of laying stone on its natural bed in order to withstand lamination and the effects of corrosion, and the present disfigurement of much early work is entirely due to this cause.

The internal divisions in many of the earlier eighteenth-century houses are formed by thin partitions of wainscotting, but most of the large houses erected during the period in which the Woods practised have internal walls solidly built of stone. In the later terrace houses it is usual to find that only the structural walls, bearing staircases and dividing the principal rooms of the lower floors, are of stone, all non-structural partitions being formed in lath and plaster on studded grounds.

Staircases were constructed in wood until round about 1750, but the first houses built shortly after that date in The Circus bear witness to the change then being made, when the use of cantilevered staircases of Painswick or other hard stone became the standard practice in Bath.

The general building methods of the time were followed in constructing floors and roofs, and up to the beginning of the nineteenth century the latter were usually of double mansard or 'M' form to accommodate the attic story. The graduated stone tiles with which many roofs were originally covered have generally been replaced with a lighter covering of slates, although stone ridge cappings continue to be used. Basements were paved with flagstones and entrance halls are often floored with thin slabs of stone or marble laid upon filler joists.

Windows were invariably fitted with sliding-sashes, said to have been introduced into Bath in 1696 by a chairman and lodging-keeper named Taylor. In the early examples subdivision into small panes is effected by use of heavy glazing bars, but the glass sizes were gradually increased and the bars correspondingly reduced in section until the limits of practicability were reached in the early nineteenth century houses, where window openings giving access to balconies are often 12 feet high and 4 feet wide and are fitted with unequally divided sashes glazed with a total of only 15 large panes.

Only those houses built during the early nineteenth century have balconies forming part of the original design, although they were

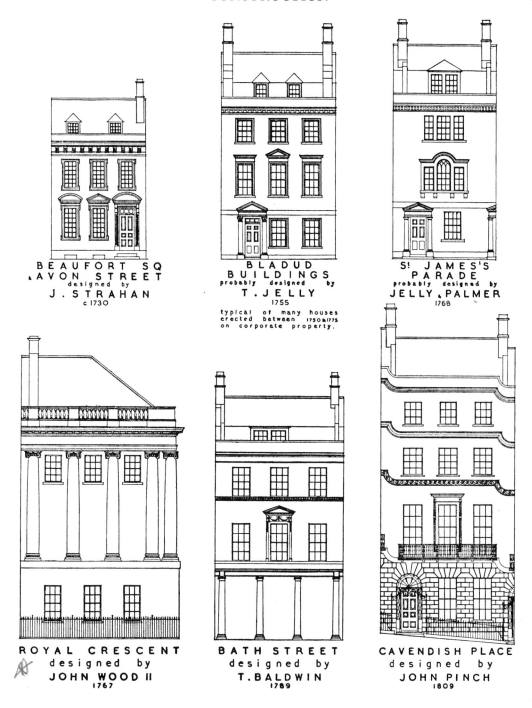

BEAUFORT SQ
& AVON STREET
designed by
J . STRAHAN
c 1730

BLADUD
BUILDINGS
probably designed by
T . JELLY
1755
typical of many houses
erected between 1750 & 1775
on corporate property.

S! JAMES'S
PARADE
probably designed by
JELLY & PALMER
1768

ROYAL CRESCENT
designed by
JOHN WOOD II
1767

BATH STREET
designed by
T . BALDWIN
1789

CAVENDISH PLACE
designed by
JOHN PINCH
1809

EXAMPLES of TERRACE HOUSE ELEVATIONS
erected in BATH during the GEORGIAN era

scale of 10 5 0 5 10 15 20 25 30 35 40 45 50 feet

Fig. 27.

frequently added to buildings of earlier date. The covered verandas are mostly additions, sometimes made to contemporary houses such as those in Cavendish Place, masking the architectural surrounds of the first-floor middle windows. They have now been removed.

REPRESENTATIVE BUILDINGS OF THE PERIOD
1700–1725

The Cold Bath House, Widcombe (demolished 1966)

The Cold Bath House in Claverton Street, Widcombe, was built round about 1704 by Thomas Greenway, the stonemason, whose yard was situated nearby. The property included an excellent cold mineral water spring, and Greenway, intending to profit by the recommendation of cold bathing contained in the first Dr. Oliver's *Practical Dissertation on the Bath Waters*, formed in 1707 a plunge-bath in the ground-floor room fronting on to the forecourt. For nearly a century this bath was resorted to by persons of quality, but fell into disuse round about 1820, and the building, after being used as a workshop and tenement, was demolished in 1900.

This was one of the first buildings in Bath to show a competent use of Renaissance motifs and details, and, apart from the added roof story, the elevations were remarkably free from alterations. The two stories were defined by cornice-string courses, and the rectangular window openings were uniform in size and dress, with bolection-moulded architraves rising from moulded sills, these resting on consoles flanking the panelled aprons. The bath

The Cold Bath House. Detail of entrance front.

Chapel Court. Early 18th Century houses.

entrance was framed by a bolection-moulded architrave, flanked by panelled pilasters with plain consoles supporting a broken segmental pediment. The window over the doorway was flanked by raised panels, and the upper cornice was broken forward from the main building face. The interior of the bath-room was panelled in plaster, and the water flowed from the lion-mask conduit head into the stone lined plunge-bath.

Broad Street

The oldest and most important of the extra-mural streets of Bath is thus described by Wood:

'Broad Street takes its Beginning South, at the same Place with Waldcot Street; but it is much more spacious, as it contains full five and thirty Feet in Breadth: . . . and it extends as far Northwards as Werborough Church, now an Ale House, over the Cistern that receives the Water to supply the several Conduits in the upper Part of the City. This Street contains 56 Houses, among which there are some that are handsome Edifices, as well old as new.'

Broad Street, being of old foundation, has a heterogeneous appearance which is absent from the later thoroughfares. The many medieval houses existing in Wood's time have been replaced by more modern structures, but a few houses remain which date from the first two decades of the eighteenth century, with

Broad Street. Front of No. 38.

Broad Street. Front of The Saracen's Head.

fronts which are interesting examples of the standards of design then prevailing in the city.

No. 38, built in 1709, is an excellent example of a house front designed during this transitional period, despite the fact that the original ground-story has been cut away. The four equally spaced, though asymmetrically placed, windows to the first- and second-floors are set within heavy bolection-moulded surrounds, which, with the cornice stringcourses at each floor level and dripmoulds of similar profile over the gable windows, and the rustic quoins against the party wall lines, are typical Renaissance details used in conjunction with such essentially medieval features as the two crowning gables. At a short distance from this house is 'The Saracen's Head', an inn built in 1713, with a smaller scale elevation of the same transitional character.

Chapel Court

Chapel Court contains some houses of transitional type, showing by contrast with the Palladian buildings of 1727 the extent of the architectural reforms introduced by John Wood. These early houses were built round about 1710, and their excellent state of preservation and general freedom from alteration make them fully representative of a brief phase in the architectural development of Bath. The elevations are almost identical in composition and detail with the Broad Street buildings already described, with bolection-moulded surrounds to the windows; cornice stringcourses marking each floor level; and the series of gable windows lighting the attic rooms contained in the steeply pitched roofs.

Trim Street

According to Wood's description:

'Trim Street is a new-built Street, of twenty-nine Feet in Breadth, begun in the Year 1707, and contains eighteen Houses. It is situated just without the North Side of the City Wall, is parallel to it, and the Land having been the property of the above-mentioned Mr. Trim, from him the Street had its name.'

It remains to be added that George Trim, a wealthy clothier whose mother was said to have been closely related to Inigo Jones, was a member of the Bath Corporation and one of the first leading citizens to defy the general opposition towards extending the city.

The buildings of Trim Street vary in date and style, and their subsequent adaptation to serve as warehouses and workshops has completely changed the character of what was once a fashionable place of residence. On the south side is a uniform group of three houses, now much altered, built in 1724 with elevations of a severe Renaissance character, one of which still retains a fine stone shell hood over the doorway.

Architectural interest centres on the north side, in the romantic feature of St. John's Gate, or Trim Bridge, and the elaborate and fairly well preserved front of No. 5, better known as 'General Wolfe's House', which is an attractive early attempt at small scale Palladian design. The elevation is composed of two stories, similar in their proportions and general treatment, each being dominated by a central feature which on the ground-story is a doorway, framed by a moulded architrave set between fluted Ionic pilasters supporting an entablature with a pulvinated frieze, broken forward over the pilasters and surmounted by a segmental pediment. In the wall on either side of this doorway are two equally spaced rectangular windows, with plain pedestal aprons, and bolection-moulded architraves. The cornice of the doorway entablature is continued as a stringcourse across the front, which terminates with rustic quoins against the party wall lines. The middle window on the first floor, corresponding with the doorway below, is framed by fluted Corinthian pilasters and surmounted by a segmental pediment. The flanking windows have panelled pedestal aprons, bolection-moulded architraves, and plain friezes over which the lower members

Trim Street. 'General Wolfe's House' and St. John's Gate.

Green Street. Early 18th century houses on south side.

only of the crowning cornice are broken forward. The deep plain parapet is a rather unsatisfactory feature which may well be a later alteration. The fine eight-panelled entrance door is probably original, but the unequally divided sashes to the windows are of later date, as is the martial trophy decorating the tympanum of the doorway pediment. The entrance hall is panelled in stone, and leads to a fine wooden staircase with carved brackets to the strings, and a ramped handrail supported by fluted newel posts and simple twisted balusters arranged in pairs.

Nos. 1 to 3, west of St. John's Gate, were demolished in 1969, although No. 1 was a listed building (Grade II) with an Ionic doorcase similar to that of No. 5. In their place stands an office building which is utterly alien to the original character of this once interesting early eighteenth century street.

Green Street

'Green Street, so named from its being built on a Bowling Green, runs direct West from St. Michael's Church, without the North Gate, and leads towards Queen Square; it is a new-built Street, of nineteen Feet in Breadth, and contains fourteen Houses; some of which are neat and handsome Edifices.'

Although Green Street was not formed until 1716, it has much of the character of a medieval street, with houses differing in height and width as well as in elaboration of adornment. One of the earliest houses is set back from the north side, and its wide front of two stories surmounted by three equal gables has the the simple dignity associated with Cotswold vernacular building.

Other houses are characteristic of the transitional period, with Renaissance mouldings and details used in conjunction with steep gabled roofs, and without any assured sense of scale or proportion. The south side is dominated by the tall and narrow front of No. 14 with its elaborately treated first- and second-floor windows, of which there are three to each tier. Moulded architraves broken by plain keystones surround the openings, the unequal spacing of which is offset by the broken pediments surmounting those on the outside, segmental to the first tier and swan-necked to the second. The two windows in the third-floor gable end have moulded architraves with a cornice dripmould over.

St. John's Court (The Sawclose)

The first houses in St. John's Court were built as a uniformly fronted group by Thomas Greenway in 1720, and were described by Wood in his *Essay* as being 'the richest Sample of Building, till then executed, in the City', although he qualifies his opinion when describing the whole court.

'St. John's Court is likewise new; it is fifteen Feet broad, contains four Houses, and was formerly the Town Mixen, till the Right to the Land was recovered, in favour of St. John's Hospital. In the Return of the Building of this Court, next Berton Lane, there is a fifth House which

makes the present Habitation of the King of Bath, whose former Palace, to the South of it, is so profuse in Ornament, that none but a Mason, to shew his Art, would have gone to the expense of those Enrichments.'

The earlier group of four houses does indeed suffer from an excess of moulded decoration, as Wood asserts, but its effect must have been impressive before the execrable addition of the present entrance to the Theatre Royal was grafted on to it. Greenway's building is of three stories with a roof attic, and the main and return frontages have respectively six and five regularly spaced windows to each upper tier. All the windows originally had bolection-moulded surrounds, and those to the ground and first-floor tiers have panelled pedestal aprons. The first-floor level is defined by a cornice stringcourse, and its windows are given additional prominence by breaking forward over them the architrave and pulvinated frieze of the main entablature, the top members of the cornice being carried in an unbroken line round the two main elevations. Rusticated quoins mark the angles of the building, and the attic story is crowned with a cornice, broken forward over the corner quoins and surmounted by a widely spaced balustrade with panelled dies, largely a conjectured restoration of the vanished original. Nothing of note remains within the building, part of which has been gutted to accommodate the staircases of the theatre. The bust of David Garrick, placed over the entrance to the public house, is an early nineteenth century work of Lucius Gahagan.

To the north of the group already described stands a detached house containing two stories and a roof attic, which is a later and more refined example of Greenway's building. The narrow entrance front is given importance by the central doorway, with a window on either side and three first-floor windows to correspond. The return front has two tiers of five equally spaced windows, some of which are blind, all with wide plain architraves. Horizontal emphasis is provided by the moulded stringcourse at first-floor level, the continuous plain sills underlining both tiers of windows, and the crowning entablature. The most interesting feature is the elaborate doorway, which might have been added later. The rusticated surround to the arched opening, with its moulded impost and keystone carved with a lion's head, forms a ground for two engaged

Buckler shows them to have been adorned by various figures, vases and eagles, all of which were typical productions of the Greenway family's famous yard in Claverton Street (Fig. 28).

The house is well preserved, both externally and internally, and retains the original eight-panelled front door and the heavy barred sashes to the windows. The internal arrangements are simple but well planned. The en-

Sawclose. Houses forming St John's Court.

three-quarter columns, with plain shafts and Corinthian capitals, which support the rich entablature with its frieze adornment of floral paterae. Centred over the columns are panelled pedestals with eagles perched on hemispheres. The gable end over the entrance front and the return parapet are now quite plain, but the drawing made round about 1836 by J. C.

trance door gives direct access to a small hall, separated by a wide arch from the fine balustraded staircase rising to the left. Opposite the front door is the entrance to the principal apartment, and there is a small room leading off to the right. This arrangement is repeated on the first-floor, where the principal chamber measures 25 feet in length, 19 feet in width and 12 feet in height. The room is lit by windows on both of its long sides, and the wall opposite the entrance contains the fireplace. The wainscot lining is arranged in tall fielded panels, some of which conceal cupboards, and there is a fine enriched wooden cornice surrounding the plain plaster ceiling.

Fig. 28. 'Beau Nash's House, St. John's Court.

St. John's Court is forever associated with its most famous resident, Richard Nash, who left his house in the earlier group to occupy the one just described, where he lived until his death in 1761.

Abbey Church Yard

Wood's *Essay* contains the following brief description:

'The Abbey Church Yard is an open Area that has little to recommend it, besides its Situation, in the very Heart of the Town. It is one hundred and twenty three Feet in Length, by fifty five Feet in Breadth; it contains twelve Houses; and

it lies obliquely before the West Front of St. Peter and Paul's Church.'

There can be little doubt that Wood's opinion was conditioned by his desire to open up and rebuild this part of the city to form what would now be termed a 'civic centre', but his ideas in this direction never materialized and some of the houses he wished to sweep away still remain on the north side of the area.

The most important building in this group is the large house built round about 1720, and once occupied by General Wade. The front is probably the earliest example in Bath of the Palladian use of a giant order. A fine Regency shop-front has replaced the original ground-story, which provided an arcaded base to the order of fluted Ionic pilasters, set on moulded pedestals, dividing the upper part of the front into four equal bays. Bolection-moulded architraves rising from plain sills surround the first- and second-floor windows, and the spaces between the tiers are adorned with freely carved festoons and pendants of ribbons and garlands. The order is crowned by a fine entablature with a pulvinated frieze and modillioned cornice, above which is a disproportionately high attic-story, with panelled piers centred over the pilasters, and window architraves of a different profile, indicating that this story might be a later addition. The attic finishes with a simple cornice and low parapet, with carved vases placed on projecting dies over the centre and end piers. The traditional ascription of this front to Lord Burlington has no further basis than the fact of that noble architect having designed Wade's London residence in Cork Street.

On the right of General Wade's House is an interesting building, possibly by Greenway, where an immature use is made of superimposed Doric, Ionic, and Corinthian pilasters, spaced so that the five-windowed frontage is divided into a narrow central bay flanked by two wide ones. The ground-story openings have three-centred arches, and the semicircular headed middle windows to the first- and second-floors are surmounted by pediments, of triangular and segmental form respectively. The full entablature is only used over the pilasters, the cornice being continued across the front as a stringcourse to each floor level. The upper part of this front is a later and badly related addition.

No. 3 St. James's Street South (demolished)

The elimination of St. James's Street South brought about the destruction of several interesting pre-Wood houses, the most important being No. 3. A large double-fronted house, it contained a semi-basement, three stories, and a lofty attic, the rooms being arranged in pairs flanking the hall and staircase. This arrangement found expression in the symmetrical front, with its narrow central feature flanked by gabled bays, each two windows wide.

The ground story was dominated by the central doorway, dressed with plain pilasters and consoles, carved as beasts holding cartouches, which supported the flat stone hood

Fig. 29. No. 3 St. James's Street South.

projecting from the first-floor bandcourse. The window above the doorway was flanked by fluted pilasters capped with plain consoles supporting a projection of the moulded stringcourse to the second floor. Fluted pilasters also flanked the arch-headed window in the middle of the third story, where the crowning cornice was turned to form a segmental pediment over the window. In the two side bays the windows were dressed alike with corbelled sills, and moulded architraves broken by keyblocks. The attic stage of each side bay formed a pedimental gable and contained a segmental-arched window (Fig. 29).

This house was the most important surviving example of the work of William Killigrew, who also designed the very similar Weymouth House, destroyed earlier, and the old Blue Coat School (page 88). While the finely panelled rooms and handsome staircase of No. 3, had suffered deterioration through long misuse of the premises, the exterior stonework could have been carefully taken down and re-used to give some distinction to the new buildings hereabouts.

No. 41 Broad Street

This house, built round about 1720, is an early attempt at Palladian design and bears a marked affinity with authenticated work by William Killigrew. The front is four windows wide, but asymmetrical emphasis is given to the design by framing the doorway, which is the second opening on the left, with Ionic pilasters supporting a projecting entablature. The first-floor window over the doorway is similarly set between fluted pilasters, capped by wide consoles supporting a triangular pediment. All the first-floor windows have panelled pedestal aprons, with moulded sills from which rise orthodox architraves broken by plain keystones, and the second-floor windows have similar but unbroken architraves rising from plain sills. The party wall lines are marked by rusticated quoins, and cornices are

Abbey Church Yard. North side, with 'General Wade's House'.

carried across the front as stringcourses marking each floor level. The attic-story, probably consisting of twin gables, had been considerably altered and has been removed.

REPRESENTATIVE BUILDINGS OF THE PERIOD 1725–1750

Widcombe Manor

In the village of Widcombe, now contiguous to Bath, is a distinguished group of buildings belonging to Widcombe Manor, of which the most important is the Manor House, partly rebuilt for Philip Bennet round about 1727. In the absence of any evidence pointing to its designer, the late Mowbray Green expressed his opinion that the house was probably the work of Thomas Greenway, but if this is the case then Greenway displays here considerably greater skill in architectural composition and rectitude of detail than is shown in any of his Bath buildings. In fact Widcombe Manor House, both in design and execution, bears the impress of the cultivated mind of someone well

Fig. 30. The garden house at Widcombe Manor.

acquainted with the earlier and somewhat French manner used by Vanbrugh in designing Castle Howard.

The principal front facing south is adorned with a giant order of pilasters, with fluted shafts and foliated Ionic capitals, arranged in pairs to form a central feature with subsidiary

Widcombe Manor House. Principal front facing south.

wings. Plain Doric columns supporting an entablature and segmental pediment form a porch to the central doorway, which is flanked by arched windows set in rusticated masonry. On the first-floor above are three small windows, the middle one arched with a plain archivolt broken by a keystone carved with a floriated monogram. Each wing has two tiers of two windows, identically treated with moulded sills on corbels, and moulded architraves broken by keystones carved with grotesque masks. The main entablature has a pulvinated frieze and modillioned cornice decorated at each end with an armorial cartouche, and is broken forward to receive the tringular pediment which crowns the central feature. The stone tiled roof is partly masked by a pedestal parapet, with balustrades between plain dies, stopped against the pediment, of which the tympanum is decorated with an oval window flanked by garlands pouring from cornucopiae. The east front is largely modern work, but is excellently related to the earlier portion, and the enclosed forecourt and terraced gardens form an exquisite setting to the house.

The manorial buildings include a lovely garden house, with an open loggia forming the ground-story, its front of three arches being decorated with an engaged order of Doric columns supporting an entablature, while single Ionic columns flank the group of three windows to the upper floor and carry the crowning entablature (Fig. 30).

Ralph Allen's Town House

Allen's first residence in Bath was a large house of transitional type in Lilliput Alley, to which a north wing was added in 1727, its principal front facing east, overlooking a large garden and commanding a fine view of Claverton Down, upon which Allen built later his 'eyecatcher' of 'Sham Castle'. After Allen's removal to Prior Park, the garden was subjected to successive building encroachments, and the almost hidden house degenerated into a tenement.

Wood states that: 'While Mr. Allen was making the Addition to the North Part of his House in Lilliput Alley, he new fronted and raised the old Building a full Story higher; it consists of a Basement Story sustaining a double Story under the Crowning; and this is surmounted by an Attick, which created a sixth Rate House, and a Sample for the greatest Magnificence that was ever proposed by me for our City Houses.'

The narrow east front of the extension is an early example of an elaborate Palladian frontispiece, probably inspired by Wood but lacking the finesse of his work. The rusticated ground story contains a wide arch centred between two narrow flat-arched openings, the intermediate piers being finished with a moulded impost, originally returned into all the openings. The arch keystone projects beyond the face of the first-floor platband, while the adjoining voussoirs die into it. Above this rustic base rises the giant order of four engaged three-quarter columns, having moulded bases on plain pedestals, plain shafts, and Corinthian capitals. These columns divide the upper part of the front into three bays, the wide middle one being dominated by an arched window, with its moulded archivolt springing from an impost moulding which is continued above the rectangular window in each narrow side bay. Below these first-floor windows are blind balustrades, continuing the lines of the column pedestals. Architraves are omitted from the second-floor windows, but below those in the side bays are richly carved festoons of fruits and flowers, and the sill to the middle window is broken into by the carved keystone of the arch below. The main entablature has a modillioned cornice surmounted by a steeply pitched triangular pediment, with a tympanum decoration of elaborately scrolled foliage surrounding a small circular opening, and acroterial ornaments of stone balls (Fig. 31).

The north wing now forms part of a house in Church Street, and has become isolated from the original building in Lilliput Alley, of which the garden front was refaced to provide

Fig. 31. 'Ralph Allen's Town House'. The garden front.

a suitable foil to the elaborate Palladian elevation just described. Here the order is omitted but architectural relationship is established by the use of similar floral festoons, decorating the spaces below the second-floor windows, and a corresponding treatment of string-courses and cornice.

St. John's Hospital, Chapel Court House, and Chandos Buildings

The complex story of John Wood's relations with the Duke of Chandos is related fully in *The Life and Circumstances of James Brydges, First Duke of Chandos*, by C. H. C. and M. Baker (O.U.P. 1949). It is felt that a summary account will suffice here.

Sensing Bath's growing development as a fashionable spa, and having endured the discomfort of the best available lodgings, the Duke decided to speculate in creating improved accommodation near the baths. In

1726 he bought the leases of Mrs. Anne Phillips's house in Chapel Court, together with her lodgings over St. John's Hospital and some adjacent premises. Intending at first only to remodel these buildings and to employ his London architect, Edward Shepherd, the Duke then negotiated with John Strahan of Bristol, and finally signed articles on January 13th, 1726/7, with John Wood who undertook to rebuild the Hospital range first and then Mrs. Phillips's house. The Hospital range was completed early in 1728, and despite his reiterated complaints to Wood of unethical practice, bad workmanship, and a disastrous failure to provide workable water-closets, the Duke continued employing Wood to build more houses. The largest and finest was Chandos Buildings, originally Mrs. Degge's Lodgings, completed late in 1729 and demolished, after a serious fire, in 1936. Altogether Wood built six houses of various sizes in or adjacent to Chapel Court, one being his own speculation.

Mrs. Phillips's house is on the north side of Chapel Court and the Hospital, with her lodgings above, forms the east side. According to his 'Essay' the Hospital front is a reduced version of Wood's intended design, he having been obliged to alter the window spacing to conform with internal divisions demanded by Mrs. Phillips. According to Wood:

'Before the Westward Rooms of the Hospital there was to have been a regular Arcade, instead of the antient Colonnade, consisting of nine Apertures to answer the six Windows of the six Rooms, and the three Gates of the three Passages; and the three middle Apertures were intended to advance before the rest, to make the Basis of a Frontispiece in the Center of the West Side of the Building: This Frontispiece was to have been finished with a Pediment; and in the Tympan of it I proposed to place the Figure of the Head of Saint John the Baptist, together with several other Ornaments that embellished the old

St. John's Hospital & Chapel Court House.

Chandos Buildings, from north-west.

Frontispiece, or rather Tower, in the Center of the East Side of the Building.'

The buildings are uniform, with elevations designed on broad Palladian lines influenced, no doubt, by Colen Campbell's houses in Old Burlington Street, London. The almshouses in the Hospital range are screened by an arcade, its massive piers, imposts, and arches being unmoulded though the plain keystones project to merge with the first-floor bandcourse. The plain ground story of the north range contains straight-headed openings for the door and windows, all without architraves but having projecting keystones like those of the arcade. A continuous sill underlines all the first-floor windows, all being dressed with a moulded architrave, pulvinated frieze, and cornice. The second-floor windows have shouldered and eared architraves, and both fronts are finished with a fine entablature having a pulvinated frieze and modillioned cornice.

The east front of the Hospital is built in rubble masonry with ashlar dressings. The fine entrance, formed by an arched opening set between pairs of free-standing columns, with plain shafts and Doric capitals, supporting a broken entablature and triangular pediment, has the combined severity and elegance of an early Florentine work.

These buildings, particularly Chapel Court House, are sufficiently free from alterations to enable one to appraise the fine qualities of Wood's more simple designs, which have in so many cases lost much of their original finesse through ill-considered alteration.

Queen Square (see also Appendix V)

In attempting to assess the measure of Wood's achievement in building Queen Square, his first great undertaking in Bath, it is necessary to know something of his original ideas and the extent of their realization, which, fully expounded in the *Essay*, are here summarized.

Queen Square is sited to the north-west of the old city boundaries, on the high southward sloping ground which Robert Gay granted to John Wood in a series of 99 years' leases. Having made his plans, Wood sub-let parcels of the land for a term of 98 years, to such persons as were willing to build in direct or near conformity with his designs. On December 10th, 1728, the builders began excavations for laying the foundations of four houses, three of these fronting to Wood Street, the first stone being laid at the corner of Wood Street on January 27, 1729. The last house in the Square was finished seven years later, during which period several changes had been made to Wood's original plans.

From the engraved plan here reproduced it will be seen that Wood first intended to build round an open area measuring from north to south 350 ft., and from east to west 300 ft. This area was to be laid out with a formal garden 200 ft. square, surrounded with 50 ft. wide roadways on the north, east, and west sides, and a grand parade 100 ft. wide on the south, all these roadways being projected as subsidiary streets leading from the Square. As built, the Square measures from north to south 316 ft., and from east to west 306 ft., the 206 ft. square garden being placed in the same relationship as before. Wood also intended levelling the site, but in order to save some £4,000 he decided to build in conformity with the natural fall of the land.

Wood envisaged the north, east, and west ranges of building as forming a palace forecourt, the ensemble to be viewed from the south side. The magnificent north front, elaborately modelled to gain the fullest advantage of light and shade offered by a south aspect, fully realizes the body of this supposed palace, to which the east and west sides were to form wings, simply but symmetrically treated, with plain ground-stories, and superstructures dressed 'with such Ornaments as are proper to the Ionick Order'. While the east side was carried out to this design at an early date, circumstances arose later which prevented Wood from building the complementary range. The buildings on the west side eventually took the form of a large mansion, set back

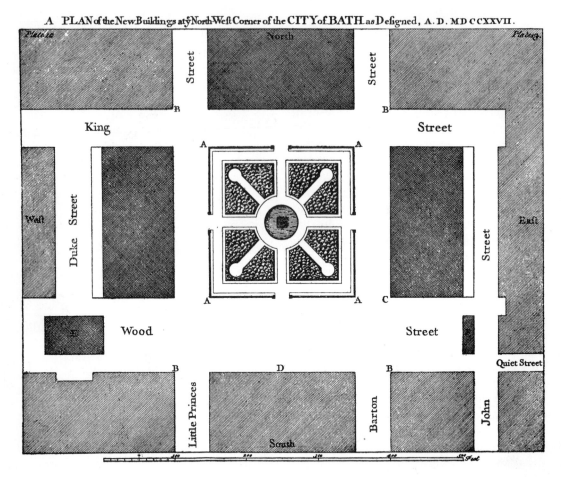

Fig. 32.
(from Wood's 'Essay towards a Description of Bath' 1749)

from the frontage line, with its enclosed fore-court flanked by two equally imposing buildings, each uniting two houses into an elaborate composition. The south side was built more or less in accordance with Wood's original intentions.

A low balustraded wall enclosed the garden, which was entered in the middle of each side through iron gates, 20 ft. wide, set between stone piers. The enclosure was bordered and crossed by gravel walks, dividing the space into four parterres and leading to a walk surrounding the central basin, 45 ft. in diameter, from which rose the tapering obelisk. The parterres were planted with flowering shrubs and enclosed by espaliered limes and elms, and

each was penetrated diagonally by a grass path leading to a small circular plat (Fig. 32).

The obelisk, of which Wood was inordinately proud, originally terminated in a sharp point at the height of 70 ft., and set into its south face, on eye level, was a marble slab with the following inscription, concocted with no great show of willingness or inspiration, by Alexander Pope:

IN MEMORY
OF HONOURS CONFERR'D
AND IN GRATITUDE
FOR BENEFITS BESTOW'D
IN THIS CITY
BY HIS ROYAL HIGHNESS
FREDERICK,

PRINCE OF WALES,
AND HIS
ROYAL CONSORT,
IN THE YEAR MDCCXXXVIII
THIS OBELISK IS ERECTED
BY RICHARD NASH, ESQ.

The magnificent north front dominates the Square, as Wood intended it should do. The seven large houses of varying size are grouped so that they form a symmetrical composition, with a central pavilion of five bays, flanked by wings and terminal pavilions of six and three bays respectively. The rusticated ground-story is enlivened by the bold impost moulding marking the heads of the window and door openings, and is terminated by a plain platband. The first- and second-floors are embraced by the giant order of engaged three-quarter columns to the central and end pavilions, with corresponding pilasters to the wings. The columns and pilasters, which have moulded bases, plain shafts, and Corinthian capitals, rise to support a richly decorated entablature with a modillioned cornice, surmounted by a plain parapet broken against the great triangular pediment crowning the central pavilion, with its acroterial ornaments of three floriated vases. The end pavilions are surmounted by disappointingly meagre attic stories. The tall windows to the first-floor are dressed as 'tabernacles', with moulded architraves, originally rising from projecting balustraded pedestals, and plain pilaster strips with

consoles supporting alternate triangular and segmental pediments. The square windows to the second-floor are set within architrave surrounds (Fig. 33).

Although the north front has suffered no major alteration, the proportions of many of the windows have been adversely affected by enlargement and re-sashing which has involved the removal of the balustraded pedestals at first-floor level. The stone balustrading originally surrounding the areas has long since been replaced by iron railings. Fortunately the excrescence against the end house on the left is more damaging to the return frontage than to the principal elevation, but its removal is called for.

The buildings on the east side of the square, intended as a foil to the elaborate north front, are consequently much less interesting. This range consists of six houses, those at either end having their principal fronts in the adjoining streets. The intermediate houses have wide double-fronted elevations, each house being stepped down to accord with the fall in ground level. Apart from the centrally placed doorway, each front is identically treated and consists of a plain ground-story, with two widely spaced windows on either side of the doorway, terminating in the platband at first-floor level. The five windows to the first-floor are underlined by a plain continued sill, subsequently cut away when many of the windows were enlarged, and the moulded architraves are

The ELEVATION, to the South, of the principal Pile of BUILDING of QUEEN-SQUARE in BATH,
as defigned by John Wood, Architect, A.D, 1728.
P. Fourdrinier Sculp.

Fig. 33.
(from Wood's 'Essay towards a Description of Bath' 1749).

Queen Square. General view from north-west corner.
(*water-colour drawing by S. H. Grimm, c.1773*)

Queen Square. General view of north and west sides.
(*water-colour drawing by T. Malton, jr. c.1784*)

Queen Square. Pedimented centre (No. 24) of north side 'Palace front'.

finished with narrow friezes and cornices. The second-floor windows are framed by moulded architraves broken in at the sides, and the fronts are terminated by a modillioned cornice and a plain parapet. It seems highly probable that the doorways, which are of coarse baroque character, were left to the taste of individual builders responsible for erecting the houses.

The west side originally consisted of two symmetrically treated groups of houses flanking the forecourt of the large mansion occupying the central site. The elevation of each of these end groups is subdivided to form a central feature flanked by slightly recessed wings. The ground-story of the central feature consists of three rusticated arches, framing rectangular door and window openings set within architraves in plain walling, while the wings are similarly rusticated and the two windows in each are framed by broken architraves alternately surmounted by segmental and triangular pediments, their bedmoulds broken by the massive projecting keystones. The first-floor windows rise from the plain platband, the three in the central feature being 'tabernacles', having Ionic pilasters and pedimented entablatures, segmental between triangular. The two windows in each wing are simply framed with architraves surmounted by narrow friezes and cornices. All the windows to the second-floor are set within architrave surrounds, and the front terminates with a modillioned cornice and plain parapet over the wings, broken against the triangular pediment surmounting the central feature, its acroteria being originally furnished with floral vases. The return frontages are similar in general lines of composition, although less elaborately detailed.

These buildings have also suffered from the indiscriminate cutting down of window sills, but the principal change to this side of the Square was effected by the addition of a central block in Greek Revival style, designed

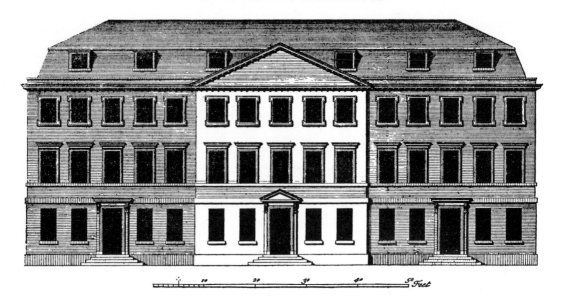

The ELEVATION, to the South, of one of the Side BUILDINGS of QUEEN-SQUARE in BATH,
as defigned by John Wood, Architect, A.D. 1728.
P. Fourdrinier Sculp.

John Wood's design for the houses forming the north side of Wood Street.
(from Wood's 'Essay towards a Description of Bath' 1749).

by the younger Pinch in 1830, which, although fine in itself, is out of keeping with the character of Wood's buildings.

The façade of the south range, originally containing nine houses, is a simple astylar composition. The central feature, three windows wide, has an arcaded ground-story, and is finished with a triangular pediment surmounting the main cornice. The houses forming the wings are distinguished by doorways similar in the manner of their execution to those on the east side, and of an even more baroque character. The destruction of the east part of this range, during the raids on Bath, was the only serious damage sustained by the buildings of the Square. Regrettably, some later alterations were perpetuated in the post-war rebuilding.

The interiors of the houses vary in interest, and almost all contain good staircases with apsidal landings. Special reference is made to the planning and important decorative features of Nos. 15 and 24, possibly the finest houses in the Square, under the appropriate headings.

There is little to say of the central garden, for Wood's formal layout of parterres disappeared long ago, and gave place to a motley of odd planting. The removal of railings, installation of water tanks, and various underground burrowings left the garden in a chaotic state, but the area has been re-grassed and enclosed with iron railings of Georgian design. The restoration of Wood's original scheme of formal planting would further enhance the appearance of the Square.

Gay Street

The survey of Bath, made by the elder Wood and dated 1735, shows a single line of houses facing west and extending from the north-east corner of Queen Square, as far north as George Street. At first regarded as a continuation of Barton Street, and then for a brief period called Montpelier, this street was extended soon after 1755 to form the principal approach to the King's Circus, and was renamed Gay Street in honour of Robert Gay, on whose land the Upper Town was sited.

Queen Square. The north group of houses on the west side.

The most interesting house is No. 41, forming the north-east angle of Queen Square, its exterior now cleaned and restored to its original appearance. While the fronts to Gay Street and Old King Street were designed to conform with the other houses in those streets, the corner to Queen Square is splayed off to receive an elaborately decorated bow. The ground story contains a large window of one wide and two narrow side lights, dressed with moulded architraves rising from a balustrade pedestal and broken by rustic blocks, while the voussoirs of the flat arches break forward in successive projections to die into the cornice below the first-floor platband. Above this is an equally elaborate venetian window, with a balustrade pedestal from which rise Ionic columns, arranged in pairs between the lights and coupled with pilasters on the outside, carrying an entablature which is returned into the arched middle light. The order, entablature and archivolt moulding are all broken by rustic blocks. Above the bold cornice at second-floor level are three windows, uniformly set within moulded architraves. The modillioned main cornice is surmounted by a plain parapet on which are set three gadrooned vases, one in the centre and one on each side of the bowed feature. The doorway in Gay Street is adorned with engaged three-quarter columns, with plain shafts and Ionic capitals, supporting an entablature and framing an arched opening, of which the moulded archivolt is broken by a keystone carved into a satyr's mask. Some notes on the planning and decoration of this house will be found under the appropriate headings.

John Strahan, and the Kingsmead developments of 1734–36

Wood's *Essay* contains the following para-

Gay Street. View of No. 41 from
Queen Square.

graphs relating to the Kingsmead developments:

'Beaufort Buildings line out a Piece of Ground that is partly a Street, and partly a little open Area, of one hundred and thirty seven Feet in Length, by eighty six Feet in Breadth, situated at the back of the Buildings, on the South Side of Queen Square, and consists of two and twenty Houses: The Place was so named from one of the Lessees of the Land, the above-mentioned Mr Hobbs of Bristol, who from having a Share in the Navigation of the River Avon, thus denominated it in Memory of his Grace the Duke of Beaufort's Father, for his getting, at his Cost, an Act of Parliament to make the River Navigable from Bath to Bristol; and the Buildings are the Piratical Architecture of his Friend Mr. Strahan.

'King's Mead Square is almost South of Beaufort Buildings; it is in Length one

Beauford Square. Houses on east side.

hundred and forty eight Feet, in Breadth one hundred and twenty one Feet, and contains twenty two Houses. The Name arises from its being executed on a Piece of Ground called King's Meadow; and the Houses of this Square, as well as those of Beaufort Buildings, may be very justly said to owe their Birth to the Restrictions the Builders of Queen Square were put under by me, in Respect to the Form and Size of their Houses, and the Use to which they should be put, when built.

'This Controul, so unnatural to the Taste of Mankind in general, drove the Capricious, as well as some of our poorest Workmen, to exercise their Building Faculties in King's Mead Square, and Beaufort Buildings; the Houses whereof bear the strongest Testimony of this Evident Truth: But, nevertheless, they far exceed the common Buildings of any Place that I have yet seen. And as the Ground of Beaufort Buildings, and King's Mead Square is of the same Tenure, so Mr. Strahan was, of Consequence, the Architect of both; but the Builders were least observant to his Draughts in the latter Place, than in the former; and therefore Beaufort Buildings have a Sort of Regularity to recommend them; but the Houses in King's Mead Square have nothing, save Ornaments without Taste, to please the Eye.'

Kingsmead Square. Houses on the south side.

Although Wood's writing always shows his natural bias against the work of professional rivals, he was particularly vindictive in his criticism of Strahan, and chose to ignore the positive merits of the uniform fronts designed by Strahan for the houses in Beauford Square (originally Beaufort Buildings) and Avon Street, where he was presumably able to control the builders.

In 1736 there were twenty-five houses rated in Avon Street, and twenty-four in Beaufort Square and Buildings, now Beauford Square. Avon Street has completely gone, but enough of Beauford Square survives to show the charm and dignity with which these uniform house-fronts were invested. Each house has two tiers of rectangular sash-windows, almost equal in size and proportion, and having the same setting of wide-moulded architraves broken in at the sides. Those to the ground-floor are further enriched by the addition of pulvinated friezes and cornices, originally intended to be surmounted by triangular and segmental pediments, arranged in alternating sequence with the larger segmental pediments which project on consoles over the doorways. There is no intermediate stringcourse, but the elevations are finely terminated by a Doric entablature with triglyphed frieze, and a plain parapet. Some of the houses retain the original eight-panelled front-doors, and the small paned, heavy barred sashes.

In 1736 there were ratepayers for nine houses in Kingsmead Square, including Mr Rosewell and John George, innholder of the Mitre. On the south side of the irregular 'square' is a terrace of six houses with generally uniform fronts, three stories high and three windows wide. The two houses at the west end have doorcases surmounted by triangular pediments, regularly spaced windows framed by moulded architraves, and cornice string courses defining the floor levels. The other houses in the range have doorways with flat projecting hoods supported on scrolled consoles, and although the window architraves are of the same profile, they are broken by keystones dying into plain stringcourses con-

tinuing the lines of the cornices. The fine main cornice is continued across the whole range, and surmounted by a dwarf parapet.

The west side of the Square is dominated by the large house forming part of a group built in 1736 by Thomas Rosewell, reputedly from designs by Strahan. The building is conventional enough in essentials, with piers dividing the front into three almost equal bays, the centre containing the doorway and a single window to each of the upper floors, and the side bays two windows to each floor. It is in the exuberantly baroque character of its detail that this building is unique in Bath, having more in common with certain buildings in Bristol and Bradford-on-Avon, where German-Flemish influence on design was very strong. The central bay begins modestly and conventionally with a porch of detached Ionic columns supporting an entablature with a triangular pediment, but the elliptical-headed window over is flanked by grotesque male

Kingsmead Square. Front of
Rosewell House.

terminal figures, and the second-floor window is surrounded by a scrolled and foliated architrave, broken by a large plain keystone supporting the cartouche (bearing the builder's rebus and the date of erection), which enriches the tympanum of the segmental pediment. The first-floor windows to the side bays are framed by elaborately formed architraves, rising from moulded sills supported on consoles, and broken by keystones carved with human masks which support projecting sections of the cornice stringcourse. The second-floor windows are similarly framed with broken architraves carrying frieze blocks, from which consoles rise to the corona of the main cornice.

Prior Park

If Wood's account is to be fully believed, his building of Prior Park for Ralph Allen owed its inception to the prejudice against Bath freestone generally held by architects at that time, which led to the rejection in 1726, by Campbell, James and Hawksmore, of Allen's tender for the stonework at Greenwich Hospital. Allen's desire to prove that this prejudice against his stone was unreasonable, and was probably fostered by rival interests,

'brought him to a Resolution to exhibit it in a Seat which he had determined to build for himself near his Works, to much greater Advantage, and in much greater Variety of Uses than it had ever appeared in any other Structure'.

The site chosen for the buildings was one of great beauty, being near the head of the vale called by Wood 'The Widcombe of Camelodunum', and commanding an exquisite prospect to the north, down the shelving slopes towards the village of Widcombe, with the city lying beyond. The first design was made for a mansion

'wherein the Orders of Architecture were to shine forth in all their Glory; but the Warmth of this Resolution at last abating, an humble Simplicity took place,'

and if the buildings eventually erected were considered by Wood to express this last quality, then his original conception must have been magnificent in the extreme. Wood's description of the site, and of the geometrical basis for his layout, are quoted from the *Essay*:

'The Comb in which this Village (Widcombe) is situated sinking into the North Side of Camelodunum, extends almost to the Summit of that Hill, and terminates itself in the Shape of the Head of a vast Niche, with natural Terrasses rising above one another, like the Stages between the Seats of a Roman Theatre; and on one of those Terrasses Mr. Allen, one of the Citizens of Bath, hath lately built himself a Seat, consisting of a Mansion House in the Center, two Pavilions, and two Wings of Offices: All these are united by low Buildings; and while the chief Part of the whole Line fronts the Body of the City, the rest faces the Summit of Mars's Hill.

'By the following Print [Fig. 35] the general Plan of this Seat, as it was first intended may be conceived; the House being marked with the Letter A, the Pavilions with the Letters B, C, and the Wings of Offices with the Letters F, G: H is a Bason of Water; and the Extent of

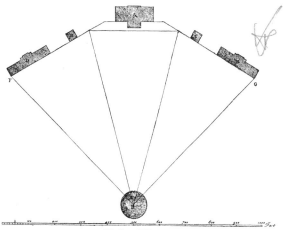

The General PLAN
Of Mr Allen's House and Offices, in the Widcomb of Camalodunum, near Bath;
I Wood Arch.   as it was first Designed.   T. Fourdrinier Sculp.

Fig. 35.

the Seat from F to G was proposed to answer that of three Sides of a Duodecagon, inscribed within a Circle of a Quarter of a Mile Diameter: But in the Execution the Wing of Offices, marked with the Letter D, was joined on to the Pavilion B.'

Work was begun round about 1735 on the west wing, containing the stables and granaries, after which the west *porte-cochère* pavilion and the mansion house were built in that sequence, the greater part of these buildings being finished under Wood's superintendence by 1748. Soon after that date Wood's volatile temper caused him to quarrel with Allen over various details of construction and decoration, and the work passed into the far less competent hands of Richard Jones, Allen's clerk of works, who altered the east wing in execution and destroyed the symmetrical balance of Wood's design. Jones is a mysterious figure, who left a garrulous and partly incomprehensible account of his life and works, wherein he claimed credit for having designed the Palladian Bridge and several buildings in Bath reputed to be the work of others.

In a letter dated May 10th, 1763, Samuel Derrick, then Master of Ceremonies in Bath, records his impressions of Prior Park:

'This gentlemen's house, which is a very noble structure, stands on the brow of a very pretty high hill, with a north view of this city, which it deliciously commands. It consists of a good dwelling and a wing of offices united to it on each side by a most elegant corridor. It has a spacious hall and a handsome staircase.

'I am no great admirer of a gallery up one pair of stairs, which runs almost the whole length of the house and is in my opinion too narrow; its terminations are an apartment in which Mr. Allen sets to dispatch business, and a good gallery or pew looking into one of the neatest chapels I ever saw, where the family constantly attend divine service.

'There is no kind of conveniency that a man can wish for, but is here to be found. Before the house is a handsome lawn with a statue of General Wade, upon a pedestal, in a Roman habit, grasping a truncheon. The ground about is charmingly disposed and improved; the gardens well watered and laid out in taste, and Mr. Allen has planted a vast number of firs in the neighbourhood, which thrive well. The ride bordering round the grounds is miles in extent in which the views of the city, river, and adjacent country, are every minute so varied, that to me it wears the appearance of fairy-ground; nothing can be more enchanting.'

The house (Fig. 36a) was stripped of its original furnishings and all removable decorative features within a few years of Allen's death in 1764, but the structure remained substantially unaltered until 1829, when the property was acquired by Bishop Baines, the founder of Prior Park College. He caused the east and west wings to be entirely reconstructed and heightened, to provide accommodation for the colleges of SS. Peter and Paul, and commissioned Henry Goodridge to design the great staircase leading down from the portico to the lower terraces. The changes made at this time to the interior of the mansion were of a minor nature, and were designed to form a processional way to the chapel, but after the fire of May 29th, 1836, had almost gutted the building, it was reconstructed to a partially altered plan, probably under the supervision of Goodridge. The interior decoration was designed to incorporate many beautiful specimens of late eighteenth-century decorative art, including a magnificent staircase in oak and mahogany; several sets of fine mahogany veneered doors; some richly carved doorcases, pilasters, and cornices; mantelpieces in marble and wood, and a series of plasterwork panels and ceiling centrepieces of markedly similar character to the work in Baldwin's Guildhall. All of this material was brought from Hunstrete, near Marksbury, when the great mansion built by Francis Popham was dismantled. From this

Prior Park. The mansion. Entrance front facing south.

Prior Park. The mansion. Principal front facing north.

Prior Park. The mansion, east front.

house came also the vigorous sculpture now ornamenting the tympanum of the east wing pediment, together with two oval medallions on either side of the venetian window below, and some statues ranged about the portico and terraces. The last major alteration to the buildings was undertaken just previously to 1844, when the west *porte-cochere* pavilion was demolished to make way for the fine Church of St. Paul, designed by John Joseph Scoles and completed many years later by his son.

It will be realized from the foregoing paragraphs that Prior Park, except for the exterior of the mansion house, now differs considerably from Wood's original conception, and it is upon his drawings and the relevant passages in the *Essay* that the following description is based.

The mansion house is a rectangular building, measuring 147 ft. in length from east to west, and 55 ft. in width, excluding the projection of the engaged and freestanding portioes on the south and north fronts respectively. The house is extremely well constructed, on massive foundations in which some 800 tons of freestone were used; the basement rooms are paved and vaulted with stone; and the walls throughout the main structure are of wrought stone laid in equal courses within and without. Wood's plan of the basement shows the disposition and original allotment of the domestic offices ranged on each side of a transverse corridor, with the substructure of the great portico containing a small beer cellar and an apartment 'reserved for Water Closets, if such Conveniences should be wanting within the Body of the House'. This plan also shows the external staircases originally proposed to lead down from each side of the portico, but these are not indicated on the elevational drawing and it seems probable that the idea was abandoned at an early stage, possibly because of the threatened obscuration of light from the base-

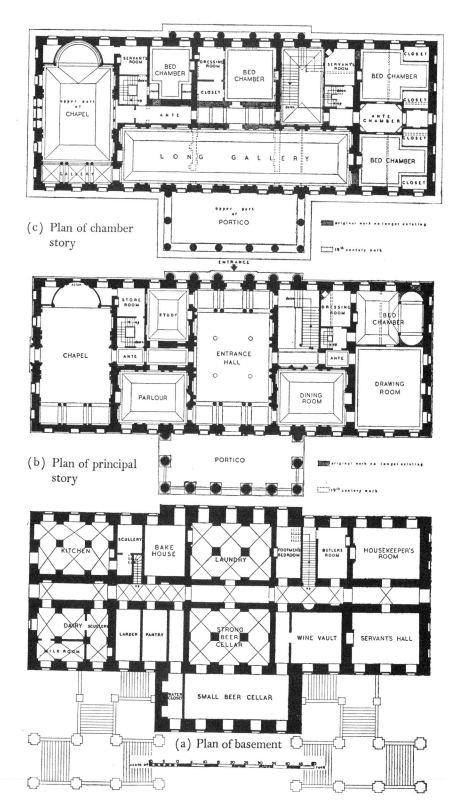

(c) Plan of chamber story

original work no longer existing

19th century work

(b) Plan of principal story

original work no longer existing

19th century work

(a) Plan of basement

Fig. 36. Prior Park

ment windows. The present disposition of rooms on the ground floor differs only in minor details from Wood's original plan (Fig. 36b). The large entrance hall in the centre extends the full width of the building. On its east side a doorway gives access to a corridor leading to the parlour on the north front; a study, service stair and storeroom on the south; and the two-story chapel occupying the east end of the house. The corresponding doorway on the west side leads into the main staircase hall on the south front, which gives direct access to the dining room on the north front; and through a lobby with a service stair to the drawing room and great bed-chamber on the west front. The first-floor, or chamber-story, has been considerably altered, for the original plan (Fig. 36c) shows that the landing at the head of the main staircase gave access on the west side to a long antichamber, with a bed-chamber on either side, while to the

east was a corridor, running between the long gallery overlooking the north front, and further bed-chamber suites on the south front, and leading to the small gallery on the west side of the chapel.

Wood's sectional drawings of the chapel and main staircase show the character of his original decorations. The larger rooms on the ground-floor were ceiled over at a height of 16 ft., while those of the chamber-story rose to a height of 20 ft., with garrets for servants contrived in the spaces above the lower ceilinged bedrooms. The elaborate wall treatment was carried out in stonework up to the crowning member of the cornices, above which the rooms were generally finished with plain plaster coves rising to flat ceilings, except in the case of the main staircase hall which was ceiled with a plain barrel vault. To Wood's manifest disgust, Allen caused the parlour and dining room walls to be stripped of their stone

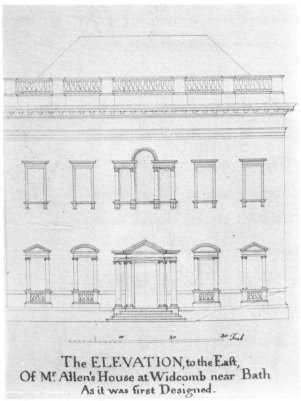

Prior Park. The mansion. John Wood's drawing for the east front.

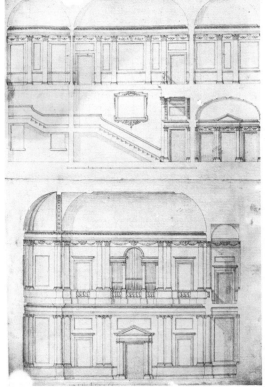

Prior Park. The mansion. John Wood's drawings for the great staircase and chapel.

ornaments and lined with wainscotting. The chapel contains all of Wood's decorations that were spared by the fire of 1836. It is a rectangular apartment, two stories high, with a gallery at the north end and an apse containing the high altar at the south end. The two stories are clearly defined by their adornment of superimposed columns of the Roman Ionic and Corinthian orders, rising from pedestal bases and carrying full entablatures. A fine venetian window in the centre of the upper tier on the east side, is balanced by the small gallery on the opposite wall. The original ceiling, formed by a segmental cove rising to a flat centre, was destroyed and has been replaced with a plaster vault of three-centred section.

The exterior of the mansion as built differs in some minor details from Wood's original designs, but realizes in full the magnificence of the original conception, which was intended to rival, if not surpass, Colen Campbell's first design for Wanstead. The four fronts are perfectly related in character and general lines of composition, while varying in degree of decorative richness. The entrance front faces south and is the most severe in expression, presenting a great wall face of smooth ashlar, broken by two uniform tiers of fifteen openings without architrave surrounds, and rising from a simple pedestal course to terminate in the splendid entablature with its modillioned cornice. The five middle openings of each tier are embraced by the giant portico of six engaged half-columns, with moulded bases, plain shafts and Roman Ionic capitals, supporting the entablature which is broken forward and surmounted by a great triangular pediment, against which the solid pedestal parapet is stopped. The wide bay in the centre

Prior Park. The mansion. The chapel, looking north.

Prior Park. The mansion. The chapel, looking south.

of the portico contains the high arched entrance doorway, leading directly into the great hall. The seven ground-floor windows on each side of the doorway are underlined by a deep continued sill forming the top member of the pedestal, while the fifteen windows of the upper tier have plain individual sills. The plain frieze of the main entablature was originally broken at regular intervals by oblong windows lighting the garrets, but these have generally been filled in.

Of the return frontages, that facing east was built in almost complete accordance with Wood's drawing, although the total height has been reduced and the proportions of the venetian window altered. The only considerable deviation occurs in the treatment of the pedimented central doorway. The ground floor windows are dressed as 'tabernacles', with blind balustrades between pedestals, from which rise Ionic plain-shafted pilasters supporting entablatures crowned alternately by triangular and segmental pediments. In the middle of the first-floor tier is a venetian window, its side lights framed by plain pilas-

ters and an entablature of the Corinthian order, while the two windows on each side are set within moulded architraves, surmounted by friezes and cornices, and all have moulded sills resting on consoles.

The principal front faces north and gains immediately by the fall in ground level which brings the basement-story into full view. This fine rusticated base, pierced by square windows with projecting keystones dying into the deep platband, projects from the main body of the building, for about one-third of its length, to carry the great hexastyle portico, with its return flanks of two full inter-columniations ending with engaged half-columns against the building face. In this portico Wood has used a giant order of columns, with moulded bases, plain shafts and Roman Corinthian capitals, supporting an entablature and triangular pediment identical with those of the south front. The fenestral arrangement is also identical with that of the south front, except that here the windows are enriched. It will be seen from Wood's elevational drawing (Fig. 37) that although he intended the ground story

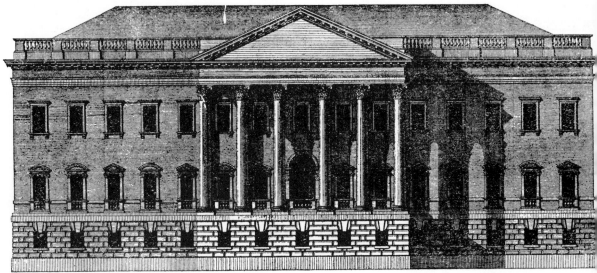

The ELEVATION, to the North,

Of Mr. Allen's House, in the Widcomb of Camalodunum, near Bath,
with the Windows Dressed according to the Original Design.

I. Wood Arch.   P. Fourdrinier Sculp

Fig. 37.
(from Wood's 'Essay towards a Description of Bath' 1749)

windows to be dressed as 'tabernacles' in the same manner as those of the east front, they were executed with blind balustrades, moulded architraves, friezes, and cornices crowned alternately by triangular and segmental pediments, while the friezes and cornices were omitted from the architraves surrounding the first-floor windows. The balustraded parapet, with solid dies centred above the piers between the windows, is returned round the flanks of the portico and stopped against the pediment.

The basement is continued on either side of the north front, by rusticated arcades ending with quadrant sweeps against the east and west ranges of building. Wood had originally intended that these arcades should be surmounted by open colonnaded galleries linking the mansion with the *porte-cochere* pavilions, with pedestals bearing vases or statuary placed in the intercolumniations, but this extravagant proposal was abandoned at an early stage.

The detached *porte-cochere* pavilions were designed to form the chief architectural incidents in the transition from the great house to the less imposing office wings. The east pavilion, which was built adjoining the office wing, survives in an altered form, but Wood's drawing shows the original design for the principal front of these rectangular structures. The massive corner piers, set on plinths and relieved by semi-circular arched niches, were finished with a plain impost from which rose a three-centred arch with a triple keystone, the spandrels being relieved with sunk rectangular panels over the niches. The modillioned cornice was surmounted by a dwarf attic story, with an oblong opening in the centre and similar sunk panels at either side. The angles of the roof were splayed off to effect the transition from the square building to the crowning octagonal lantern, with its cupola crowned with a ball and baluster vane (Fig. 38).

Only the west range of offices was built under Wood's direction, and to a revised design, but even this has now disappeared under the weight of nineteenth-century acre-

The ELEVATION, to the North, of the Square Pavilion to Mr. Allen's House In the Widcomb of Camalodunum, near Bath. For Coaches to Stop under, &c.   P. Fourdrinier Sculp

Fig. 38.
(from Wood's 'Essay towards a Description of Bath' 1749)

tions. It will be seen from the original design how rightly subservient to the splendour of the mansion these wings would have appeared, had they been carried out according to his wishes, but in this he was over-ruled and the perfection of his great design ruined in consequence. Wood's allegiance to the pure Palladianism of Inigo Jones is nowhere more completely demonstrated than in this design for the west wing, where the great scale and simplicity of detail, the bold Tuscan portico, and the wooden eaves cornice of great projection, all serve to remind one of St. Paul's, Covent Garden (Fig. 39).

The Palladian Bridge over the fishponds at the foot of the estate was built about 1755 and closely resembles the famous bridge at Wilton, designed by the 9th Earl of Pembroke and Roger Morris. Although more true to its prototype than is the later copy at Stowe, certain changes have been introduced into the design of the Prior Park example, for whereas at Wilton all the intercolumniations of the gallery are equal in width, here the middle one is

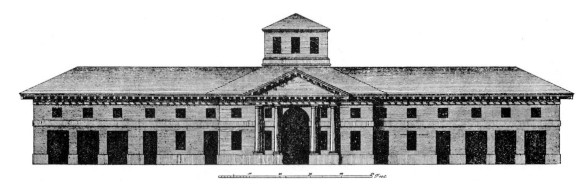

The ELEVATION, to the South,
Of the Weftward Wing of Offices to Mr. Allen's Houfe in the Widcomb of Camalodunum, near Bath,
with the Roof as it was Originally Defigned.

I. Wood Arch.

P. Fourdrinier Sculp.

Fig. 39.
(from Wood's 'Essay towards a Description of Bath' 1749)

Prior Park. The Palladian bridge.

wider than those on either side. Inside the gallery the difference is even more marked, for instead of the richly carved entablature and coffered ceiling of Wilton, the former is quite simply treated and the ceiling is of plain plastering.

The Parades (see also Appendix V)

In 1730 Wood contemplated building in the Abbey Orchard, then leased by Humphrey Thayer from the Duke of Kingston. Although subject to flooding, this ground was conveniently situated and, with Thayer's approval, Wood prepared plans to build his Circus there. This scheme failed to find support but the basic plan for the King's Circus of 1754 was foreshadowed in Wood's layout for St. James's Triangle, now the Parade Gardens.

With Queen Square nearly completed, Wood again turned his attention to the Abbey Orchard and on April 25th, 1738, he entered on a treaty for the land, planning to develop it as part of his proposed Royal Forum. Although the Corporation were now more favourably disposed towards enlarging the city, they rejected Wood's proposal, objecting that the ground was marshy and difficult of

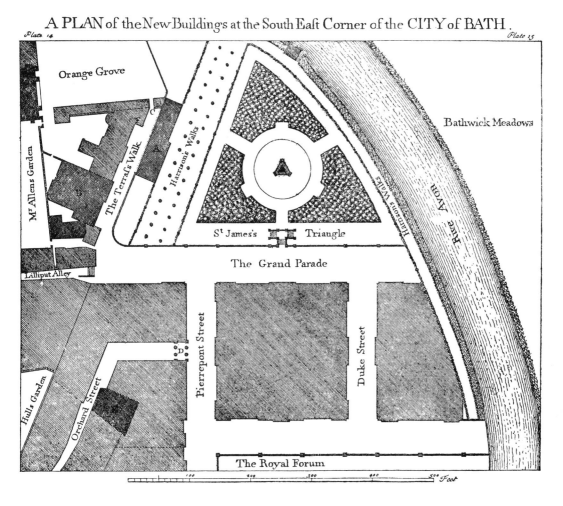

Fig. 40.
(from Wood's 'Essay towards a Description of Bath' 1749)

...ccess. Their opposition was overcome with
...he aid of Beau Nash and on May 22nd, 1739,
Wood became 'an absolute Contractor for the
Ground of the Abbey Orchard'. An indenture
of July 3rd, 1739, records that Evelyn Duke of
Kingston conveyed to John Wood and James
Leake, a bookseller and Wood's publisher, 'all
that piece or parcel of ground . . . known by
the name of the Abbey Orchard containing by
estimation four acres or thereabouts . . . being
within the suburbs of the city of Bath'. After
the customary peppercorn lease, the Duke and
his heirs were to be paid a yearly fee farm rent
of £100 tax free and a further fee farm rent of

8s. 4d. payable to the King's Majesty his heirs
and successors. Rents of the Grand Parade
houses amounting to £100 were reserved to the
Duke in full satisfaction of the said yearly rent
of £100 reserved under the indenture.

Wood now finalised his plans, which originally included building a grand assembly-
house (see Appendix IV), and a common sewer
was constructed to drain the site. Building
leases to tradesmen and others willing to construct the houses were granted between 1739
and 1751, five sites of varying frontage being
taken by Ralph Allen.

On March 10th, 1740, the first stone was

laid of the houses fronting the Grand, or North Parade, and some six months later the whole range was ready for roofing. Subsequent progress was more slow and the first stone of the buildings overlooking the Royal Forum was not laid until January 27th, 1743. The plan reproduced from Wood's *Essay* (Fig. 40) shows the original layout and includes the beginning of a further range of houses on the east side of the Royal Forum. Although this part of the project was abandoned by Wood, its revival as Kingston Square led to the erection of the early nineteenth-century houses between Pierrepont Street and Henry Street.

Having been forced to modify his design for the 'palace' treatment proposed for Queen Square, and to omit the grand parade planned for its southern side, Wood transferred these features to his new scheme, which was to consist of a great quadrangle of houses, some 220 ft. square, bounded on the north by a terrace walk, 525 ft. in length, and 52 ft. 6 ins. in breadth, to be called The Grand Parade; on the south by a similar terrace overlooking the proposed Royal Forum; and on the east and west by Pierrepont and Duke Streets with their subsidiary blocks of houses. The terraces and streets before the houses were to be raised some 18 ft. above the original ground level, and the retaining walls of the terraces were to have formed a series of recesses framed by a rusticated arcade, corresponding to the fenestration of the houses above. The quadrangular block in the centre was to have had its north and south fronts treated with all the richness lavished on the north side of Queen Square, with a giant order of Corinthian columns and pilasters, to which the subsidiary ranges were to provide plain foils. Although the builders to whom Wood granted

The Grand (North) Parade. General view looking west.
(*water-colour drawing by T. Malton, jr. c.1777*)

sub-leases had covenanted to build the frontages in strict conformity with his designs, it was not long after the work had begun that 'a Scheme, contrived by one of the Tenants, broke out, to lay aside the Ornaments; to alter the Proportion of the Walk; and to erect the Terrass Wall with Rubble Stone, so as to have no Reference to the Building above'.

Wood had proposed elevations for the subsidiary blocks of houses similar to those he had already used on the east side of Queen Square and in Wood Street. This treatment was subsequently imposed on all the frontages, with some modifications to that of the South Parade, with a resultant severity of aspect that has been accentuated into dull heaviness by the later maltreatment of many of the windows.

The Grand (North) Parade has the same compositional basis as the north side of Queen Square, with slight forward breaks in the building face forming a central feature, five windows wide, flanked by wings and end pavilions, respectively seven and three windows wide. The doorways, generally of rectangular form, with moulded architraves and triangular pediments supported on carved consoles, relieve an otherwise plain ground-story in which the windows are set without architraves. A deep platband marks the first-floor level, and a plain continued sill originally underlined the range of first-floor windows and provided a stop for their architraves, which are surmounted by friezes and cornices. The smaller windows lighting the second-floor have similar architrave surrounds rising from plain sills, and the modillioned main cornice is surmounted by a solid parapet, broken against the great triangular pediment which crowns the central feature.

The general details of the front to the South Parade are similar, but the composition is improved by the introduction of a central feature, vertically divided into three equal parts each three windows wide. The triangular pediment crowning the middle division is smaller and consequently lacks the oppressive heaviness of that to the North Parade. The

effect of lightness is enhanced by the open balustrade surmounting the main cornice. Pedestals above the end pavilions and on each side of the pediment were originally surmounted by gadrooned vases.

The elevational treatment of North Parade is repeated in Duke Street and Pierrepont Street, although Wood intended to decorate each pedimented central feature with a venetian window at first-floor level. On the west side of Pierrepont Street is St. James's Portico,

Duke Street, looking north.

skilfully contrived to give access to Orchard Street without breaking the uniformity of the street façade. The portico forms the ground-story of the middle houses, the upper part of the building being carried on four massive Tuscan columns, dividing the opening into a carriage-way and two footways, the middle intercolumniation being 10 ft., and the side openings each 5 ft. in width.

The Parades have suffered more from indiscriminate alteration than any other of Bath's major architectural ensembles. Modern shop-fronts have been inserted into some houses, and the proportions of many windows have been spoilt by cutting down the aprons, splaying reveals, and removing the sash-bars. Parapets have been cut away, terminal vases removed, and the central feature of the east side of Pierrepont Street was refaced in bad taste. The areas in front of the houses were originally surrounded by stone balustrades, but these have long since given way to iron railings. While the balustrading to the north terrace has been replaced, stone vases of poor

profile and cast-iron standard lamps have taken the place of Wood's stone obelisks, a substitution which is no improvement.

The houses, which vary in size, were planned and decorated in a similar manner to those of Queen Square, but internal changes have spoiled the clarity of the original arrangements and caused many features of decorative interest to be removed. Many of the fine staircases still remain, constructed of oak and mahogany and having the deep apsidal half-landings that are typical of the period.

Fountain House

Although Fountain Buildings, the double-fronted houses at the junction of London and Lansdown Roads, were mostly built in 1775 by William Phillips and others, the group incorporates an earlier mansion, described as Fountain House on the survey of Bath made by Thomas Thorpe in 1742.

Towards Lansdown Road, Fountain House presents a wide three-storied frontage, vertically divided to form a narrow central feature set slightly forward from flanking wings, each two windows wide. The original ground-story of the wings has been cut away, but the central feature retains the wide doorway, now subdivided, set with deep reveals in a bold rusticated arch, its keystone dying into the platband. The first-floor is dominated by the fine venetian window in the central feature, with consoles supporting the moulded sill from which rise Doric pilasters, framing the side lights and carrying an entablature which is returned into the arched middle light and provides a springing for the moulded archivolt. The two windows in either wing have similar sills, and are framed by moulded architraves surmounted by pulvinated friezes and cornices. The five square windows lighting the second-floor are uniformly set within moulded architraves broken in at the sides, and the front is finished with a bold cornice surmounted by a plain parapet, which is stopped against the triangular pediment above the central feature. Apart from the alterations to

Pierrepont Street. St. James's portico.

Fountain Buildings, Lansdown Road.

Nos. 1 and 2 The Terrace Walk

the ground-story, this front has suffered little change other than the obliteration of some detail by corrosion.

The Terrace Walk

The first houses fronting on to The Terrace Walk were built soon after 1728 from Wood's designs, and the range was extended to the south when the Parades were formed. During the early years of the nineteenth-century the Walk was widened and York Street formed, improvements which necessitated demolishing Wiltshire's Assembly House and refronting the earlier houses.

These alterations did not affect the later houses, Nos. 1 and 2, which were probably built round about 1750. While the upper parts of their elevations were designed in accordance with the accepted Palladian conventions of the time, and call for no detailed description, the ground-stories of both houses are of interest. No. 1 still preserves a stone shopfront of remarkable beauty, with four engaged half-columns, having plain shafts and Ionic capitals, supporting an enriched entablature with a modillioned cornice, and framing three arched openings of which the moulded archivolts are broken by keystones carved with human masks. The spandrels of the side arches are adorned with formalized floriated ornament, while drapery festoons ornament those of the wide elliptical arch in the centre. Although the joinery work is modern it is in excellent taste, and the whole front has been carefully restored.

Crowbrow House, once famous as The Parade Coffee House, has a fine doorway, placed off-centre, its arched opening being framed by engaged half-columns, with plain shafts and Ionic capitals, supporting an entablature which is surmounted by a triangular pediment, broken in the centre by a small pedestal. On the right of the doorway is a barrel-bowed window, an excellent modern replacement of an original which was rather larger in scale.

North Parade Buildings (formerly Gallaway's Buildings)

On a 'Map of the dissolved Abbey or Priory of Bath belonging to His Grace the Duke of Kingston', dated 1750, the site of North Parade Buildings is shown and described as 'a Tenement and Garden granted to Wm Gallaway' at a reserved rental of £17 per annum. The fee simple of the property was conveyed to Gallaway, an apothecary, on July 3rd, 1738,

North Parade (Gallaway's) Buildings. The west side.

but he did not begin his building development until about 1750 when John Wood, by an indenture dated May 3rd, 1750, granted certain 'privileges, easements, and advantages' to Gallaway who was then building eight houses 'on the said Garden, intended to be known as

Gallaway's Buildings'. Two more houses, making up the street's total of ten, were built by Henry Fisher, a Bath rough-mason, who purchased the plots from Gallaway. Boddeley's *Bath and Bristol Guide* for 1753 described Gallaway Street as 'neat and new built' and 'consisting chiefly of Lodging-Houses'.

Entered from Lilliput Alley, the street is a paved cul-de-sac extending southwards between two terraces of houses, that on the west side being broken by a short passageway leading to Abbey Green. The south end is open but railed, as the ground beyond lies at a lower level. Although the houses vary in frontage, they share uniform elevations to a Palladian design possibly by Richard Jones but more probably by Thomas Jelly, who was associated

with Jones and Henry Fisher in several Bath developments outside of Wood's undertakings. These three-storied fronts are of ashlar masonry with long-and-short quoins marking the corners of each range. A plain bandcourse defines the first-floor level, and the crowning block cornice is surmounted by a plain parapet. Most of the houses have fine doorcases with plain-shafted Corinthian columns or pilasters supporting entablatures and triangular pediments. All the windows have moulded architraves but those to the first floor also have friezes and cornices, with a triangular pediment to emphasize each alternate window. A front of very similar design, though with a more imposing doorcase, can be seen nearby in Abbey Street. This street was formed about 1756 and was partly sited on the old Abbey House which was demolished to make way for the Kingston Baths, designed and built by Thomas Jelly.

REPRESENTATIVE BUILDINGS OF THE PERIOD 1750–1775

The Circus and Gay Street (see also Appendix V)

An indenture dated November 1st, 1754, enrolled January 21st, 1755, records that Thomas Garrard and Margaret, his wife, conveyed to John Wood of Queen Square, Bath, eldest son and heir of John Wood, then deceased, and to Samuel Purlewent as trustee 'all that piece or parcel of ground containing by measure 9 acres lying together and being part of a certain pasture called the Hayes', subject to an annual rent charge of £163. On this ground the upper part of Gay Street, the Circus, and part of Brock Street were built. Although the elder Wood had already agreed to buy the nine acres, by a contract dated December 18th, 1753, he died before any conveyance was made. By his will 'all his estate and hereditaments in Walcott' were left to his wife Jenny. However, the conveyance of the Hayes ground was made to the younger Wood,

Abbey Street. Houses on west side.

it being 'apprehended that the estate and interest which the said John Wood, the father, acquired in Equity in and to the said premises comprised in the said contract did not pass by the said will, but devolved in a course of descent upon the said John Wood as heir at law to his father'.

Despite persistent ill health, the elder Wood must have conceived the plan and overall design for the King's Circus, perhaps leaving his son to work on the detailing. It was a masterly conception, translating the external grandeur and detailed multiplicity of a Roman amphitheatre into terms of domestic architecture. Evidently the project soon found support from Bath's leading builders and others, as the building leases for the Gay Street sites, except for seven on the east side, were all granted by the younger Wood on January 3rd, 1755. The plots for houses in the 'west wing' of the Circus were granted at various dates, the first on January 3rd, 1755 and the last on December 31st, 1765. Similarly, those in the 'east wing' were granted between October 2nd, 1762 and August 9th, 1766, and those in the 'north wing' between June 19th, 1764 and July 29th, 1766.

Gay Street provides a sober transition from the grandeur of Queen Square to the magnificence of the Circus. Except for No. 8 on the west side, the house-fronts are of a standard design architecturally related to the east side of Queen Square, being uniformly three stories high but varying from two to four windows in width. To accord with the rising ground, each house steps up above its southern neighbour and the first-floor bandcourse and crowning cornice are returned at the party-wall lines. The doorcases vary in design according to the taste and purse of the builder.

The front of No. 8, known as The Carved House, must reflect the taste and profession of its first leaseholder Prince Hoare, the sculptor. Here a different fenestration pattern has allowed the doorway and two ground-story windows to be grouped within a setting of four plain-shafted Corinthian pilasters and their entablature, the lintels above the openings being carved with garlands. This framing is repeated round the three first-floor windows, the middle one being accented with a triangular pediment. The three second-floor windows are now without architraves, and the crowning cornice matches those of the adjoining houses.

Although John Wood the elder died on May 23rd, 1754, he lived to see the foundation stone of his King's Circus laid. According to *The Gentleman's Magazine* for February 7th, 1754

> 'the first stone of the building which is to be called the King's Circus, and which is to consist of 33 elegant houses, was laid. It is to be a circular area of 318 ft. diameter surrounded by 3 equal and similar piles of building, in theatrical style. In the centre is to be an equestrian statue of His Majesty, and 3 streets 52 ft. wide are to lead to it, each terminated with a fine building.'

The buildings surround a circular area of 318 ft. diameter, corresponding to the north-south dimension of Queen Square. The grouping of the houses into three equal segments is a brilliant contrivance of planning, designed to give the effect of a continuous range of building confronting the spectator and closing the vista from each of the entering streets. The south-west range contains 11 houses, the south-east 12, and the north 10. Though varying in size all the houses contain three principal stories, with basements and attics, and have a uniform frontage height of some 42 ft.

The elevations 'in theatrical style' are of the most elaborate description, a *tour-de-force* of external decoration clearly designed to impress the beholder at close quarters. The three stories are enriched with superimposed orders of Roman Doric, Ionic and Corinthian plain-shafted three-quarter columns, carrying their appropriate entablatures. These engaged columns are arranged in pairs, 108 to each complete tier, and frame the rectangular windows which are set without architraves in the main wall face. The Doric entablature has its frieze decorated with triglyphs, alternating with

Gay Street. No. 8. 'The Carved House'.

Miles's Buildings, from George Street.

The Circus. The north segment.
(*water-colour drawing by T. Malton, jr. c.1780*)

The Circus, looking south to Gay Street.
(water-colour drawing by S. H. Grimm, c.1773)

carved motifs emblematic of the arts, sciences, and occupations, but the friezes to the second and third entablatures are left unadorned. Each bay of the main wall face above the third-story windows is decorated with a frieze carving of a female mask, linked by garlands with the Corinthians capitals, and underlined by a continuation of the astragal moulding at the head of the column shafts. The pedestal parapet is broken forward over each pair of columns to form bases for the crowning ornaments of stone acorns.

Fortunately, Wood's dominant use of the three orders had rendered insignificant the various minor changes that have been made to the Circus façades. These include the enlarging of window openings, especially in the first two stories, and the addition of iron guardrails at first-floor level. Now that the stonework has been cleaned and restored, and the windows generally refurnished with barred sashes, the Circus has regained much, if not all, of its original splendour.

The houses behind these uniform façades show extremely diverse planning arrangements, which find expression in the picturesque garden elevations of the buildings. Some notes on the planning and decoration of the more interesting houses will be found under the appropriate headings.

A water-colour drawing made in 1773 by Samuel H. Grimm shows the original appearance of the King's Circus, with its broad pavement ringed by tethering-posts and mounting-steps, and a roadway of cobbles radiating from the covered reservoir in the centre, upon which there were three iron lampholders. Five immense plane trees form a group in the middle of the enclosure, but their presence is to be deplored, for they only serve to destroy the scale of the buildings and to interrupt the vista from each entering street.

Bladud's Buildings. London Road front.

Bladud's Buildings

Bladud's Building, erected in 1755 on some Corporate property described as Cockey's Garden, was the first to be built of the three great terraces lining the east side of London Road. The fifteen houses were built by various speculating builders, who conformed to a prescribed elevation. No architect's name has been recorded in connection with this design, and it may therefore be assumed to have been produced for the Corporation's approval by either Jelly or Atwood, both of whom built in this terrace. They were competent architects and their assimilation of the broad principles of Palladianism, from study of the many available pattern-books, led them to design buildings which compare favourably with the less spectacular achievements of the Woods.

This building is probably unique among the Bath terraces in that both elevations, facing east and west, were regarded as being equal in importance, and were similarly composed and ornamented. The open nature of the site encouraged the designer to treat the middle and each end house as slightly projecting pavilions, but otherwise the houses are uniformly fronted with the standard elevation, three stories high and three windows wide. The doorways have pedimented surrounds of varying richness, but all the windows are set within moulded architraves rising from plain sills, those to the first-floor having friezes and cornices, with a triangular pediment emphasizing the middle window of each house. The first-floor platband and bracketed main cornice are continued across the fronts, which finish with a pedestal parapet stopped against the triangular pediment crowning the middle house.

The balance of the London Road front has unfortunately been impaired by the addition of a semi-circular bay to No. 6, the second house on the right of the pedimented centre, and the insertion of shop fronts into the ground-stories of several houses in the southern half of the range. No. 6 retains the original dormer windows to the attic-storey, and part of the stone tile roofing once common to all the houses.

Milsom Street

In 1755 the Bath Corporation granted a lease of the land north of George Street, called the Town Acre, to Daniel Milsom, a wine cooper, at a yearly rental of £100. He already held Milsom's Garden, a large tract of land extending southwards from George Street, and his intention was to develop the two properties for building purposes, but finding his plans frustrated by the presence of the Poor House, then standing on the site now occupied by Somersetshire Buildings, Milsom repeatedly applied to the Corporation for an abatement of part of his rentals. The Corporation's Minutes for September 20th, 1760, record their decision 'to let Mr. Milsom take all rents and profits of his Garden and Town Acre for 35 years, and at expiration to deliver up all right and title in both estates and the rents thereof forever. They to join with him in building leases for 99 years agreeable to a plan to be settled by both parties, Mr. Milsom to be at all expense of making Common Sewer and to prepare the ground for building.' At their meeting on February 20th, 1761, the Corporation approved the plans and elevations for the proposed buildings, which were produced by John Horton, who was empowered to act, with the Mayor and Walter Wiltshire, on behalf of the Corporation and to grant, in conjunction with Milsom, the building leases for 99 years. Typical of these leases was one granted in 1763, as between the Mayor, Aldermen and Corporation, of the First Part, Charles Milsom, Wine Cooper, of the Second Part, and Walter Wiltshire, Gent, of the Third Part, for a building site in Milsom's Street, 26 ft. in front and 92 ft. deep, the rental being reckoned at four shillings per foot frontage. As neither the lease nor the Corporation's records name a surveyor, it can be assumed that it was made a condition that the house fronts should

be uniform and similar to those adopted for Bladud Buildings.

When Milsom Street was laid out, George Street was lengthened eastwards with Edgar and Prince's Buildings forming the north side. The nine houses of Edgar Buildings were built on the southern part of the Town Acre, under leases granted by the Mayor and Corporation on September 29th, 1761. Those who leased sites and built houses included John Ford, mason, and Samuel Sainsbury, tyler, both participants in the building projects of the Woods. Prince's Buildings, a terrace of seven houses, was built between 1764 and 1770 on part of 'Close No. 58'. This scheme was promoted by Prince Hoare, the sculptor, who purchased the site from Thomas and Daniel Omer under an indenture dated May 31st, 1764.

All of the houses comprised in these developments were given fronts of a standard Palladian design, similar to Bladud Buildings but more refined in details. Every house is three stories high and three windows wide, all the openings except those in the ground story having moulded architraves. Those to the tall first-floor windows rise from sills resting on consoles, and are finished with friezes and cornices, that of the middle window being returned to form a triangular pediment. The second-floor window architraves have eared heads, and all the fronts are finished with a modillioned cornice and plain parapet. The Milsom Street houses are stepped up to conform with the rising ground, but Edgar Buildings is raised on a level pavement and treated as a balanced composition, with a slightly projecting house at each end, and a pedimented centre which provides an effective termination to Milsom Street. Prince's Buildings differs in that there is a pediment to each alternate first-floor window.

The intended uniformity of Milsom Street was disrupted when Thomas Baldwin built, in 1781–83, the imposing group of Somersetshire Buildings on the old Poor-House site, and a heterogeneous collection of shopfronts has completely obliterated the orderly succession of windows and pedimented doorcases depicted by William Watts and Thomas Malton.

Brock Street (see also Appendix V)

The east end of Brock Street, with six houses on the north side and five on the south, was built on part of the nine acres of ground conveyed on November 1st, 1754, to the younger Wood, who granted leases of the eleven house plots between October 4th, 1763 and June 26th, 1767. By this time Wood and Thomas Brock, his brother-in-law and trustee, were already negotiating with Sir Benet Garrard for a further conveyance of nineteen acres on which to build more houses. This conveyance was made by an indenture dated December 20th, 1766, and as a first step Brock Street was lengthened to provide an appropriate link between the Circus and the intended Royal Crescent.

The Brock Street houses are of medium size and scale, their fronts plainer than those in Gay Street. Most have a pediment-crowned Doric or Ionic doorcase, or porch, and two windows in the ground story, a venetian window to the first floor, and a straight-headed window of three lights above, all being without architraves. The younger Wood lived at No. 12 on the south side, where some houses are double-fronted, No. 7 being an excellent example. An Ionic porch projects between two venetian windows similar to those of the first floor, and the second floor has three single-light windows. The crowning modillioned cornice and plain parapet continue unbroken across the neighbouring houses. Additions and alterations have impaired the unity of the south side, but the intended effect of the street can be seen in the north side terrace west of Margaret's Buildings, where three single-fronted houses extend from each side of a narrow centrepiece. This originally marked

Brock Street, looking west towards the Royal Crescent.

the entrance to Margaret Chapel, and the first-floor window of three lights is handsomely dressed with an Ionic order of pilasters and columns, the latter supporting a pediment extending above the middle light.

The Royal Crescent (see also Appendix V)

The younger Wood's Royal Crescent is, beyond question, the summit of the Palladian achievement in Bath, providing a splendid climax to the monumental sequence begun with Queen Square. Approached from the Circus through Brock Street, with its relatively modest houses, the full majesty of the Crescent, with its superb sweep of Ionic columns facing an open prospect, creates an overwhelming impression.

The site was acquired under an indenture dated December 20th, 1766, whereby Sir Benet Garrard, subject to a yearly rent charge of £220, conveyed to John Wood, of Brock Street, Walcot, and Thomas Brock, of Chester (as Trustee), nineteen acres of meadow or pasture ground in the parish of Walcot. This ground comprised certain closes called the Hayes Furlong and the Hayes Lower Furlong, being bounded north by the road from Walcot to Weston, west by the Town Common, south and partly east by a line drawn in range with the fronts of houses in Brock Street. Wood convenanted to build within ten years 'good stone messuages or houses and construct streets in connection therewith, according to a plan annexed to the said indenture'. While building the Crescent he had permission to set up a stone survey pillar on Garrard's land to the south 'in order that Wood and his workmen might resort thereto to take views for the better forming the buildings intended to be built in the said Crescent'.

The *Bath Chronicle* for Thursday, May 21st, 1767, records that 'on Tuesday last the foundation stone was laid of the first house of the intended new building above the Circus, called the Royal Crescent'. No. 1, the east end house leased in 1769 to Thomas Brock, was built first, presumably to serve as a model for later builders to follow. Several sub-leases were granted by Wood and Brock between February, 1770 and December 1771, mostly to various building tradesmen who collaborated in building the houses. These sub-leases contained several clauses framed to ensure that the standard of building was high, and, above all, that the front elevation was executed in strict conformity with John Wood's design which, to quote from a standard sub-lease—'shall not after the same is built and finished at any time or times afterwards be ever altered or varied'. When each house was finished its builder undertook to 'cleanse and tone down the Stone Work on the Outside of the sd. Mess'ge to the End no Crack may appear and the whole Building may be of one Colour'.

The thirty houses form a concave semi-elliptical building, fronting a great lawn but separated from it by a wide flagged pavement and a roadway of granite setts. The semi-ellipse has a major axis of 538 ft. east to west, this dimension being prolonged by the 48 ft. wide return fronts of the end houses. Every house contains a basement, three stories, and roof garrets, but they vary in size. Most have a frontage width of 24 ft. 9 ins., comprising three bays of the great colonnade, but Nos. 14 to 17, in the middle of the range, occupy four bays each, as does No. 30. This house, like No. 1, also has the advantage of a return front, five bays wide.

The noble front of finely worked freestone masonry rises some 47 ft. from the pavement level to the capping of the crowning balustrade. The elements of the composition are simple but so skilfully used that the total effect is extremely grand. The ground story face is quite plain, the windows and doorways not differentiated but spaced at equal intervals in square-headed openings without architraves. Above a deep bandcourse rises the giant Roman Ionic order of engaged three-quarter columns, having plain shafts decreasing in diameter from 2 ft. 6 ins., and diagonally voluted capitals. These columns, 22 ft. 6 ins high, are spaced at 8 ft. $4\frac{1}{2}$ in. centres to divide the upper two stories into bays, each one

The Royal Crescent. General view from south-west.
(*water-colour drawing by S. H. Grimm, c.1773*)

The Royal Crescent. General view from south-east.
(*water-colour drawing by T. Malton, jr. c.1780*)

The Royal Crescent. Restored front of No. 1.

window wide, the openings also without architraves. There are, in all, 114 columns supporting an entablature appropriate to their order, having a moulded architrave, plain frieze, and modillioned cornice. Here it may be observed that there is a different spacing of modillions above the paired columns at each end of the building, the most satisfactory spacing being that adopted at the western end which was the latest to be built. Above the crowning cornice is a stone balustrade having dies centred above the columns.

Paired columns emphasise each end of the semi-elliptical colonnade as well as the central bay, where the first-floor window is arch-headed. This provoked a critic to write, in *The Stranger's Assistant* and *Guide to Bath for 1773*, that

'the wretched attempt to make a centre to the Crescent where none is necessary is absurd and preposterous, in a high degree. The pairing of the pillars is too small a difference to be noted in so large a building, as is the window intended to be the centre. . . . Had the centre been desired, it would surely have been more eligible, as a chapel for divine service was wanted in that part of the town, and is now building but a few yards off, to have made that the centre'.

It remains to add that the colonnade is continued across each return front for a further five bays, the middle one being widened for emphasis. The doorway placed centrally below is handsomely dressed with a pedimented Doric doorcase.

The bold architectural scheme of the Crescent has survived relatively unimpaired, although many window openings have been enlarged, notably those of the first floor. Original sashes with glazing bars survive only in some basement and garret windows, while the front doors vary considerably in design and finish. However, the effect originally intended by Wood can now be studied in the east end house, No. 1, which has been scrupulously restored by Philip Jebb for Bernard Cayzer, who generously presented it to the Bath Preservation Trust to serve as their offices and as a typically patrician Georgian house.

Some interesting features of the planning and decoration of the houses are commented on under the appropriate chapter headings, and illustrated. Here, as in Queen Square and the Circus, internal arrangements and finishings varied according to the requirements of the leaseholders, so that while some houses were beautifully decorated to suit an individual taste, others built for casual letting were given only the stock finishings and plaster ornaments then in current use.

St. James's Parade

Book 8 of the Bath Corporation Minutes has this entry for September 30th, 1765: 'Messrs. Richard Jones, Thomas Jelly and Henry Fisher have liberty to pull down the Boro' walls next to the Ambry gardens in order to build new houses there'. The houses referred to formed the south side of Lower Borough Walls, and were built as part of a general development of the Ambry or Amery ground. The best houses were located in Thomas Street, later St. James's Parade, mostly built about 1768 and for many years maintained by its residents as a private close. Harcourt Masters' map of c.1810 shows that the houses fronted a wide paved walk enclosed at both ends by bollards.

The Royal Crescent. The west end.

St. James's Parade. Houses on north-east side.

Although Jelly and Palmer probably built the houses, their fronts closely resemble those designed by the younger Wood for Miles's Buildings, Brock Street and Rivers Street, where venetian windows are used in the principal story. In St. James's Parade, the venetian windows have band architraves that rise from sills on bold consoles and finish with cornices, turned over the arched middle light. The stone doorcases are of the usual type, with a pedimented entablature supported by two columns, generally, but not invariably, Roman Doric. At Nos. 39 and 40 the adjacent entrances share a doorcase composed of three columns, with 'Tower of the Winds' capitals, supporting an entablature having a festooned frieze, and a large triangular pediment. There is some evidence to suggest that the houses to which this shared doorcase belongs was built by John Eveleigh.

The Paragon

The Corporation's Minutes for February 24th, 1767, record the appointment of a committee 'formed to propose a plan and elevations of a building to be erected on Mrs. Hooper's ground and the Chamber land adjoining Bladud's Buildings', and on July 18th, 1768, a 99 years' building lease of the whole site was granted to Thomas Warr Atwood, at a rental of four shillings per foot frontage. The records show that on September 7th following, the plans and elevations of the building proposed for Atwood's ground were produced and signed as approved by the Mayor, William Chapman, subject to certain restrictions governing the stables or other buildings which were to front the lower London Road.

Upon this long and narrow site, sloping between two curving roads of different levels, Atwood built the fine crescent of twenty-one houses which he named Paragon Buildings, a costly speculation involving a massive substructure of retaining walls and vaults which were intended for coach-houses and storage. As in the similarly sited range of Belmont, the houses were planned with staircases rising towards the street front, so that the principal rooms at the back overlooked the extensive prospect of the Avon valley.

The building relies for its effectiveness upon the use made of good classic detail and the excellent scale of its parts, the proportions being somewhat larger than those of the two adjoining terraces. The three-story fronts to the houses, each of which is three windows wide, are uniformly treated with the standard elevation adopted for buildings sited on Corporate property. Except for one house at each end of the range, which is set slightly forward to form a terminal pavilion and has a ground-story of three rusticated arches framing the rectangular door and window openings, every house has a doorway framed by Doric pilasters supporting a triangular pedimented entablature. The first-floor platband and bracketed main cornice are continued along the whole front, and a triangular pediment serves to emphasize the middle window of the three to the first-floor of each house. It is evident that this terrace front was crowned with a balustrade.

Walcot Parade

Walcot Parade is a picturesque range of houses raised on a high terrace above the north-west side of the London Road, and was built as Swithin's Terrace and Butler's Buildings round about 1770. The houses originally commanded an uninterrupted view over the river, and were then inhabited by people of rank and fashion.

Built on sloping ground, the houses have a complicated sub-structure of cellars and basements, with three principal stories and a roof attic above. Although the elevations were all designed and detailed in a similar manner, according to the accepted Palladian convention of the time, they vary in width and height and it is very evident that the various builders responsible made no attempt to produce a balanced composition.

The Paragon. General view.

The Paragon. Houses at the south end.

Walcot Parade. General view.

Belmont, Lansdown Road. View from Bennett Street.

Belmont

Sited on the east side of steeply rising Lansdown Road, this impressive range of twenty houses was built in stages between 1768 and 1773, and originally designated 'Bellemont Row'. Each of the houses, numbered from 1 to 12, is stepped up, with the raised pavement ramping up to the terrace in front of the remaining houses, which were built to a uniform level. Some of the houses were planned in pairs sharing common chimney stacks, and all have staircases rising towards the street front, to allow the principal rooms to be placed at the back, overlooking the Avon valley.

Every house in this range is fronted with the standard type of three-story elevation, having three equally spaced windows to each upper floor. Many of the doorways are set in a framing of engaged Doric three-quarter columns supporting a triangular pedimented entablature, and a triangular pediment emphasizes the middle window to the first-floor of each house. Malton's drawing of the Assembly Rooms shows the Belmont houses with continued sills below the first-floor windows, but these have generally been removed and the windows cut down to floor level. The fronts of Nos. 5 and 6, and 16 to 20 have been heightened to include the attic-story, and to the return front of No. 1 has been added an exquisitely detailed porch of serpentine plan, which bears every evidence of having been designed by Thomas Baldwin.

The Streets surrounding the New Assembly Rooms

The area of ground bounded on the east by Lansdown Road, and on the west by the Circus, was probably laid out for building round about 1770, with new streets planned in parallel alignment with the New Assembly Rooms and the recently finished buildings in George Street, rather than in axial conformity with the north-east exit from the Circus.

Although most of the leading speculative builders of the time, men such as Beale, Fielder, Ford, Hensley and Hewlett, participated in this development, it is evident that they worked together on a general layout devised by the younger Wood, and generally conformed to the typical elevations prescribed by him.

The majority of the houses in these streets belong to a standard terrace type, with a basement, three principal floors, and an attic contained in the double-mansard roof. The elevation most generally used is one three windows wide, with two on the ground-floor set without architraves in a plain wall face, which is relieved by the doorway with its surrounding architrave and projecting cornice supported by consoles. Several of the houses in each street show the structural peculiarity of a flat arch common to both ground-floor windows, with voussoirs radiating from a centre

Rivers Street. Houses on south side.

located in the intermediate pier; obviously the idiosyncrasy of one particular builder. The tall first-floor windows, many of which have been lengthened, are uniformly framed by moulded architraves, which rise from moulded sills resting on consoles, and are surmounted by plain friezes and cornices. No attempt has been made to vary the rhythm by introducing pediments at intervals. The second-floor windows are smaller and more simply treated, with moulded architraves rising from plain sills. The first-floor platband, the modillioned main cornice, and the solid parapet provide horizontal emphasis and are continuous where the houses are built upon level ground, but are returned and stopped against the party wall divisions where the houses are sited on rising ground.

Alfred Street

Alfred's Buildings, first referred to in the rate-books for 1772, may be identified with the east terrace of houses on the south side of Alfred Street. This range of seven houses is the only example of a compositional group to be found in these new streets, and is markedly similar to the south side of Queen Square. The wide middle house, set slightly forward, is adorned with an arcaded ground-story and a triangular pediment crowning the main cornice. Except that each end house is set forward to form a responding pavilion, the remaining houses are very similar to those in the other terraces, the difference being in matters of decorative detail, such as the eared architraves, and the doorways framed by Doric pilasters supporting tringular pedimented entablatures.

The eight houses opposite the Assembly Rooms are uniformly fronted with the standard elevation already described, but No. 14 is distinguished from the others by its elaborately decorated doorway. This has a moulded and enriched architrave, on either side of which are jambs decorated with pendants of husks and bearing consoles, carved with acanthus leaves, which support an enriched cornice. The frieze between the consoles is adorned with festoons of husks looped over paterae, and the cornice is crowned with poppy-head vases flanking a pediment-like pedestal carved with acanthus scrolling, which supports a bust representing King Alfred. Before this doorway is a fine wrought-iron lamp overthrow, with link extinguishers on the standards.

The houses on the north side of Alfred Street, with the return range of Oxford Row, occupy a site which can be identified with the 'Hand and Flower' ground which Warr Atwood obtained in 1773 by dispossessing the original leaseholder, one Rogers, and afterwards re-leased the plots at great personal profit.

Bennett Street

First figures in the rate-books for 1773, and presumably derives its name from one of the principal leaseholders, Francis Bennett, who was Mayor of Bath in 1773. The first houses to be built were those on either side of Russell Street, the remainder of the north side and the terrace on the south side being completed round about 1776. The few houses at the extreme west end of the street may be properly regarded as forming the return frontages to the Circus.

Russell Street

Built in 1773, rises from the north side of Bennett Street, axially opposite to the Assembly Rooms, to join with Rivers Street. Each house is stepped up to accord with the rising ground, and except for those houses on the west side nearest Bennett Street, which have simple venetian windows to the ground- and first-floors, the standard three-window front is used. This street is most effectively terminated to the south by the Assembly Rooms, and to the north by a fine house with a three-sided bay in Rivers Street.

Alfred Street. General view looking west.

Bennett Street. South side with the Assembly Rooms.

Bennett Street. North side.

Russell Street. General view looking north to Rivers Street.

REPRESENTATIVE BUILDINGS OF THE PERIOD 1775–1800

Northumberland Buildings, Wood Street

The houses numbered 1 to 7 Wood Street, and forming Northumberland Buildings, were built in 1778 as a speculation by Thomas Baldwin, who had leased the site from Dr. Henry Harington.

The seven houses form a balanced composition, in which each end house and the middle one are treated as pavilions, set slightly forward from intermediate wings, each containing two houses. While the six equally spaced rectangular openings containing the doors and windows to the ground story of each wing are left unadorned, the middle window of the centre house is set within a blind arched surround and the opening on either side has a rectangular architrave framing, this arrangement being reversed in each end house. A pedestal course originally underlined the whole range of first-floor windows, which have plain surrounds except for the middle window to each end house, and the three to the centre. These latter are given prominence by a framing of architraves, flanked by pilasters with composite capitals supporting an entablature, which has its frieze broken above each window by a tablet carved with festoons. A band of Vitruvian scrolling continues the lines of this entablature across each wing and the side windows of the end pavilions. Here it is used to form an impost for the blind arch framing the central window, which is dressed with architrave, frieze, and triangular pedimented cornice, while the arch lunette is fringed with carved festoons depending from the moulded archivolt. The second-floor windows are all equally plain, but the wall face below is decorated with oval paterae of varying size and design, centred above the windows in the three pavilions, and over each alternate pier in the wings. The delicate main entablature is surmounted by triangular pediments placed over each pavilion, the main wall face being carried up to form a high attic-story terminated by a secondary cornice and plain parapet. The attic windows, which were originally oblong and alternated with panels of the same form, have in most cases been lengthened.

Somersetshire Buildings

For many years after the formation of Milsom Street, the site of the Poor House on the east side remained unbuilt on, but shortly after 1780 a lease of the ground was granted to Thomas Baldwin, who in 1782 erected thereon the group of five houses originally bearing his name, but later designated Somersetshire Buildings. His position as city architect enabled Baldwin to depart from the standard elevation hitherto prescribed for buildings sited on Corporate property, and his work has a scale and magnificence surpassing the earlier houses in the street.

The fine elevation clearly shows that Baldwin was influenced as much by Chambers as by Adam, and although Baldwin's design lacks the final refinements distinguishing the work of those masters, the following criticism, taken from Dallaway's *Observations*, is not deserved:

> 'Milsom Street, from its being built on an ascent, is very striking, and the junction in the middle, of several tenements under one design, is not without an appearance of grandeur. Yet the ornaments are merely such as a builder, uninstructed in the Palladian school, might capriciously have invented.'

The five houses are brought together into an elaborate composition, wherein the wide central house, with its segmental bowed front, and the end houses form pavilions flanking the more simply treated intermediate houses. The ground-story was built with uniformly treated door and window openings forming a rusticated arcade, broken forward to provide a base for the giant order of engaged three-quarter columns, having plain shafts and Corinthian capitals, embracing the two upper stories of the pavilions. There are six columns to the central house, dividing the segmental bow into three equal bays, with a further bay on each

Northumberland Buildings, Wood Street.

Somersetshire Buildings, Milsom Street.
(*water-colour drawing by T. Malton, jr. c.1780*)

side to serve as a respond to the end pavilions of three bays. The three first-floor windows to the bow, and the middle window of each of the remaining houses, have architrave surrounds rising from a pedestal continued below all the windows to this floor and decorated with blind balustrading below each light. Tablets, decorated with rams' heads and festoons, break the architraves and friezes of the enriched windows, which are finished with cornices. The second-floor windows are without architraves, but are underlined by a moulded sill continued between the columns. The fine entablature to the order is returned at the ends of each pavilion, and carried across the intermediate houses. The frieze is decorated with lion masks, centred above the columns and over the windows of the intermediate houses, and the cornice is enriched with dentils and carved modillions. A triangular pediment surmounts each end pavilion, while the remaining houses are finished with an open balustrade having solid dies centred above the columns and piers, and stopping against the pediments, each of which has a pedestal at its apex, originally bearing a vase. The beautiful and accurate delineation of these buildings, made by Thomas Malton, shows how much of the original effect has been lost by the substitution of unrelated shopfronts for the original aracading of the ground-story.

The interiors, although generally well finished, have been altered for commercial uses, but the ground-floor front room in the central house, now the National-Westminster Bank, contains an elaborately decorated ceiling to which full reference is made in the section of this study which deals with decoration.

Portland Place

Ascending steeply northwards from Julian Road, formerly Cottle's Lane, Burlington Street leads to the triangular area of Portland Place, of which the north side forms a uniform range of ten houses, fronting on to a raised terrace. Building appears to have begun round

about 1786 when No. 5, the largest house, was erected for P. C. Crespigny, Esq., to form the centre of the range. Some of the flanking houses were built for Cross, the banker, by John Eveleigh, who probably designed the frontage for the whole terrace.

The elevation of this north range forms a composition which is three stories in height and some 300 ft. in length, and consists of a pedimented central feature flanked by long wings and terminal pavilions treated with an unusual severity of architectural expression.

Portland Place. General view of
north range.

The rectangular windows and arched doorways to the houses in the wings and end pavilions are set without architraves in a plain wall face, which is subdivided horizontally by the platband above the ground-story; the plain continuous sills underlining the two upper tiers of windows; and the crowning entablature with its modillioned cornice. Such decorative interest as there is has been concentrated on the treatment of No. 5, the five-window wide house forming the central feature, in which slight forward breaks in the wall face are used to effect three vertical divisions. That in the middle is three windows wide, and is enriched by rustic quoins carried up to the main entablature, which is surmounted by a triangular pediment. The centrally placed doorway is arched and surrounded by a moulded architrave broken with rustic blocks. The platband is continued across the central feature, as originally was the first-floor sill, but that to the second-floor was omitted. It will be noticed that the outer bays are splayed slightly outwards from the middle three, and their breaks against the wings are enriched with rustic quoins only up to the underside of the platband. The front is finished with a plain parapet stopped against the central pediment.

The broad flight of steps descending from the paved terrace to the roadway, is broken in front of the central house by ramps leading left and right, and providing access for chairs. The iron railing is terminated by stone obelisks, originally carrying lamps, and there are fine overthrow lampholders to Nos. 3 and 9.

The balance of the composition has been impaired by the addition of a further story to three houses on the right of the centre. Minor alterations have been made to the parapet and most windows have lost their glazing bars. It is probable that the aprons to the first-floor windows of the central house were cut down when a veranda was added in the early years of the nineteenth century. This is shown in a lithograph of that time, but has since been removed, although a veranda has been subsequently added to No. 6.

Camden Crescent

Camden Crescent forms only part of a large unfinished project begun round about 1788 on the south-east slope of Beacon Hill. On this site, with its magnificent and airy prospect, the promotors intended to build a great crescent with wings, forming Upper Camden Place, having before it a large garden sloping towards a terrace of houses, and Lower Camden Place, forming a tangent to the crescent. The site was cleared and levelled at considerable expense and rapid progress had been made with the building of the upper crescent, when a series of alarming landslips brought the work to a standstill. That part of the building

which was sited on solid rock was completed, but no further progress was made with the remaining houses, which were eventually demolished. For some years the north-east pavilion of the crescent remained as an isolated and picturesque ruin perched on a crag of rock, and can be seen as such in the drawings by Nattes and others.

Two prominent Bath physicians, Caleb Hillier Parry and John Symons, were actively concerned in this building project, and they leased many of the plots to John Morgan, carpenter, and Mark ffowles, plasterer, whose names figure on some of the original leases. There can be little doubt that John Eveleigh was employed to give the designs for the plans and elevations, for in his ledger for 1788 there is an entry against Morgan in respect of the plans and elevations drawn on two agreements for houses in Camden Place. Apart from this important evidence, the elevation has certain

Camden Crescent. Detail of pedimented centre.

distinctive touches personal to Eveleigh's work, and to that original and unconventional architect should be accorded a design which has been variously ascribed to Chambers, his pupil Willey Revely, and the younger Wood, and by reason of these attributions, over-praised at the expense of Eveleigh's other and more original designs.

Upper Camden Place, now Camden Crescent, was originally planned to consist of thirty-two houses, of which twenty-two were to form the crescent proper, with its great Corinthian order, the remainder composing the flanking wings, their simply treated eleva-tions being stepped down to overcome the sharp falls in the ground level. Because of the landslip only eighteen houses of the crescent, together with the whole of the left wing, were completed, so that the pedimented centre has only four houses on its right, but even in this truncated state Camden Crescent forms a beautiful and impressive landmark in any prospect of Bath from the east.

The elevation shows a use of purely Palla-dian motifs which is most remarkable in a building erected at so late a time, and the only serious solecism committed was in placing a column centrally in the pedimented feature. The centre and end pavilions, respectively four and three bays in width, have arched door and window openings to the ground-story, deeply set in rusticated arcades which form bases for the giant order of engaged three-quarter columns, with plain shafts and Corin-thian capitals, which embrace the two upper stories and support the entablature. This has a modillioned cornice which was originally sur-mounted by an open balustrade with pedestals

Camden Crescent. General view from north.

above the columns and pilasters. The intervening houses are more simply treated, with richly
framed doorways relieving an otherwise plain
ground-story, while pilasters of the giant order
divide the upper stories into bays. In order to
conform to the rising ground level, the windows are stepped up towards the centre in
groups of three, while the first-floor platband
and the crowning entablature rise gradually
from each end pavilion towards the central
feature, which is surmounted by a triangular
pediment. This last has its tympanum
enriched by the sculptured coat-of-arms of
Charles Pratt, Marquis Camden, the politician
and Recorder of Bath after whom the buildings were named, and his crest, an elephant's
head, is used to adorn the keystones of the
doorways to the intervening houses.

Thomas Baldwin, and the development of Bathwick

In 1777 Robert Adam was commissioned by
his friend and patron, William Pulteney, to
prepare plans for the new quarter proposed to
be built on the Bathwick estate, which had
been laid open for development by the construction of Pulteney Bridge in 1770. A second
scheme was evolved by Adam during 1782,
but it would appear that strong local prejudice
must have influenced Pulteney's daughter
Henrietta Laura, to whom the estate had
passed, to set aside Adam's plans and employ
Baldwin to design the general layout and elevations which were adopted when in 1788 she
began to grant building leases for 99 years.
The formation of Argyle Buildings, Laura
Place and Great Pulteney Street proceeded
rapidly, with houses built by Baldwin,
Eveleigh and others for personal speculation,
but when bankruptcy overtook these builders
the work came to a standstill. No serious effort
was made to complete Baldwin's ambitious
layout until during the early nineteenth century, when some streets and terraces were
built to the designs of John Pinch.

Although there are some surprising
gaucheries in the planning, Bathwick generally
exhibits Baldwin's considerable skill in the
layout and composition of urban scenery. Collectively the buildings are effective and group
well, but individually they are disappointing
and exhibit a decadent taste, and close examination of their elevations will reveal many
faults in composition and detail. In particular,
the use of single pilasters, and half-pilasters, at
wide and varied intervals, is most unfortunate.

Argyle Street

Argyle Street, formerly Argyle Buildings,
was built to serve as a link between Pulteney
Bridge and Laura Place, and forms a most
unworthy entrance to Bathwick. The elevations are so weak in composition that doubts
are at once raised as to whether Baldwin's
designs were strictly followed. While the north
side has been considerably altered, the south
side remains much as it was originally
designed. The pedimented terminal features,
which are used as recurring motifs throughout
the principal succession of streets in Bathwick,
bear little relation in scale and character to the
intervening houses, and rise a full story
higher. There are, however, some fine contemporary shopfronts on the south side, which
bear eloquent testimony to the joiner's skill.

Laura Place

Laura Place was planned as an irregular
octagon, to join four streets of different width
and contain four terraces of houses, built out
of parallel alignment but of equal length. Each
elevation is similarly treated to form a balanced composition continuing in line and
detail the adjoining ranges of Great Pulteney
Street. The ground-story, containing flat-
arched door and window openings, forms a
rusticated base to the giant order of fluted
Corinthian pilasters, embracing the first- and
second-floors, and carrying the main entablature, which has a modillioned cornice and is
surmounted by a plain parapet. The eight
pilasters are grouped into pairs which divide
the wall face into three wide and four narrow

Great Pulteney Street. Central feature of middle range on south side.

bays, arranged in alternating sequence and containing respectively three and one of the windows to each of the upper floors. These windows are without architraves, but both tiers are underlined by moulded sills continued between the pilasters, and in each wide bay the middle window at first-floor level is given prominence by its decorative framing. That in the centre of the front is flanked by paired pilaster-strips, with consoles supporting a decorated frieze surmounted by a triangular pediment, while the arched window in the middle of each side division has a framing of single pilaster-strips and consoles supporting a decorated frieze and cornice.

Great Pulteney Street

In many ways the most impressive street in Bath, Great Pulteney Street owes its effectiveness to its regularity and great dimensions, it being 1,100 ft. in length and 100 ft. wide between the buildings, and the vaults and made ground upon which it is built bring it to a uniform level throughout.

The north and south sides are divided by tributary streets into two and three blocks respectively, with pedimented features placed to form effective closures to the vistas from the opposite streets. The central block on the south side contains the largest and loftiest houses in the street, and has the finest elevation. Above the ground story of uniformly arched door and window openings, recessed with plain margins in a rusticated arcade, the main wall face is adorned in the middle and at each end of the range with a giant order of fluted Corinthian pilasters, equally spaced

Great Pulteney Street. Perspective view of north side.

between the windows to form end pavilions, each of three bays, with two respondent bays on each side of a pedimented central feature of five bays. All the windows are without architraves but are underlined with moulded sills, which, with the band of Vitruvian scrolling at second-floor level, form stringcourses continued between the pilasters. The crowning entablature, with its modillioned cornice, projects forward above the pilastered bays, with a secondary break to receive the triangular pediment, with the Pulteney arms carved in the tympanum, crowning the central feature. The houses are generally finished with an open balustrade, having pedestals centred above the pilasters and piers.

The flanking ranges are less impressive in scale and treatment. Again the ground-story is rusticated, but the door and window openings have flat arches, and the wall face at each end of the range is broken slightly forward to provide a base for a terminal pavilion, containing in its upper part two tiers of three windows, of which that in the centre of the first-floor tier is an arched light, framed by pilaster-strips with consoles supporting a decorated frieze and cornice. The main wall face between the pavilions is formed into three divisions by fluted Corinthian pilasters arranged in close pairs, with half-pilaster responds against the return breaks of the pavilions. The middle division is eighteen windows wide, and each side division six. The windows are without architraves but each tier is underlined by a moulded sill continued between the pilasters. The main entablature

Sydney Place. North-west range.

has a modillioned cornice, which is surmounted by a dwarf pedestal stopped against the triangular pediments crowning each terminal pavilion. The two ranges on the north side of the street are decorated in a similar manner to the foregoing, the various motifs being used to compose architectural groupings of great length and balanced diversity which the eye cannot possibly take in completely.

Nos. 1 to 14 Sydney Place

Baldwin planned Sydney Place with eight terraces of houses fronting on to the road surrounding the hexagonal pleasure gardens, but only the range on the west side, lying between Great Pulteney and Bathwick Streets was built to his designs.

The fourteen houses are grouped to form a balanced composition, with slightly projecting pavilions at each end and in the centre. The division into three stories is strongly defined by the plinth below the first-floor windows, the plain sill underlining the second-floor windows, and the simple crowning entablature. On the ground-story arched doorways, dressed with vermiculated rustications, form every third opening from either end, meeting to form a pair in the central pavilion. The windows are set in groups of three to each house and generally have plain surrounds, but decorative interest is provided at first-floor level by the elaborate setting of the middle windows in each pavilion, and those above the doorways to the intermediate houses. In each of these last the window is framed within a moulded architrave, surmounted by a plain frieze and cornice, and flanked by half-pilasters with plain shafts and composite capitals lining up with the frieze. In each end pavilion the window surround is composed of paired pilaster-strips, with consoles supporting a frieze decorated with ribboned festoons below a cornice, while the two windows in the central pavilion are resolved into a centrepiece by their setting of three composite pilasters, which rise from the platband to support a frieze decorated with ribboned festoons between paterae, below a cornice. The centre and left-hand pavilions have triangular pediments, that to the right having only a dwarf parapet similar to that which finishes the intermediate houses. Other alterations, including removal of sills to allow for the insertion of cast-iron window guards, and the splaying of many window reveals will doubtless be amended by restoration.

Bathwick Street

On the north-east side of Bathwick Street are two groups of houses built round about 1790 and having elevations from Baldwin's designs. Nos. 1 to 8 have uniformly treated fronts in which the three stories are strongly defined by the moulded stringcourse at first-floor level; the plain continuous sill underlining the second-floor windows; and the diminutive main entablature, which is surmounted by a plain parapet, all of these horizontal members being continued by concave quadrant ramps wherever the houses are stepped up to conform with changes in ground level. Every house has a three-light window to each story, but that to the first-floor is emphasized by framing each light by pilaster-strips with decorated consoles supporting a frieze and triangular pediment, the former bearing a panel carved with festoons above the wide middle light. The ground- and second-floor windows are without architraves and the entrance doors are recessed within plain arches, arranged in pairs, the houses being so planned that each pair shares chimney-stacks.

Marlborough Buildings

The great range of houses forming Marl-

Bathwick Street. General view of Nos. 1–8.

borough Buildings, which appears from the rate-books to have been built just before 1790, is sited along the eastern boundary of the common land, now Victoria Park, and lies at a right-angle to the main axis of the Royal Crescent. It is probable that these houses derived their name of Marlborough Buildings from the Muddle-brook which originally flowed just beyond their gardens.

No architect has been named in connection with the design of the elevations, but Nos. 13 to 15, which are treated to form a group closing the vista across the Crescent from Brock Street, are of the scale and character usually associated with Baldwin's work. It was, however, John Palmer, in association with Charles Davis, James Beale and William Mullins, who petitioned the Corporation for the grant of a 99 years' lease of a strip of common land on which they proposed building two further ranges of houses in continuation of Marlborough Buildings. Although Palmer and his associates had the support of many freemen of the city, the lease was not granted.

The uniformly treated elevation of Nos. 13

Sydney Place. Central feature of north-west range.

Marlborough Buildings. Nos. 13 and 14.

to 15 has a ground-story in which the door and two window openings of each house are treated to form a rusticated arcade, the nine arches springing from piers with moulded imposts, and having slightly projecting keystones dying into the first-floor platband. This last is now partly obscured by the early nineteenth-century balconies added to Nos. 13 and 14, but served to underline the range of nine tall windows to the first-floor. Though these are equal in size and spacing, the middle window of the three to each house is given prominence by its architrave framing, which is surmounted by a plain frieze and triangular pediment, and set within a shallow recess with an arched head rising from a plain impost continued between each arch, one course above the heads of the intervening windows. The middle window of the central house has a larger pediment resting

on consoles and is set in a wider arch than those of the flanking houses. Moulded panels, carved with ribboned garlands, are placed on either side of the arches, in the wall face below the second-floor windows, which are uniformly spaced in plain surrounds. The crowning entablature has a plain frieze and dentilled cornice, and was originally surmounted by an open balustrade or which only the pedestals remain between the houses.

The houses to the left of the central group are stepped down the steep declivity of the site and except for No. 1, which has a frontage two windows wide, each house has a rusticated ground-story containing two windows and an arched doorway, and two upper tiers of three windows, set in plain surrounds but underlined by continued sills. The first-floor platband is returned to form a vertical margin between the rusticated ground-stories, and the main entablature is returned and stopped against each party-wall division. The elevations to the houses on the right of the centre have similar elevations but the platband, sills and entablature are continuous throughout. These houses were planned with staircases rising towards the street front and the principal rooms facing the gardens, and the fronts to many of them have suffered from the addition of projecting porches with sanitary accommodation contained in annexes above.

Bath Street

One of the purposes for which the Bath Improvement Act of 1789 was obtained was to effect some necessary clearances in the older part of the city and generally improve the approaches to the baths. Baldwin's principal undertakings in this direction included widening and refronting Cheap and Stall Streets, and forming Union and Bath Streets. While the buildings in the first two streets are of no particular distinction, and the early nineteenth-century fronts to Union Street have been altered or rebuilt, Bath Street, by far the most beautiful of Baldwin's street designs, has fortunately suffered little change. The *Bath Chronicle* for March 31st, 1791, contains this notice—

'This day at noon was laid the first stone of the new street to be called Bath-

Bath Street. Segmental return fronts at west end, with the Cross Bath.

street, in which is the following inscription (in Latin): "For the honour and dignity of this City, these works were conducted by Commissioners by Parliament appointed for its improvement, 1791. John Horton, Mayor; T. Baldwin, Architect."'

Bath Street is a short segmental-ended thoroughfare, designed to form covered promenades between the baths in Stall Street and the Cross Bath, these buildings forming its axial terminations. The two ranges of shops and houses have uniform frontages, distinguished by the treatment of the ground-story in which the shops are set back behind colonnaded walks beneath the upper stories. Ionic columns, similar to those used in the porticoes of the Pump Room and New Private Baths, are spaced out at equal intervals to carry the wood lintels, which are treated to form a frieze with moulded fascia panels corresponding to each three bay house, and are capped by a stone cornice. The first-floor windows are underlined by a continuous plain sill and are without architraves, but the middle window of the three to each house is emphasized by its setting between plain pilaster-strips and carved consoles supporting projecting frieze blocks decorated with oval paterae, which flank a tablet carved with ribboned festoons and surmounted by a triangular pediment. The second-floor windows are also without architraves and are underlined by a continuous band of Vitruvian scrolling. The sharply moulded entablature and plain parapet form an effective finish to these elevations. The segmental return fronts at either end of the street show minor variations in the spacing and treatment of the decorated window at first-floor level. The north-east segment lost its two north end bays when the White Hart Hotel was demolished in 1869.

Lansdown Cresent

The building of Lansdown Crescent was largely due to the enterprise of Charles Spackman, a property valuer who had amassed considerable wealth as a coachbuilder and from whom the crescent received one of its early names, Spackman's Buildings, other's being The Upper Crescent and Lansdown Place. John Palmer was employed to design the layout and elevations for the houses, most of which were erected between 1789 and 1793 by various speculating builders, some of whom, such as William Wheeler, were ruined by the bank failures of 1793.

The concave crescent and its convex wings form a serpentine line of buildings following the curving contours of the south-east slopes of Lansdown, and are one of the most conspicuous elements in the Bath scene. The houses of the two wings are stepped up towards the crescent, and while their fronts vary in width from two to four windows, they conform to a

Bath Street. Interior of north colonnade.

Lansdown Crescent. General view.

uniform height of three stories. The windows, and in most cases the doors also, form simple rectangular openings in a plain wall face relieved only by the first-floor platband, and a modillioned cornice surmounted by a plain parapet.

The twenty houses of the crescent are arranged in a segment forming nearly one-third of a circle of approximately 300 ft. radius. Their fronts are treated to form a balanced composition in which the two middle houses are skilfully united into a pedimented central feature, between wings of eight houses terminated by pavilions formed by the very large house at each end of the range. All the houses are three stories high, and those forming the wings and central feature are almost identical in size and plan, with frontages three windows wide. Each end house has its entrance at the side, the main frontage being set

well forward from the general building line, and of the five windows to each story, three are contained in a centrally placed segmental bow. The ground-story is rusticated throughout and the window and door openings, except for those in the pavilion features, form equally spaced flat-arched openings with keystones dying into the platband. The adjacent doorways of the two middle houses are united by an engaged portico of three bays, with Doric columns supporting an entablature, the central bay being filled by an arched niche set in a rusticated surround. The first- and second-floor windows form two tiers of regularly spaced rectangular openings, set without architraves in a wall face which is horizontally divided by the plain sill, continued below all the first-floor windows except those to the end houses, which are carried down to the platband; and a band of guilloche moulding one stone course above their heads. The second-floor windows have separate sills and are set high up in the front, which is terminated by an entablature with a plain frieze and modillioned cornice, surmounted by an open balustrade with solid dies above the piers. Slight breaks in the wall face serve to set the two middle houses forward from the wings, and the rusticated ground-story is again broken forward to provide a base for the giant order of four pilasters decorating the central feature. These pilasters have moulded bases, plain shafts and Ionic capitals, and are spaced to form one wide and two narrow bays, the latter enclosing one and the former two windows of each story, those on the first-floor being resolved by an arched recess between them, probably intended to be treated as a dummy light. The first-floor window sill is continued between the pilasters, as also is the guilloche moulding which is turned over the arched recess. The main entablature is broken forward above the order and crowned with a triangular pediment. The pedestals at the breaks in the balustrade over each end pavilion are surmounted by elegant vases of which all four remain at the east end, but only one at the west end. The basement areas are surrounded by ornamental railings and there are very fine wrought-iron lampholders to all but the end houses, the majority consisting of standards filled with honeysuckle and other ornaments, which are crowned with vase profiles and support serpentine curved over-throws decorated with scrolls.

Though this front has been very little altered, some of the balusters have been removed and the roof of No. 7 reconstructed to admit of a second attic-story. The provision of venetian shutters and their guides, though not a structural change, has tended to confuse the horizontal emphases of the design. Many windows retain their original glazing bars, but some openings have been lengthened. The small amount of damage inflicted by German bombs has now been made good.

The interiors are extremely well finished, with good joinery, plaster friezes and cornices of Adamitic detail, and in many cases fine mantlepieces, but they contain nothing of outstanding note. Reference to the planning will be found under the appropriate heading.

Lansdown Crescent. Detail of
west end pavilion.

St. James's Square

In March 1790, Sir Peter Rivers Gay, Lord of the Manor of Walcot, granted to Richard Hewlett and James Broom, a 99 years' building lease of some land to the north of the Royal Crescent. This land consisted of orchards and gardens which at the time were tenanted by various residents of the Crescent, among them Christopher Anstey, whose annoyance at being given notice to quit found expression in the oft-quoted epigram:

> Ye Men of Bath, who stately mansions rear
> to wait for tenants from the De'il knows where,
> Would you pursue a plan that cannot fail,
> Erect a Madhouse, and enlarge your Jail.

To which came the riposte:

> Whilst crowds arrive, fast as our streets increase,
> and our Jail only proves an empty space.
> Whilst health and care here court the grave and gay,
> Madmen and fools alone will keep away.

St. James's Square. General view of north side.

St. James's Square. General view of east side.

The lease had been granted to Hewlett and Broom on the condition that they would lay out a sum of at least £10,000 'in erecting buildings and finishing stone messuages', and they engaged John Palmer to design the layout and elevations for a large residential square with four tributary streets. Building was begun as soon as the site could be cleared, and most of the houses had been finished by 1794. John Fielder and Thomas King were among the more prominent builders associated with the project.

The houses of St. James's Square enclose a quadrangular area measuring some 360 ft. from north to south, and 250 ft. from east to west, in the centre of which is a large informal garden containing some very fine trees. Palmer's treatment of the buildings follows the precedent created by the elder Wood in dealing with Queen Square on a similar sloping site. Thus the north and south ranges are given architectural predominance by composing the houses into uniform groups, while the houses forming the east and west sides are treated as individual units identical in design, stepping down in order to overcome the considerable fall in ground level from north to south.

The north and south sides contain seven and eight houses respectively, and their elevations are very similar in composition to Lansdown Crescent, which Palmer had just previously designed. The disposition of elements is virtually the same, but they are treated with greater simplicity. Interest is again directed on to the end and central houses, the latter being enriched by a giant order of four Corinthian pilasters with plain shafts, which form three bays equally one window wide, and support the projecting entablature and its triangular pediment. Each end house is distinguished by a segmental bow, flanked by single pilasters of the order, and containing a simple venetian window at first-floor level, with a corresponding three-light window above and below. The windows and doorways, most of the latter having arched heads, are set without architraves in a plain wall face, horizontally divided by a pedestal sustaining the order and under-lining the tier of first-floor windows; a moulded stringcourse just above their heads, which is turned over the arched lights of the venetian windows and that in the middle bay of the central feature; and the main entablature with its plain parapet. It may be noticed that the central feature is one bay out of centre on the south side, due to an even number of windows at each floor level.

The fifteen houses forming the west side are uniformly three windows wide, as are thirteen of those on the east side where the remaining house is a double one, with two upper stories, five windows wide, carried over the segmental arched entrance to St. James's Place. This small difference apart, the fronts are identical in composition, the houses being stepped down from north to south in accordance with the fall in ground level. Each end house, and that in the centre, is treated to form a pavilion, with a rusticated ground-story containing two windows and a doorway forming equal flat arched openings with keystones dying into the platband. The three first-floor windows are framed by plain shafted composite pilasters, which rise from a sill supported by fluted consoles, and carry an entablature which is surmounted by a triangular pediment above the middle window. The three second-floor windows are without architraves, and the main entablature of each end house is surmounted by a plain parapet, while the central house is crowned with a triangular pediment. The intervening houses are uniformly treated, each with a ground-story containing two windows without architraves, and a doorway with an architrave framing flanked by plain jambs, with consoles supporting a projecting cornice. The three equally spaced windows to each of the two upper stories are also without archit-raves, but the first-floor tier is underlined by a plain sill, which, like the first-floor platband and the crowning entablature, returns and stops against the party-wall divisions. The iron railings to the areas of the houses on the north and south sides, and the pavilion features, are of a more elaborate pattern than those to the remaining houses.

The exteriors generally are free from alteration, although there has been wholesale removal of glazing bars from the windows, and the general effect has not been improved by the pernicious practice of painting in bright colour the ground-story to some of the houses.

The houses are well finished internally, and decorated with the delightful neo-classic plasterwork and reeded architraves of the period, and in some reception rooms there are fine mantelpieces of white statuary marble, with coloured inlays and carved metopes illustrative of classic and fabulous subjects (see page 219).

Somerset Place

The serpentine range of buildings formed by Lansdown Crescent and its wings, is continued to the west by a further crescent of houses, Somerset Place. The masonry jointing indicates the possibility that this crescent may have had its beginnings in a pair of houses which form the centre of the composition. These houses, crowned by a great segmental pediment, were designed by John Eveleigh, and are clearly shown as an isolated feature in the plate entitled 'Crescent and Lansdown', engraved by William Watts from a drawing made by him at some time during 1791–93. Somerset Place was to have consisted of twenty houses, an various speculating builders, John Fielder and James Beale among them, had leased plots and begun to build houses, when their efforts were generally brought to a stand-

Somerset Place. General view.

still by the wave of economic depression which swept over England during the last years of the eighteenth century. Some of the houses remained unfinished until round about 1820, and only five were built in the west wing, although the ground had been cleared and the cellars constructed for two more.

The crescent is dominated by the central feature, a design of great beauty and originality, combining two houses each three windows wide and three stories high. Of the six openings to the ground-story the middle pair form rectangular doorways, framed within plain architraves broken by rustic blocks and emphasized triple keystones, the centre carved with an icicle-work mask, and finished with a cornice projecting on moulded consoles ending in carved leaves. The two windows to each house are without architraves but have emphasized triple keystones. A plain platband marks the first-floor level, and a plain continued sill originally stopped the moulded architraves to the first-floor windows, which form two equally spaced groups of three, and are surmounted by plain friezes and cornices. The wide pier between the groups contains an arched niche of semi-circular plan, surmounted by an open-bed pediment with its cornice returned above those to the windows on either side, and a tympanum decorated with ribboned festoons and pendants. A continued sill stops the moulded architraves to the second-floor windows which are spaced to accord with those below, the wide intervening pier being decorated with a garland of husks looped over paterae lining up with the architrave heads. The modillioned cornice of the main entablature is returned and continued over the great segmental pediment up to the points where reversed curves break the tympanum, to unite under the moulded base of the central vase. The exquisite decoration carved in the tympanum is composed of festooned drapery caught up by pegs and rings, and looped by ribbons over three paterae, a large one of oval form decorated with radiating acanthus leaves in the centre, and a smaller one of circular form filled with radiating fluting centred above the middle window of each house (Fig. 41).

Fig. 41. Somerset Place. Central feature of elevation

The flanking wings are very simply treated, with doorways varying only slightly from those in the centre, and windows without architraves. The continued platband and entablature are laid with a gradual rise towards the central feature, and the windows are stepped up in groups of three. The terminal houses were designed to form slightly projecting pavilions having a rusticated ground story.

Somerset Place was severely damaged during the German raids of 1942, when the three houses at the west end were destroyed and Nos 10 to 13 gutted. Fortunately, the central feature escaped serious damage, and great care was taken to restore Eveleigh's façade to its original appearance when the destroyed and gutted houses were rebuilt to serve as a students' hostel.

Seymour Street and Green Park

A considerable extension of the city, southwards into the riverside area of Kingsmead, was planned soon after 1790. One of the

Green Park Buildings. The west side, looking towards Seymour Street.

Norfolk Crescent. General view from north.

principal features of the layout was the formation of Green Park, a wedge-shaped open space lying between two great terraces of houses converging on Seymour Street, designed as wide continuation of the existing Charles Street. Although the architect's name has not been recorded, there is no doubt that John Palmer was closely concerned in developing this area, in which he and his associates had long held property interests. Seymour Street was built during the period 1792–96, together with an approximate half of each range of Green Park Buildings, of which the southernmost houses date from the early nineteenth-century. Unfortunately time has dealt hardly with this fine urban development, for the whole of the west side of Seymour Street made way for the Midland Station, erected in 1869, and the east side was demolished during the 1950s, several of its houses having been gutted in the German raids of 1942, when the entire east range of Green Park Buildings was also destroyed.

Each side of Seymour Street consisted of nine single-fronted houses, their fronts combining to present a balanced composition. All shared a pedestal-course below the first-floor windows, and a crowning entablature which was surmounted by a balustraded parapet above all but the house at each end, which was broken slightly forward and crowned with a triangular pediment. Every house was similar in the ground story, having a two-light window without an architrave, and a doorway dressed with an architrave, narrow frieze, and a cornice on consoles. Each end house had a venetian window for the first floor, dressed with a wide moulded architrave and a cornice turned over the arched middle light. The straight-headed three-light window above was dressed with a narrow architrave. In each story of the adjoining front there were two widely-spaced rectangular windows, dressed to correspond with the three-light windows in the next house. These two systems of fenestration were repeated alternately throughout the nine houses, with charming effect. Some delicately carved festoons and paterae provided a decora-

tion on the shaped aprons below all the first-floor windows.

The elevations of the contemporary houses in Green Park differ but little from many others built during this time. The frontages, three stories high and three windows wide, are uniformly treated, with rectangular door and window openings of equal height set in the rusticated ground-story, and a plain wall face

Seymour Street. Detail of end houses on east side (demolished).

above containing two tiers of windows without architraves. Horizontal emphasis and relationship is established by the continued plinth below the first-floor windows, and the main entablature with its surmounting parapet. The early nineteenth-century houses show a considerable increase in scale, and their fronts have more decorative detail. The rusticated ground-story of each house contains two rectangular windows and a wide segmental-arched doorway, and while the windows of the two upper stories are generally without architraves, the plain wall face is relieved by the setting of the first-floor central window. This consists of a moulded architrave frame, flanked by plain jambs which curve outwards towards the base, and a plain frieze surmounted by a triangular pediment supported on scrolled consoles. The three houses nearest the earlier group on the west side form a composition of marked similarity to the central feature of Marlborough Buildings.

Norfolk Crescent

The formation of a crescent of nineteen houses, originally to be called Norfolk Place, with Surrey Street entering at a right-angle opposite its centre, was an important feature of the late eighteenth-century developments planned for the Kingsmead area. The land was leased in 1792 to Richard Bowsher, an attorney, whose associates in this speculation were the builders James Broom and Thomas King. Plots were re-leased to various craftsmen who undertook to build houses in the crescent, but the ensuing financial crisis brought work to a standstill. Only the nine houses north of the centre had been finished by 1810, when Bowsher opened a tontine subscription to raise the necessary funds to complete the crescent. Although this scheme failed at the outset, the return to more stable conditions brought about the eventual completion of Norfolk Crescent, but Surrey Street was abandoned and its site laid out as an informal garden.

The architect's name is not recorded, but the elevational treatment suggests that Palmer was again employed by Broom and King, as in the case of St. James's Square, while the joinery and ironwork details indicate that the buildings were finished by John Pinch, at that time a bankrupt whose affairs were in Bowsher's hands.

Norfolk Crescent contains nineteen houses of equal size set out to form the segment of a circle having a radius of approximately 420 ft.

The frontages, four stories high and three windows wide, are united into a composition in which the three middle houses, and one at each end, form pavilion features between balancing wings. The ground-story presents a rusticated face in which the door and window openings form equally spaced flat-arched openings, with projecting keystones dying into the moulded stringcourse which marks the first-floor level. Vertical breaks in the wall face serve to set the three middle houses slightly forward from the general building line, and further breaks provide a base for the giant order of pilasters used to decorate the central and end pavilions, dividing them into five and three bays respectively. These pilasters, consisting of moulded bases, plain shafts and Ionic capitals, are set upon a plain plinth-base and rise through the first- and second-floors to carry projecting sections of the main entablature, which is continued across the building. The first-floor windows form a continuous range of tall rectangular openings, set without architraves in a plain wall face. Each house has at first-floor level a stone slab balcony with a wrought-iron front formed by panels of varying fret designs, possibly added to the earlier houses when the crescent was completed. The second-floor windows form a tier corresponding to those below, but less high, and are underlined by a plain sill continued between the pilasters. Above the main entablature is an attic-story with a similar range of windows, some of which are dummy lights. This attic is finished with a cornice of slighter profile than that to the main entablature, and surmounted by a plain parapet which stops against the triangular pediment crowning the central feature. Two of the houses have wrought-iron overthrow lampholders, of identical design to those in New Sydney Place, and there is a charming stone watch-house of circular plan at the north-east corner of the wedge-shaped open space.

Although the industrial quarter nearby has effectively blighted this once fashionable residential area, it is pleasant to record the City Council's enterprise in restoring the façade of

Norfolk Crescent and rebuilding, albeit for a different purpose, the seven houses that were gutted in 1942.

Nelson Place, the terrace of houses on the north side of the open space, was begun soon after 1800. Although the houses share a front which is architecturally related to that of Norfolk Crescent, the houses are smaller and the story heights less. At the east end is a pavilion dressed with an Ionic order of pilasters dividing the upper two stories into three bays. For more than 150 years this terrace was unfinished, but recently the City Council have added a west end pavilion matching that at the east end.

REPRESENTATIVE BUILDINGS OF THE PERIOD 1800–1830

Widcombe Crescent and Terrace

Widcombe Crescent and Terrace were built around 1805, almost certainly to the designs of Charles Harcourt Masters, who is named in some of the original leases and was actively concerned in various building enterprises on the south side of the Avon. Crescent and Terrace combine to form one of the most attractive minor ensembles in Bath.

The fourteen houses of Widcombe Crescent, except for one at each end, are grouped to form six pairs sharing common chimney stacks, and are planned with staircases rising towards the principal front, which overlooks the carriage road and enclosure to the east, while the largest rooms face west to command a fine view of the valley and city beyond. Each pair of houses share a common front, bounded by thin pilaster-strips and designed to form a repeating unit in the composition of the elevation. The ground-story is distinguished by the charming and original manner whereby the arched doorways to each pair of houses are enclosed within a wide three-centred arch of shallow recession, its lunette decorated with a floral boss centred above the pier between the doorways, and with ribboned festoons of husks dependent from the soffit of the arch,

which has a plain keystone breaking into the first-floor platband, this last bearing the beautifully cut inscription WIDCOMBE CRESCENT above the middle arch. There is also a single rectangular window set between wide piers to the ground-story of each house. The fenestration of the two upper stories of each pair of houses follows a similar pattern, with a threelight window, of which the middle light is blind, though glazed, centred above the arched feature, and a single window on either side. All the windows are without architraves and while those to the first-floor have individual sills, the second-floor windows share a continued sill stringcourse. The main cornice, with boldly moulded profiles typical of the early nineteenth-century work in Bath, breaks round the pilaster strips and descends with concave quadrant ramps where changes in ground level have caused a corresponding drop in the floor levels. The crowning parapet is enriched with sections of open balustrading, corresponding in width and position to the windows below. The doors, containing six fielded panels, are of an earlier type than one might expect to find, and several of them are adorned with fine knockers. The iron railings surrounding the areas are of the simplest description, but there is a fine wrought-iron overthrow lampholder at No. 1. Altogether this front is singularly free from alteration, and most of the windows retain their original quota of glazing bars. While the west elevation is very simply treated, it exhibits a number of fine treillage verandas.

The six houses of Widcombe Terrace have their principal fronts facing west, and are separated by a paved terrace from their gardens on the sloping hillside. Although these houses are considerably smaller than those of the Crescent, their fronts are treated with even greater architectural distinction, and form part of a composition in which each end house is set slightly forward from the others. Every house has a wide window to the ground- and first-floors, contained within a high arch slightly recessed between wide piers, which are rusticated up to the first-floor platband and contain

Widcombe Crescent. Main front facing north-east.

Widcombe Terrace. Main front facing south.

Widcombe Terrace. North end front.

New Sydney Place. West return front.

the arched entrance doorways, set to one side and having a blank window to correspond on each floor above. The platband and simply moulded impost are returned into, and carried across the arched recesses, which have plain lunettes. The second-floor windows, arranged in pairs above each arch, are underlined by a plain continued sill, and the cornice of similar profile to that of the Crescent is surmounted by a plain parapet. This basic treatment is continued round the return frontage facing the Crescent, gaining in richness of effect by its application to two segmental bows. In addition the impost moulding carried across the first-floor window heads is adorned with a Vitruvian scroll, and the parapet is surmounted by three finely carved vases.

New Sydney Place

Proposals for building a second range of houses in Sydney Place were announced by advertisements appearing in issues of the *Bath Chronicle* during September 1804, offering to let plots of ground for the erection of elegant residences to plans and designs by Thomas Baldwin. Contemporary plans of the city show the sites for these intended houses to have been on the north side, forming part of the grounds of Bathwick Villa. This project appears to have been abandoned in favour of an extension to the south, and John Pinch, as architect to the Darlington estate, was employed to design the range of fine houses which were completed and offered for sale during 1808. A contemporary account praises the building as 'a specimen of the architectural perfection that may be formed of Bath stone. It was all brought from one quarry, and the houses raised gradually together, tier after tier, thereby forming one compact building in which not the least flaw or settlement, or different shades of colour can be seen.' The stone has weathered to a beautiful tawny gol-

New Sydney Place. General view from east.

den colour, and the building merits the highest praise for its subtle design and the excellent craftsmanship it displays.

The fronts of the eleven houses are uniformly four stories high, including the attic, and three windows wide, and they are grouped to form a balanced composition in which the large house at each end, and that in the middle, are treated to form pavilions set slightly forward from the main building face. The ground-story is arcaded throughout the range, each house having a group of three arches springing from piers with moulded bases and imposts. In all but the end houses the left-hand arch is wider than the others and of segmental form, containing in its recessed opening an eight-panelled entrance door framed by reeded architraves, with trellised side-lights and a fan-light of delicate metal-work. The centre and right-hand arches frame plain marginal surrounds to the ground-floor windows, which have fan glazing in their upper sashes. The three rectangular windows to each of the upper stories are spaced at equal centres to form balanced groups, their dimensions are decreased with each successive story and all are without architraves. The plain wall face is horizontally divided by an entablature-like stringcourse at first-floor level; a moulded band carved with Vitruvian scrolling at second-floor level; a moulded sill underlining the second-floor windows; and by the boldly profiled main cornice below the attic-story, this last being finished with a secondary cornice and plain parapet. In the four houses of each wing concave quadrant ramps are used to continue these horizontal members where each house is stepped up to accord with the rising ground. This general arrangement is repeated in each pavilion, with the following variations: the ground-story to each end house contains three equal windows; and the first-floor central window is emphasized by a frame of plain pilaster-strips with carved consoles supporting

New Sydney Place. Detail of
central house.

a frieze decorated with festoons between oval paterae, surmounted by a cornice. The string-courses and cornices are returned and stopped against the main building face, and the attic-story cornice is continued to form a triangular pediment above each pavilion, that in the centre containing the Vane family arms carved in bold relief in its tympanum. Each pavilion has a wide balcony at first-floor level, formed of stone slabs with wrought-iron fronts of elaborate treillage designs, and each first-floor window of the intervening houses has a balcony railing of similar character, but of segmental plan. Before the doors to all except the end houses are wrought-iron overthrow lamp-holders of an elegant serpentine form with trellised standards.

The return fronts are set at different angles to the main frontage, to which they are skil-fully related by segmental bows. Each end house has a projecting Doric porch, that to No. 93 being surmounted by a charming con-servatory, with sash-windows and delicate segmental fan-lights set in reeded frames, and corner posts supporting a tent-shaped roof, with bells depending from the eaves.

The houses are well planned on conven-tional lines, with fine stone staircases and well proportioned rooms. Some reference to the interior decoration will be found under the appropriate heading.

Cavendish Place

John Pinch designed several of the fine ranges of houses sited on the southern slopes of Lansdown, of which the first to be built was Cavendish Place, begun during 1808 but not completed until after an interval of nearly eight years had elapsed.

The thirteen houses are sited on steeply rising ground, facing west and overlooking the High Common, and were originally approached by way of Park Place and Park Street, the north-west exit from St. James's Square. The transition from the smaller scale of the houses in Park Street, built by John Palmer, has been skilfully effected by increas-ing the size and scale of each subsequent house of Park Place and Cavendish Place until the wide curving front of No. 3, the wedge-shaped corner house, is reached. The remaining houses, Nos. 4 to 13, are built with the floor levels of each house stepped up an equal distance above those of its right-hand neigh-bour.

Each house is uniformly fronted with a well composed elevation, four stories in height and generally three windows wide, decorated with crisply modelled detail which responds well to effects of weathering and light or shade. The ground-story is of V-jointed rusticated masonry, with flat-arched windows in the centre and to the right, and a wide arched opening to the left containing the entrance door with side- and fan-lights. The three rectangular windows to each upper story are

Cavendish Place. Front of No. 3.

Cavendish Place. General view from south-west.

spaced at equal centres but graduated in width and height, and though all are without architraves that in the centre of the first-floor tier is emphasized by a frame of reeded pilaster-strips, with fluted and foliated consoles supporting a returned frieze and straight cornice. Strong horizontal emphasis is given by the platband and balcony at first-floor level; the wide stringcourse decorated with Vitruvian scrolling just below the second-floor window sills; and the main and secondary cornices below and above the attic-story. Quadrant ramps are used to connect the string-courses and cornices from house to house, and unify the whole terrace. The stone slab balconies at first-floor level have reeded fascias and delicate iron railings, and most were surmounted by lofty verandas. In the earlier houses the doorways have side- and fan-lights of similar design to those in New Sydney Place, and in front of them are wrought-iron overthrow lamp-holders.

The houses are planned with a conventional arrangement of large and lofty rooms. While the decorations call for no special comment, being drawn from stock sources, the detail is generally in the best Regency tradition, with reeded architraves, marble mantelpieces of simple design, and crisply moulded plasterwork of Hellenistic derivation.

Fire caused by German bombs destroyed the interiors of Nos. 6 to 9, necessitating the partial demolition of their fronts. Fortunately, this handsome terrace has now been fully restored, and all the verandas have been removed.

Cavendish Crescent

Cavendish Crescent was designed by John Pinch for William Broom, a speculating builder who in 1815 was living at No. 3, and was

Cavendish Crescent. General view from west.

adjudged bankrupt in 1825. Although the first houses were begun only a few years later than those in Cavendish Place, Nos. 10 and 11 were still unfinished when offered for sale in 1829.

The contours of this site appear to have dictated the use of a crescent formation, and the eleven houses of equal size are set out to form a quadrant. There is a slight rise in the floor levels of each house from either end towards the centre.

The fronts of the houses are identical, and combine to form an elevation of simple elegance, the general treatment being rather more austere than in Pinch's earlier buildings. Except for No. 11, where a side porch gives access to the hall and staircase, the entrance doors are set within arched openings, emphasized by surrounds of long and short rustications, to the left of each pair of ground-floor windows. The three upper stories are lit by windows arranged in groups of three, spaced out at equal centres but graduated in width and height, with a scarcely perceptible rise in each group towards the central house. All the windows are without architraves, but that in the centre of each first-floor group has a framing of narrow pilaster-strips, with fluted and foliated consoles supporting a returned frieze, with paterae over the consoles, and a straight cornice. The elevation is unified by the strong. horizontal lines provided by the first-floor platband; by the entablature-like stringcourse at third-floor level; and by the boldly profiled main cornice and crowning parapet. All of these members rise slightly towards the centre, and are continued in a modified form across the return frontages. Most of the first-floor windows have segmental balconies of trellis design in ironwork, but the veranda of three arches supporting a tent-shaped roof, added to No. 9, although charming in itself, impairs the balance of the composition.

The interiors of the houses are planned and finished in much the same manner as those in Cavendish Place.

Winifred's Dale

The semi-detached villas, Nos. 1 and 2 Winifred's Dale, sited between Cavendish Place and Crescent, were almost certainly designed by John Pinch. Their fronts are combined to form a charming composition, with a double porch of the Doric order curving forward between two wide segmental bows, which are carried up for the full height of the three-storied front. Horizontal emphasis is provided by the platband and sill below the first-floor windows, and the main and secondary cornices below and above the second-floor windows. The bows are flanked by pilaster strips moulded in the manner of early nineteenth-century architraves.

Sion Hill Place

The last of the Lansdown terraces to be built from designs by John Pinch was Sion Hill Place, situated amidst surroundings of park-like beauty on the high ground of Sion Hill. The earliest houses in the terrace, Nos. 1 to 4, were built on part of the Summerhill estate of Dr. Caleb Hillier Parry, whose trustees granted the first leases in 1810 to William Cowell Hayes, described as a painter, who probably erected the houses round about 1818. The central house, No. 5, was built about 1820 by Daniel Aust, and the others are of much the same date. The elevations were built to an agreed design, but the houses differ slightly in their dimensions and internal finishings.

The simple elegance of the elevation is reflective of the best contemporary taste. The nine houses are combined to form a balanced composition in which the central house, slightly broken forward and crowned with a pediment, is flanked on either side by a wing

Winifred's Dale. Nos. 1 and 2.

containing three houses, terminated by a responding break and the wide segmental bow emphasizing the large house at each end. The masonry of the ground-story has the horizontal joints and arch voussoirs rusticated, and while the central house has flat-arched windows in the centre and to the right, and a narrow arched doorway to the left, the houses in the left-hand wing each have one wide flat-arched window set off-centre to the right and a narrow arched doorway to the left, this order being reversed in the right-hand wing. The segmental bowed front of each end house contains three flat-arched windows of equal width, both houses originally having side entrances formed by projecting porches with Tuscan columns flanking a segmental arched doorway, and supporting a decorated entablature. The windows to each of the three upper stories are arranged to form groups of three to the central house and the segmental bows, and of two to each house in the wings. These rectangular

Sion Hill Place. General view from south-west.

windows are all set without architraves in a plain wall face which is horizontally divided by the first-floor platband; the plain continued sill below the second-floor windows; the moulded stringcourse decorated with Vitruvian scrolling between the second and third-floor windows; and by the crowning entablature and plain parapet, this last stopping against the triangular pediment which crowns the central house. Each house has a balcony at first-floor level, most of these being formed of stone-slabs with reeded fascias, which are supported on iron brackets and have iron railings of very simple design. The balcony railings surrounding the bow to No. 9 is of cast-iron, and was originally continued by standards of honeysuckle ornament to form a veranda with a tent-shaped roof, it apparently being the intention of the architect to decorate the end and central houses with these features.

While the exteriors generally have been spared alteration, the interiors of Nos. 1 and 9 have been partially reconstructed and lavishly redecorated in the style of an earlier period than that to which the houses belong. A splendid Palladian façade, originally in Chippenham, has been re-erected to form the west front of an extensive addition made to No. 1. Although a part of this addition has been detailed to accord with the early nineteenth-century elevation, the proportions have been changed and the original balance of the composition irretrievably spoiled.

Some reference to the internal planning and decoration will be found under the appropriate headings.

Claremont Place

Claremont Place, consisting of four pairs of semi-detached small houses, has the building date of 1817 incised on the front of one pair.

Claremont Place. Typical pair of houses.

Doric House, Sion Hill.

The refined charm of these elevations suggests that John Pinch designed them. Each pair of houses presents a uniform front containing two tiers of three widely spaced windows, those in the centre being dummy lights. The segmental-headed windows to the ground-story are set without architraves in wide marginal surrounds of the same form, slightly recessed from the plain wall face. The rectangular windows to the first-floor are also without architraves, but a plain continued sill underlines them and stops against a tall pilaster, decorated with incised lines ending in frets, at either end of the front. The delicate entablature is returned round these pilasters and surmounted by a solid parapet, which rises with stepped breaks to a panelled tablet in the centre, and has segmental-headed stops above the pilasters. The window glazing is given an added elegance by the use of narrow marginal panes, and it was intended that the pattern should be reproduced in the dummy lights, where the stonework is cut back to conform with the sashes.

Doric House, Sion Hill

Doric House, sited on the steep slope of Sion Hill, was built round about 1810 by Charles Spackman, to serve as a picture gallery and residence for his friend and protégé Thomas Barker, one of Bath's most distinguished resident painters. Joseph Michael Gandy, A.R.A., the friend and disciple of Soane, was commissioned by Barker to design the elevation, which is one of the most original and beautiful small works of the Greek revival.

Gandy's first design, exhibited in 1803 at the Royal Academy, was for a building of one lofty story, raised on a massive plinth and presenting a windowless wall divided into five equal bays by an order of fluted Doric columns, with plain antae at each end. The upper part of the wall face was to be decorated with a sculptured frieze continued between the columns, and the building finished with an entablature and plain parapet, this last partly masking the roof and its large lantern-lights.

The completed building consists of a principal story, set upon a plain basement plinth and surmounted by an attic. The windowless wall face to the principal story is set immediately behind a colonnade of four detached columns equally spaced between engaged antae. The plain shafts of the columns are surmounted by concave Doric capitals with massive square abaci, which carry an entablature with a boldly projecting modillioned cornice. A superimposed colonnade of dwarf columns with orthodox Doric capitals fronts the attic story, which contains three windows corresponding to the middle intercolumniations. The attic entablature has a cornice of slight projection which is surmounted by a low parapet, broken by curious acroterial ornaments centred above the columns. Both entablatures are returned round the side elevation, which faces south and contains a three-light window centred in its principal story, and a single light in the attic, the whole being crowned by a triangular pediment.

The interior contains a fine curving staircase with a delicate wrought-iron railing, and the lofty picture gallery is dominated by Barker's fresco of 'The Massacre at Chios', contrasting with the placid elegance of the Greek revival plasterwork and a fine mantelpiece of white marble, with its shelf supported by Egyptian terminal figures.

Camden Terrace and Lower Camden Place

These terrace houses in Camden Road, named Camden Terrace and Lower Camden Place, date from the third decade of the nineteenth century, and were possibly designed by John Pinch. Their fronts illustrate the considerable degree of architectural distinction with which even small houses were invested at that time.

Camden Terrace, built on the rising ground of Beacon Hill and set back from the west side of the roadway, contains six terrace houses with their fronts combined into a balanced composition in which two houses are treated to form a slightly projecting central feature.

Camden Terrace. General view.

Lower Camden Place.

Every house has a small projecting porch placed to one side, formed by thin screen walls of stone supporting a flat hood, and each story contains one centrally placed window. These form equal rectangular openings, set without architraves at regular intervals in a generally plain wall face, which is partially relieved by rustication of the horizontal jointing to the ground-story masonry of the central feature, and the voussoirs of the first-floor windows. Horizontal emphasis is provided by the first-floor platband to the central feature; the plain continued sill underlining the second-floor windows; and the simple main entablature which is surmounted by a plain parapet stopped against the triangular pediment above the central feature. The tympanum of the pediment contains a carved shield bearing the arms of Charles Pratt, Marquis Camden.

The houses of Lower Camden Place contain basement, ground- and first-floors only, and are stepped to accord with the rising line of the road frontage. The houses are uniformly fronted with simple two-storied elevations separated by plain pilasters. The ground-story contains a window and doorway, both equal in width and height, forming flat-arched openings in a wall face of which the horizontal joints and voussoirs are emphasized by rustication. Above the first-floor platband the plain wall face contains two rectangular windows without architraves, centred over the ground-floor openings. The main cornice of each house is returned round the pilaster on its right, and finished with a plain parapet.

Prior Park Buildings

Prior Park Buildings, erected round about 1825, is a terrace of nineteen houses set back from the east side of Prior Park Road, behind a narrow garden through which flows a stream. The frontage was almost certainly designed by John Pinch, and is a charming composition, with long wings ranged between slightly projecting end pavilions and a pedimented central feature.

The three houses forming the central feature contain three principal stories and a lofty attic. The ground-story of each house contains one centrally placed window with a doorway to one side, that to the central house being balanced by a blank opening, while the others are placed at the extreme left and right of the central feature. These uniform flat-arched openings are set in a wall face of which the horizontal joints and voussoir stones are emphasised by rustication. Th upper part of the front contains two tiers of six windows, regularly arranged in widely spaced pairs to each house,

Prior Park Buildings. Central feature.

Beckford's Tower, Lansdown.
(*engraved drawing by T. H. Shepherd, 1829*)

those to the first-floor being tall rectangular openings set without architraves in arched surrounds of shallow recession, rising from the platband and giving access to open ironwork balconies with railings of interlacing arches. The second-floor windows are also without architraves, but are underlined by a plain continuous sill. The cornice of the main entablature is returned across the face of the attic-story to form an immense triangular pediment, its apex just breaking the coping line, and its tympanum containing a large oval window in the centre and a small rectangular light placed above the second window from either end in the tier below. The houses formings the wings and end pavilions are similarly treated, but their fronts contain three stories only. The horizontal stringcourses and entablature are continued at lower levels than those of the central feature, and the arched surrounds are omitted from the first-floor windows.

Nos. 7 to 11 Quiet Street

The premises now numbered 7 to 11, on the south side of Quiet Street, were erected in 1824. No. 9 formed 'The Auction Mart and Bazaar' and contains on its first-floor a large and lofty hall originally used for exhibitions, meetings, etc., then becoming a Methodist chapel, since when it has served for a variety of purposes.

The Quiet Street elevation has such distinction that, in the absence of contrary evidence, it is not unreasonable to assign the design to Henry Edmund Goodridge. The frontage to No. 9 forms an elaborate centre to which the flanking wings act as simple foils, each containing shopfronts on the ground-story, and two tiers of three regularly spaced windows in the upper part of the front. Each first-floor window is dressed with an architrave, frieze, and boldly projecting cornice supported on consoles. The ground-story of No. 9 is formed into a wide opening between two narrow ones, by rusticated piers with fluted capitals carrying an entablature which is returned round

'The Bazaar', Quiet Street.

each pier. The upper part of the front is dominated by a large segmental arch, corresponding in width to the shopfront below, containing a three-light window and a fanlight of honeysuckle pattern. On each side is a wide pier containing an arched niche of semicircular plan, rising from a pedestal course with panels below the niches and blind balustrading beneath the three lights of the window. The impost mouldings are continued across the lintel below the segmental fan-light, which is set within a moulded archivolt, and each spandrel is decorated with a carved wreath centred above the niche. The main cornice is simple and bold in profile, and is surmounted by an elaborate attic modelled on that of the Choragic Monument of Thrasyllus, consisting of pedestal-like wings flanking a stepped centre from which rises a sculptured figure. This last is larger in scale and lacks the charm of those in the niches, which were carved by

Lucius Gahagan and represent 'Commerce' and 'Genius'.

The Corridor

The Corridor, an arcade of shops connecting High Street with Union Street, was built in

'The Corridor', High Street.

1825 by Goodridge, largely as a personal speculation. The main front towards High Street is a fine example of his earlier manner, wherein he made brilliant use of Graeco-Roman motifs.

The central portion of the front is slightly recessed between narrow pavilions. The ground-story contains a portico of three bays, and a shopfront in each pavilion, the entablature being carried by Doric columns and pilasters with polished granite shafts. The three windows to the first-floor of the central feature are of equal size, and while all are framed with architraves, the middle light is emphasized by

its setting of pilaster-strips with consoles carrying a triangular pediment. The corresponding windows to the second-floor are uniformly framed with architraves and underlined by a continued moulded sill. The side pavilions contain one window to each story, that to the first-floor having an architrave surmounted by a cornice supported on consoles, while the upper window is similar to those in the central feature except that the sill does not extend beyond the architrave. The main entablature is returned round the wall face breaks and surmounted by an attic-story, containing three semi-circular windows framed by moulded archivolts, centred over the middle window and those in each pavilion. The parapet is broken in the centre of the front against a wide pedestal, its die ornamented with a ribboned wreath.

Beckford's Tower, Lansdown

In 1822 William Beckford was forced by the critical state of his finances to part with Fonthill, and shortly afterwards he removed to Bath. For a time he lived on a comparatively modest scale in the large terminal houses of Lansdown Crescent and Lansdown Place West, which he had connected by a gallery at first-floor level. But his passion for scenic transformation soon led him to lease a tract of land rising from behind his houses towards the brow of Lansdown, which he proceeded to lay out with elaborate plantations. Here, on the highest point of vantage, he built during 1825–6 his 'Retreat', a miniature Fonthill dominated by its 154 ft. high tower. His architect, H. E. Goodridge, produced several designs, including one resembling a Gothic Lighthouse, but Beckford chose to build in the Graeco-Roman manner then fashionable, although for some reason contemporary reference was made to his 'Saxon' tower.

Lansdown Tower is most effective in silhouette, and its decoration of freely treated Graeco-Roman detail is reminiscent of Soane's manner. The square shaft is approximately 130 ft. in height, two-thirds consisting of plain masonry relieved only by the small windows lighting the stairway. The first stage terminates in a great Doric entablature, with a boldly profiled cornice supported on each side by four mutules. Each face of the second stage is divided by plain square piers into three tall rectangular openings, which frame deeply recessed arches. The entablature to this stage is suitably reduced in scale and has a dentilled cornice. The plinth-like parapet is decorated with long panels of key-fret, and the emphasized corner dies are crowned with curious square blocks ornamented with circular bos-

ses. The third stage is roughly octagonal in plan and forms a high perforated plinth for the octagonal crowning lantern. This very original adaptation of the Choragic Monument of Lysicrates, carried out in wood and with a fluted column of iron at each angle, was originally finished with colour and gilding.

The two-story building from which the tower rises is in no way remarkable externally. The interior, formerly used as mortuary chapels and offices, has now been restored for residential use.

Detail of a small cast plaster panel used as a repeated motif in the decorative border of a ceiling in No. 5 Sion Hill Place

STONE DOORCASES AND PORCHES

The illustrations on the following pages, 197–202, show something of the wide range of treatment accorded to the entrance doorways of Bath's Georgian buildings, from the immature Renaissance example once to be seen in St. James's Street South, to the elegant Adamesque paired doorways in St. James's Parade, and the Grecian Ionic porch of No. 10 Bathwick Hill. Two handsome examples of the joiner's are in constructing shopfronts are illustrated on page 202.

No. 3. St. James's Street South. Stone-hooded
doorcase (*demolished*)

Queen Square. Baroque doorcase on south side.

No. 1 Pierrepont Place. Roman Ionic doorcase.

The Circus, return front to Brock Street. Roman
Doric porch.

North Parade (Gallaway's) Buildings. Roman Corinthian doorcase with pediment.

No. 7 St. James's Parade. Roman Doric doorcase with pediment.

No. 14 Alfred Street. Adamesque doorcase and overthrow lampholder.

No. 2 Percy Place, London Road. Adamesque doorcase with pediment.

St. John's Hospital. Entrance archway dressed with Roman Doric columns and pediment.

Nos. 39 and 40 St. James's Parade Paired doorways dressed with Adamesque columns, entablature and pediment.

Great Pump Room. North front. Ionic doorcase with pediment.

No. 10 Bathwick Hill. Ionic porch of Soanic character.

Camden Crescent. Rusticated doorcase.

Somerset Place. Rusticated doorcase.

No. 1 Belmont, Lansdown Road. Porch feature of serpentine plan added to return front.

No. 103 New Sydney Place. Doric porch.

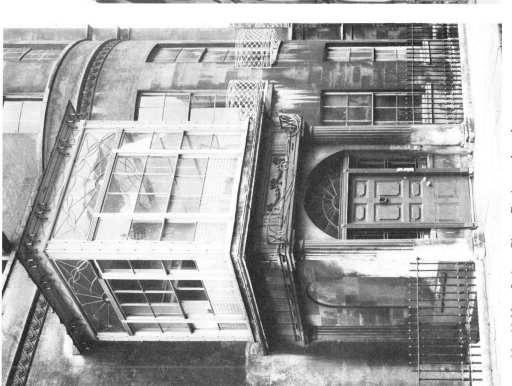

No. 93 New Sydney Place. Doric porch and conservatory.

Argyle Street. Segmental bowed shopfront on south side.

Walcot Street. Paired shopfronts and doorways to Nos. 114 and 116.

INTERIOR DECORATION

INTRODUCTORY NOTE

The decoration of Bath's Georgian houses differs but little from contemporary work in London and the great provincial centres. The influence of the carpenter and joiner predominates in the early eighteenth century until John Wood the elder introduced the Palladian manner of architectural decoration prescribed by Kent and Ware, with relief plasterwork, often baroque in character, providing the chief interest. Although less generally used, the joinery of this time is exceedingly fine, both in design and craftsmanship, and some of Wood's houses still retain staircases of oak and mahogany which are masterpieces of the joiner's art. This period is also remarkable for the introduction of richly carved marble or wood chimney-pieces of a monumental character, which give distinction to the great reception rooms.

The interiors decorated between 1760 and 1785 show many variations of style, and while some of the houses in the Royal Crescent have rooms with ceilings and friezes of distinctly rococo character, others are designed to conform with the ideas of classicism advocated by Chambers and Adam. The latter master's influence is most completely felt in the beautiful chimney-pieces of statuary and coloured marbles which fortunately remain in many of the finest interiors. Stone has generally succeeded wood as the material used in constructing the staircases, which are light and airy in character with delicate balusters of wrought iron with lead enrichments, supporting the continuous handrails of mahogany.

The later Georgian interiors show an ever increasing degree of simplicity, often with a tendency towards over-refinement and attenuation of detail. Reeded architraves with composition ornaments decorating the stops, crisply detailed cast plasterwork of Hellenistic derivation, and delicate marble or wood and composition chimney-pieces, form the stock adornments of rooms which have all the studied elegance of the contemporary furniture.

As the majority of these houses were built for speculative letting or sale, their interiors call for no special comment, although the craftsmanship displayed is usually excellent and the details were designed in accordance with the best contemporary taste. Most of the interiors selected for illustration are located in and around Queen Square, The Circus and Royal Crescent, and belong to houses which were built to meet the special requirements of wealthy and distinguished occupants and were decorated accordingly.

It is generally fallacious to ascribe the design of these interiors, down to the last detail, to the architect responsible for the exterior. Even when his services were retained in planning the internal arrangements, it is extremely doubtful whether he ever did more in most cases than advise on, or select, the decorative finishings. Of course there must be exceptions to this generalization, but it is safe to assume that the majority of the Bath interiors, even those of outstanding architectural merit, owe their beauty and uniformity to the employment of master craftsmen who had acquired their perfect knowledge and understanding of sound principles of design from the study of the numerous pattern-books then available.

STAIRCASES AND ENTRANCE HALLS

No. 24 Queen Square. Staircase, view looking from first half-landing towards entrance arch

Many of the large houses built during the period 1730 to 1760 contain fine staircases of wooden construction, of which this is a typical example, rising in two equal parallel flights between each of the principal floor levels, with deep apsidal half-landings. This staircase is constructed of oak, the treads being finished with plain brackets planted on to the strings, while simply turned balusters, of identical pattern, are spaced in groups of three to each tread and carry the moulded handrail which ramps up to the landing newels, formed in the manner of Doric columns. On the walls is a corresponding dado of large fielded panels,

with a capping to match the staircase handrail. The entrance arch is framed by wood Doric pilasters, from which a moulded archivolt rises

No. 24 Queen Square. Staircase, view looking from first half-landing towards entrance arch. *c.* 1730

No. 15 Queen Square. Staircase hall, view looking from gallery landing. *c.* 1730

to a narrow keyblock, the pilaster shafts and arch spandrels being relieved by fielded panels.

No. 15 Queen Square. Staircase Hall, view looking from gallery landing (page 204)

No. 15 Queen Square was built round about 1732–34 to Wood's design for one 'Esqre Greville', and, despite the depredations of antique dealers, enough remains to show that its interior decorations were of an unusual degree of richness. The magnificent staircase is now in Norcott Hill House, Berkhamstead, but the hall retains its splendid stucco decoration, reasonably attributed to Italian stuccadors. The hall is rectangular in plan and two stories high, and the staircase ascended round three of the walls to arrive at a gallery landing. The moulded wood fascia of this gallery is returned as a plaster stringcourse round the walls of the stair well, and the spandrel shapes formed below were simply divided into panels by an enriched moulding.

Centrally on the wall opposite to the gallery is an elaborately moulded and scrolled archway, its reveals and soffit worked in false perspective, framing a bas-relief composition of St. Cecilia playing an organ and attended by cherubs. On each side of this feature is an arched semi-circular niche, surrounded by a moulded architrave and containing a statue of a female musician. The musical motif is continued by the two bas-relief panels, representing the contest between Apollo and Marsyas with its gruesome sequel, which adorn the fields provided by the walls opposite the windows and to the gallery. Each panel is enclosed by a richly moulded architrave frame, broken into ears and returned across the head in serpentine curves which meet in elaborate scrollwork surrounding a female mask. The walls terminate in a cove, decorated with acanthus scrolls and cherubs holding cartouches.

No. 4 North Parade. Ceiling to first half-landing of staircase (page 206)

This staircase is generally similar to that in No. 24 Queen Square, already described. The first half-landing, of the usual apsidal form, is adorned with some vigorously modelled plasterwork. The curved wall face above the classical setting of the venetian window is relieved by two spandrel panels, each containing a ribboned garland framed within an egg-and-dart moulded surround. The flat ceiling is decorated with two richly foliated and scrolled branches, placed on either side of a basket of fruits and flowers and convoluting into a scallop shell. The soffit of the landing beam is modelled with a bold key fret.

No. 10 The Circus. Semi-dome above upper half-landing on staircase (page 206)

No. 10 The Circus. View of entrance hall, looking towards staircase (page 205)

The staircase at No. 10 The Circus is almost identical in design and construction with that

No. 10 The Circus. View of entrance hall, looking towards staircase. *c.* 1755.

No. 4 North Parade. Ceiling to apsed half-landing of staircase. *c.* 1740

No. 10 The Circus. Semi-dome to apsed half-landing of staircase. *c.* 1765.

at No. 24 Queen Square, and the entrance and staircase halls show a similar arrangement, but the manner of their decoration is one of exquisite refinement. The walls are uniformly treated throughout, being divided above the dado rail into tall panels, flush with the marginal surround from which they are separated by a narrow beaded moulding. A finely modelled plaster entablature with a modillioned cornice surrounds the plain ceiling of the entrance hall, while the staircase walls are finished with an enriched cornice. The arched opening connecting the entrance and staircase halls is finished in woodwork. On each face the moulded archivolt rises from Doric pilasters with fluted shafts, while the soffit, decorated with square coffers, springs from Doric pilasters with panelled shafts. The principal decorative feature is the plaster semi-dome above the upper half-landing. In this most beautiful example the radiating and diminish-

ing coffers, containing moulded bosses, are partly overlaid by a large scallop shell rising from the curving cornice, along the top of which are continued rolled scrolls.

No. 23 Royal Crescent. Staircase, circa 1770
St. James's Square. Staircase, circa 1790

No. 93 New Sydney Place. Staircase, circa 1808 (page 208)

These are typical staircases in Bath houses constructed during the period from 1775 to 1820. In each example the treads and landings are of stone, the former being cantilevered out from the walls enclosing the stair well. As in the finest wooden staircases the soffit of each tread is worked to continue the nosing and bracket profile back to the wall face, although this practice was not always followed in the latest examples. Plain and slender balusters of square section, in wood or iron, have now

No. 23 Royal Crescent. Staircase. *c.*1770.

St. James's Square. Staircase. *c.*1790.

No. 93 New Sydney Place. Staircase, *c.* 1808.

replaced the turnings used in earlier work, and are usually spaced two to each tread, alternating at close and regular intervals with narrow upright panels of wrought or cast iron, enriched with moulded lead or pewter ornaments. These panels vary in design from the elaborate delicacy of the Royal Crescent example, where two contrasting panels are used in alternation, to the elegant simplicity of the Vitruvian scrolls in New Sydney Place.

REPRESENTATIVE INTERIORS

No. 41 Gay Street. Drawing-room on first-floor (page 209)

This house, built in 1734–36 for Richard Marchant, a rich Quaker, contains some of the finest woodwork of that period now remaining in Bath. The apsidal-ended rooms on the ground and first floors are lined with panelling, the scheme in each being generally simi-

lar but different in detail. The dado is plain, but above the moulded chair-rail the walls are set out with tall fielded panels, finishing in a finely carved entablature with a modillioned cornice surrounding a plain plastered ceiling. The apses in the ground-floor room are flanked by fluted pilasters with Ionic capitals, a smaller version of this order being used to frame the fireplace. The Ionic order is again used for the doorcase and chimney-piece in the first-floor room, but the apses are flanked by three-quarter columns with fluted shafts and Corinthian capitals. The triangular pediments above the doorcases are said to have been added at a later date.

No. 1 Royal Crescent. Drawing-room and dining-room (page 210)

The beautifully restored rooms of No. 1 Royal Crescent are fairly typical of the style in which Bath's later Georgian houses were decorated. In the drawing-room the walls above the dado-rail are hung with damask, but in the ground-floor rooms the walls are finely finished in plaster, both the dado and upper face having slightly-sunk panels within enriched mouldings.

Wood is still used for door and window casings, skirtings and dado rails, and some doors are of finely figured mahogany. The wood entablatures or box-cornices of earlier times have given way to delicately enriched friezes and reduced cornices of plasterwork.

PLASTERWORK

No. 1 Pierrepont Place. Ceiling to drawing-room (page 212)

This fine house, designed by the elder Wood in 1742 for John Hutchins, plasterer, retains much of its original baroque plasterwork. The general character of the work is akin to that in several houses in Queen Square and The Parades, probably by the same hand. The drawing-room ceiling is surrounded by an enriched modillioned cornice, and adorned with large scale decorations modelled in bas-relief. Scallop shells and foliage scrolls are enclosed with the L-shaped corner panels,

No. 41 Gay Street. Drawing-room on first floor. *c.* 1735.

between which are foliated cartouches, while the oval central panel is plain except for the boss of cloud from which the chandelier is suspended.

No. 9 The Circus. First-floor front room ceiling (page 212)

An enriched modillioned cornice surrounds this ceiling, which is decorated with plasterwork of similar character to the work of the Bristol stuccoists and closely resembles another ceiling in the Royal Crescent. The central panel of oval form, surrounded by festooned garlands and pendants, is filled with ornaments of rococo character combined with flowing sprays of foliage. The narrow border panels contain foliated scrolls and are broken at each corner by diagonally flowing interlacing branches.

No. 15 Royal Crescent. First-floor front room ceiling (page 212)

A deep frieze of foliated scrolling surmounted by a richly ornamented modillioned cornice surrounds this fine ceiling, which is divided into a geometrical arrangement of compartments—in a manner reminiscent of earlier Palladian work—and decorated with scrolled branches, trophies, etc. The birds with free-standing necks and wings, and the repeating diaper pattern used for the soffits forming the main divisions, are characteristics met with in the work of the Bristol stuccoists.

No. 5 Royal Crescent. First-floor front room ceiling (page 213)

The exquisitely refined plasterwork decorating this room reflects the influence of the Adam designers, Bonomi and Pergolesi. The

No. 1 Royal Crescent. Drawing-room on first floor. *c*.1769.

No. 1 Royal Crescent. Dining-room on ground floor. *c*.1769.

frieze of wreathed honeysuckle ornaments alternating with candelabrum is surmounted by a simple cornice. A plain margin surrounds the oblong ceiling, which is reduced to a square by a narrow panel at each end, filled with honeysuckle and foliated stems ranged between husk festoons. Within the square a delicately reeded moulding forms a large circular panel which in turn encloses a strongly defined octagon, from the angles of which extended interlacing festoons of husks, the spaces thus formed being decorated with scrolls, branches and trophies. Within the octagon is a central seed, surrounded by radiating branches of honeysuckle and foliage linked by festoons of leaves.

No. 39 Milsom Street (Somersetshire Buildings). Ground-floor front room ceiling (page 213)

This is one of the finest ceilings of its period in Bath, and demonstrates Baldwin's mastery of interior decoration. Although it has a distinct affinity with the circular panels in the Guildhall Banqueting Room, this ceiling is treated with greater delicacy and freedom. A large circular panel encloses an octagon, the segmental spaces thus formed being filled with fluting. A second octagon impinges on the first, leaving triangular spaces which contain scrolled ornaments. In the angles of this inner octagon are rams' heads, linked by drapery festoons, and from them foliated branches radiate towards the centre, to end in reversed scrolls which are linked by husk festoons, the intervening spaces being enriched with husk wreaths around floral paterae. A splayed frieze of anthemion ornaments surrounds the recessed circular central panel, which is decorated with eight festoons of husks, enclosing crossed branches and meeting in ribbon bows from which depend four agricultural trophies. An enriched moulding forms a concave lozenge from each corner of which a tied ribbon bears an oval portrait medallion—all identical—while a circular panel in the centre encloses wreathed bands of husks and a boss of curving leaves.

No. 12 Royal Crescent. First-floor front room ceiling (page 215)

This fine Graeco-Roman ceiling, of late eighteenth-century date, is skilfully assembled from stock ornaments. An enriched modillioned cornice leads up to the plain marginal surround of the large panel of decoration, which is enclosed by a narrow moulding of Pompeian scrolling and dominated by a great circular motif. This is made up of husk strings radiating from the centre and bordered by husk festoons which meet in ribbon bows and interlace with the reversed curves of a beaded moulding. Four small oval medallions, of classical figure subjects, break the husk strings which are at right-angles to the walls, and in each corner of the ceiling is a quadrant ornament of radiating leaves, etc. In the centre is a large and elaborate 'rose', composed of a seed surrounded by a ring of radiating acanthus leaves and one of scrolls, palmettes, etc.

Two decorative panels above chimney-pieces

No. 8 Upper Church Street, Royal Crescent No. 28 Rivers Street (page 214)

In some of the late eighteenth-century interiors a charming feature is provided by the use of bas-relief medallions or tablets—usually of classical subjects modelled after antique gems or the highly stylized jasper tablets produced by Wedgwood and Bentley—forming focal points in the decorative panels above chimney-pieces.

At No. 8 Upper Church Street is a panel containing a fine oval medallion depending from strings of husks, which are looped and festooned over paterae. In the unusually rich and beautiful example at No. 28 Rivers Street two strings of husks and leaves are looped over paterae to form festoons meeting in a ribbon bow. From this ribbon depends an oval medallion of Athena, while chains support the large oblong central tablet, which represents a bacchanal. Scrolled cresting surmounts the tablet, below which the ornament is continued with foliated branches scrolling right and left to end in floral cornucopiae.

No. 1 Pierrepont Place. Ceiling to drawing-room. *c*. 1743.

No. 9 The Circus. Ceiling of first-floor front room.

No. 15 Royal Crescent. Ceiling of first-floor front room. *c*. 1770

No. 5 Royal Crescent. Ceiling of first-floor front room. *c*.1770

No. 39 Milsom Street. Ceiling of ground-floor front room. *c*.1782

No. 8 Upper Church Street. Decorative plasterwork above chimney-piece. *c*.1775.

No. 28 Rivers Street. Decorative plasterwork above chimney-piece. *c*.1775.

No. 12 Royal Crescent. Ceiling of first-floor front room. *c*.1775.

No. 4 Grosvenor Place. Ceiling of first-floor front room. *c*.1810.

No. 100 New Sydney Place. Ceiling *c*. 1808

No. 4 Grosvenor Place. First-floor front room ceiling (page 215)

Several of the houses in Grosvenor Place were finished during the early years of the nineteenth century, probably under the direction of John Pinch for the interior decorations reflect his curiously eclectic taste in such matters. In this room the traditional cornice has been supplanted by a small cavetto, enriched with freestanding anthemion ornaments. The ceiling border consists of plain mouldings framing a band of scrolls and curving palmettes, with corner stops, and is fringed with curious acute-triangular ornaments of Gothic derivation. These are also used on each side of the bold circle of reeding which surrounds the central rose—of almost identical design with that described above. A bead-and-reel moulding is used to form wide marginal surrounds and enclose the complementary panels which are ornamented with small circular panels of vine leaves.

No. 100 New Sydney Place. Ceiling (page 216)

The fine houses of New Sydney Place, built in 1808 from designs by John Pinch, were

decorated in the eclectic taste of the Regency, the plasterwork, in particular, deriving from both Classic and Gothic sources. The cornices and ceiling borders are generally detailed in the Gothic manner, the former sometimes suggesting vaulting of a minute scale, decorated with cusped arches or trefoiled spandrels. The ornamentation of the central roses is usually of purely Hellenistic derivation, with sharply cut acanthus and olive leaves radiating, or spirally curving, from the seed, within a circle of reeded mouldings. These relief ornaments are often fringed with the triangular ornaments noted above, which seem to be peculiar to Pinch's work.

No. 2 Sion Hill Place. Ground-floor front room ceiling (page 217)

The two ground-floor rooms in this house have ceilings of identical design, skilfully composed of stock ornaments from the plasterer's repertory. A central boss of spirally curving acanthus leaves is set in a rough octagon formed by husk festoons which continue in diminishing interlacings diagonally towards each corner of the ceiling, each interlacing enclosing an acanthus leaf patera.

No. 5 Sion Hill Place. Ground-floor front room ceiling (page 217)

A fine border surrounds this plain ceiling, with panels, containing crossed branches of palm and vine, arranged in alternate sequence and separated by blocks bearing acanthus leaves. The narrow cavetto cornice is enriched with free-standing leaves.

CHIMNEY-PIECES

No. 41 Gay Street. Wood chimney-piece in drawing-room, c. 1735 (p. 218)

This finely carved chimney-piece is designed to accord with the doorcase and window surround. Fluted pilasters and an enriched entablature of the Ionic order, with architrave slips of breccia, frame a cast-iron hob grate of late eighteenth-century date.

No. 2 Sion Hill Place. Ceiling of ground-floor front room. *c*.1818.

No. 5 Sion Hill Place. Ceiling of ground-floor front room. *c*.1820.

No. 41 Gay Street. Chimney-piece of carved wood in drawing-room. *c*.1735.

No. 7 Royal Crescent. Chimney-piece of carved wood in drawing-room. *c*.1770

No. 7 The Circus. Chimney-piece of carved statuary marble. *c*.1770.

No. 25 Royal Crescent. Chimney-piece of carved wood with composition ornament. *c*.1770.

No. 7 Royal Crescent. Wood chimney-piece, c. 1770 (page 218)

An elegantly detailed chimney-piece, enriched with carving and composition ornament. The basic form of some earlier Palladian examples is retained, but the decoration is typical of the Adam school. The frieze tablet represents Aesop's fable of the Fox and the Stork.

No. 25 Royal Crescent

This wood chimney-piece is enriched with carving and composition ornaments. The frieze tablet represents Aurora's chariot.

No. 7 The Circus. Chimney-piece of white statuary (Carrara) marble (page 218)

The handsome marble chimney-pieces still to be found in many Bath houses were typical productions of the marble-mason or statuary. They were assembled with taste and skill from a large stock of mouldings, columns and ornaments, and often incorporate frieze tablets carved with mythological or fabulous subjects.

No. 17 St. James's Square

The drawing-room chimney-piece is of white statuary marble with carved ornament and coloured marble inlay. (below)

Appendix I

A LIST OF STREETS CONTAINING GEORGIAN BUILDINGS OF ARCHITECTURAL INTEREST NOT DEALT WITH IN THE TEXT OR ILLUSTRATIONS

(Those marked with an asterisk are of considerable architectural merit)

*Abbey Green
 Ainslie's Belvedere, Lansdown Road
 Alexander Buildings, London Road
 Albion Place, Upper Bristol Road

 Barton Buildings, Queen Square
*Bathwick Hill
 Beacon Hill
 Beau Street
*Beaufort Buildings, London Road
*Belvedere, Lansdown Road
 Bloomfield Crescent, Lyncombe
 Bridge Street
 Bristol Road
*Brunswick Place, Julian Road
*Burlington Street
 Burton Street

*Catharine Place
*Chapel Row, Queen Square
*Charles Street
 Cheap Street
*Church Street
 Claverton Street
*Cleveland Place
*Cornwell Buildings, Walcot Street

*Daniel Street, Bathwick
*Darlington Street, Bathwick
*Devonshire Buildings, Lyncombe
*Dunsford Place, Bathwick Hill

*Edward Street, Bathwick

*George Street, Bathwick Hill

*Great Bedford Street
*Great Stanhope Street
 Grove Street, Bathwick

 Hampton Row, Bathwick
 Harington Place
*Henrietta Street, Bathwick
 Henry Street
*Hetling Court
*High Street
 Holloway

 James Street West
*Johnstone Street, Bathwick

*Kensington, London Road
*Kingsmead Street
*Kingston Buildings

*Lambridge—villas
*Lansdown Road

 Macaulay Buildings, Widcombe
 Manvers Street
*Monmouth Street
*Montpelier, Julian Road
 Morford Street
 Mount Beacon

*New Bond Street
*New King Street
 Nile Street
*Norfolk Buildings
 North Parade Passage
 Northgate Street

*Northampton Street
Northumberland Place

*Old Bond Street
*Orchard Street

*Paradise Row, Holloway
*Park Street
*Percy Place, London Road
*Princes Street, Queen Square

*Queen's Parade
*Queen Street

*Raby Place, Bathwick
Richmond Hill

*Sion Hill—villas
Sion Place, Bathwick Hill
Spencer's Bellevue, Lansdown Road
*Springfield Place, Lansdown Road

Stall Street
*Sydney Buildings, Bathwick

*Union Street
Union Passage
Upper East Hayes
Upper Borough Walls
*Upper Church Street

*Vane Street, Bathwick
*Vineyards, London Road

Walcot Street
Walcot Terrace
Westgate Buildings
*Westgate Street
Widcombe Hill—villas

*York Buildings, George Street
York Street

Appendix II

DIRECTORY ENTRIES OF ARCHITECTS PRACTISING IN BATH DURING THE
LATTER PART OF THE GEORGIAN ERA

1793—Bath Directory
    Palmer, John   6 Upper Charles Street
    Eveleigh, John   Grove Street
    Baldwin, Thomas   Harington Place

1800—Bath Directory
    Palmer, John   6 Charles Street
    Pinch, John   12 Chatham Row

1805—Bath Directory
    Baldwin, Mr.   Walcot Terrace
    Masters, Mr. Harcourt   39 Rivers Street
    Palmer, John   6 Charles Street
    Pinch, John   Spring Gardens

1809—Bath Directory

Baldwin, Mr.	7 Walcot Terrace
Harcourt, Mr. Charles	39 Rivers Street
Pinch, John	Spring Gardens

1813—Original Bath Guide

Basnett	Westgate Buildings
Baldwyn (sic)	Walcot
Finden	Abbey Place
Harcourt	Rivers Street
Pinch	St. James's Parade

1819—Bath Directory

Basnett, Mr. C. H.	20 Paragon Buildings
Finden, Mr.	4 Galloway's Buildings
Goodridge, H. E.	36 Bathwick Street
Lowder, Mr.	Chapel House, Lansdown Grove
Manners, Mr.	29 Rivers Street
Pinch & Son (and surveyors)	27 St. James's Parade
Viner, C.	9 Walcot Terrace

Appendix III

DRAWINGS RELATING TO BATH IN SIR JOHN SOANE'S MUSEUM

Robert Adam's design for the proposed Ball and Concert Rooms

Nos. 45 to 49 in volume 28 of the Adam drawings form a set of finely rendered drawings giving the plan, principal elevation and three sections of Robert Adam's design for the Ball and Concert Rooms at Bath. The Plan appears to have been based on that of a casino which Adam had noted during his Continental travels. The disposition of the rooms is basically similar to that of Wood's suite but the plan forms are altogether more elaborate. The core of the building is an oblong vestibule, entered from a semi-circular portico recessed into the principal front. Directly beyond this vestibule is a large rotunda, with four apses, which gives access to staircases left and right. The ballroom and concert room form parallel blocks placed left and right of the vestibule, each room being entered in the centre of its long side. From each side of the oblong ballroom extends a semi-circular exedra, one of which forms the entrance from the vestibule. The concert room is approached through a small ante-room, which has its counterpart on the opposite side, and the orchestra end of the room is semi-circular. The architectural treatment proposed for the exterior and interiors is in Adam's earlier and less personal manner, great use being made of Roman monumental trappings such as giant orders, pedimented tabernacle frames containing statues and vases, long panels of bas-relief sculpture and richly coffered ceilings.

Robert Adam's designs for Bathwick New Town and Pulteney Bridge

Most of the drawings relating to Bathwick

New Town and Pulteney Bridge are bound into volume 38 of the Adam drawings.

No. 1 is a coloured perspective study for the riverside 'crescent'—actually two balancing curved ranges of four-storied buildings, with terrace walks raised above warehouse vaults. This design, although carefully considered, does not appear to relate exactly to any of the plans mentioned below.

Nos. 2 to 5 are fully dimensioned drawings for Pulteney Bridge as executed. (Nos. 22 and 23 in volume 51 are small scale rendered elevational drawings of this bridge.)

No. 6 left is a small scale drawing showing the proposed layout for Bathwick, a copy of which was submitted to Mr. Pulteney during June, 1777. This plan shows an academic arrangement of six straight streets, equally 120 ft. wide, radiating at equal intervals from a great circus of 800 ft. diameter. The principal street is axial with the bridge, and other streets lead left and right to semi-octangular and octangular places, being crossed at right angles by other streets which converge on the bridge. In general this plan is adequately related to the existing city.

No. 8, drawn to a larger scale and in more detail than the foregoing, is a plan for the development of the Bathwick riverside immediately opposite the bridge—a copy of a drawing sent to Mr. Pulteney during December, 1782. Volume 10 contains two drawings—Nos. 81 and 82—which are elevational studies for this project. On each side of the bridge are quadrant retaining walls, finished with balustrades broken by water gates and steps between small domed pavilions. Against the river bank, at right angles to the bridge, are two ranges of two-storied buildings with basement wharfs, each range being divided into seven bays, each three windows wide, by narrow pilastered pavilions crowned by large vases, the central bay being emphasized by a domed tower. Opposite the bridge is a great crescent, broken at equal intervals by three streets designed to converge on the bridge. The principal street is 100 ft. wide and centred axially on the bridge, the secondary streets being only 30 ft. in width. This drawing shows a site for the proposed new prison, approximately in the position occupied by Atwood's building.

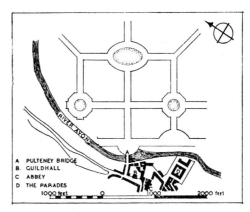

Robert Adam's sketch-plans for laying out
Bathwick.
(*re-drawn to conform with site conditions*)

No. 7 right is an alternative to the above, so uninspired in its general conception that it might well have been prepared solely to stress the obviously fine qualities of the first scheme.

No. 9 is a sketch design for the elevational treatment of the buildings for the New Town at Bath. The terrace houses to have a rusticated ground-story, the upper parts of the fronts to be plain except for the pavilions of three bays with Ionic pilasters rising through the two upper stories to support a triangular pediment.

Nos. 10 and 11 are dimensioned plans for the New Prison. This scheme was set aside in favour of Atwood's design for a much smaller building.

George Dance the younger's designs for the Theatre Royal

No. 1 is a sketch design for the 'Grand Front' in Beauford Square.

No. 2 is an alternative design for the above.

No. 3 is a study for the frieze and cornice to the grand front (as executed except for the substitution of acroterial lyres instead of the pediments to each end bay). On the reverse side of this sheet is a sketch for an 'Egyptian' treatment of the front.

No. 4 is a rough sketch for the frieze and cornice.

No. 5 is a constructional plan of the auditorium—possibly by Palmer.

Nos. 6 and 7 are longitudinal and cross sections of the auditorium. This was generally similar in form to the Theatre Royal at Bristol, but larger. The steeply raked pit was surrounded by three horsehoe tiers containing the boxes and galleries, and the flat main ceiling sloped sharply down towards the coved proscenium. The columns supporting the tiers were set back behind the balcony fronts, and those supporting the main ceiling were finished with elaborate palm leaf capitals expanding into arches.

No. 8 shows the two sections of the auditorium drawn to a small scale. On the reverse of this sheet is a study for the reeded decoration of the columns.

Nos. 9 and 10 show three alternative designs for decorating the balcony fronts (a) gilt trellis over a puce ground, (b) Roman fish-scale ornament, (c) painted festooned draperies.

No. 11 is a study for decorating the proscenium arch.

No. 12 is the setting out of the ceiling construction.

Nos. 13 and 14 are studies for the ceiling decorations, designed to incorporate the five paintings by Andrea Casali brought from the Palladian mansion of Fonthill.

No. 15 shows the decorative treatment of the coved proscenium. The jambs contained proscenium doors with decorative panels over, fan ornaments filled the spandrels, and the head was sub-divided into three decorative panels of which the central one was lettered with THE WORLD'S A STAGE.

Appendix IV

THE ELDER WOOD'S 'PROPOSALS FOR ERECTING BY SUBSCRIPTION AN ASSEMBLY-HOUSE IN THE CITY OF BATH'

During research among the archives belonging to the City of Bristol, the author chanced upon a copy of the printed proposals and plans, prepared by John Wood the elder, for an Assembly House and Theatre, designed to form the centre of the buildings on the South Parade. This scheme must have been evolved, and the proposals published, some time between 1740 and 1743, during which period the North and South Parades were built. The contents of this prospectus are summarized and partly quoted in the following paragraphs.

'The inhabitants of the City of Bath

daily increasing, as well as the Resort of Strangers for the Benefit of the Medicinal and Mineral Waters; and the Rooms for Publick Assembly being too small for that Purpose, each containing no more than 1800 square Feet upon its Area: It is Proposed, by John Wood, of the said City, Architect, that a convenient and commodious House shall be erected by Subscription, upon the North side of a Square now begun, and agreed, to be built upon the Abbey-Orchard and Ham in the said City, according to the following Designs; containing a Hall, with three Doors for six Chairs to set down at a Time; two Anti-Chambers; two Rooms proper for Billiard-Tables to stand in; a Ball-Room, with a Gallery round it, whose whole Area amounts to 4659 square Feet; a Drawing-Room, containing upon its Area 1980 square Feet; a Room Proper for a theatre, 80 Feet long, and 35 Feet six Inches broad; with convenient Apartments for a family. In the Disposition of which, the strictest Regard has been had to place the Doors and Windows, so as to prevent People from taking Cold; to contrive Apertures in the Ball-Room to let in any Quantity of Air that may be necessary in Summer; and to make the Entrance to that Room so as that People returning out of it may go through a Passage into an Anti-Chamber to cool themselves before they enter the Hall to take their Chairs, or go out into the Street to take their Coaches.

'The Expence of Building and Finishing the said House, and of making a Street before it of about forty Feet broad, amounts to the Sum of 4200L, as appears by the following Particulars, vis.'

Fully detailed estimates are grouped under the following headings:

Wall Stone, Free Stone, and Paving Stone	L1223	19	1
Rough Masons Work and Lime	607	10	1
Carpenters and Joiners Work	1706	17	0
Carving and Marble	130	11	6
Plaisterers and Tylers Work	277	12	6
Plumbers Work	121	14	0
Painting	65	2	11

It was proposed to raise this sum of £4,200 by issuing forty equal shares of £105 to intending subscribers, who were bound by covenant to make proportionate payments to Wood as the building progressed.

The three plans show basement, ground- and first-floor layouts of a building forming the centre of a range of houses fronting on to the north terrace walk of the Royal Forum; that is, the site whereon the South Parade was eventually built. The frontage of approximately 90 ft. is divided into eleven bays, the middle five being slightly advanced from the main building line to form a pedimented central feature. On the ground-story the three middle bays contain doorways leading directly into the hall, from which further doors give access to an ante-chamber on either side. The hall and each ante-chamber has a door leading to a corridor, which surrounds the ball-room on all four sides and gives access to the two billiards-rooms, placed one on each side of the ball-room block. Behind each ante-chamber, and approached from the corridor, is a staircase rising to the arcaded gallery which surrounds and overlooks the ball-room, a great apartment forming a double-cube of 26 ft. 9 ins. Above the hall and ante-chambers is the long drawing-room, forming a quadruple-cube of 22 ft. 3 ins. This room is entered from the gallery by a doorway, placed centrally between two fireplaces on one long side, and has eleven windows overlooking the terrace walk. The two staircases also provide access to the corridor surrounding three sides of the basement theatre, which is placed below the ball-room. The small auditorium is arranged to form a pit with a horseshoe of boxes. Caretaker's quarters are contained in the front basement, and there are deep vaults extending below the terrace walk.

Appendix V

A DETAILED ACCOUNT OF THE WOODS' BUILDING PROJECTS

In undertaking their ambitious building enterprises in Bath, the two John Woods had two main objectives, to demonstrate in a practical way their superior talents as architects, and to create for themselves and their families an annual income deriving from the fee farm rents charged by them on the individual houses.

Queen Square

John Wood, the elder, proceeded with caution in his first building development, Queen Square, taking a sequence of 99-years leases from the ground landlord, Robert Gay, each plot being sufficient to meet the immediate demand for house sites. The first lease, granted by Gay on November 28/30th, 1728, at an annual rent charge of £20, was for two plots. One fronted 100 ft. to the east side of Queen Square and 150 ft. to the north side of Wood Street, while the other fronted 100 ft. to the south side of the Square and 150 ft. to Berton Street, then described as 'a Way leading to Trim Street'. Between September 1729 and September 1731 Wood granted underleases for building eight houses on the first site, five being double-fronted, and four houses on the second site. Supplementary leases of two strips of ground, both five feet wide, probably for making pavements in

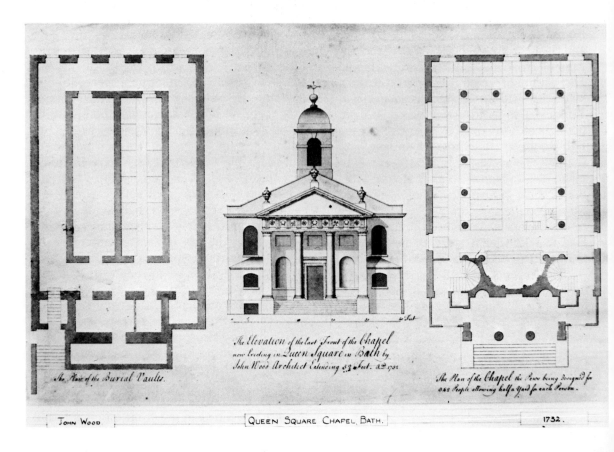

The Plan of the Burial Vaults.

The Elevation of the East Front of the Chapel now erecting in Queen Square in Bath by John Wood Architect Extending 53 Feet. A.º 1732.

The Plan of the Chapel the Pews being designed for 642 People allowing half a Yard for each Person.

JOHN WOOD   QUEEN SQUARE CHAPEL, BATH.   1732.

Wood Street and John Street, were granted to Wood on June 17th, 1730, at a rental of £8. On March 8th, 1730/31, at a rental of £21 10s., Wood leased a large plot with a frontage of 300 ft. and a depth of 150 ft., enabling him to complete the south side of the Square with five houses, and to build the twelve houses of Chapel Row. The relative underleases were granted between April 5th, 1731 and April 10th, 1732. Two more plots were leased on October 12th, 1732, at a rental of £32 14s. The larger plot, 206 ft. in front and 150 ft. deep, was for the north terrace of seven houses, forming the 'Grand Front' of the Square, while the other plot, fronting 101 ft., completed the east side with three houses. The building underleases were granted from January 30th, 1732 to July 25th, 1734. To complete the Square, Wood leased all the ground required for the west side on December 16th, 1732, at a rental of £31 6s., his underleases for five house sites being granted from December 23rd, 1732 to October 3rd, 1734.

Queen Square does not appear as such in the early Walcot ratebooks, the ratepayers being listed under Wood Street, Berton Street, Queen Street, and Prince's Street. However, the recurrent sequence of names makes it possible to identify the ratepayers with the houses as they are now numbered, in clockwise sequence round the Square, beginning at the north end of the east side. In 1734 rates were paid for the three double-fronted houses in Wood street, 1, Robert Mathews; 2, Mrs. Parker; and 3, Richard, Earl Tylney of Castlemain. Earl Tylney also paid for 2 and 3 Queen Square, and Jerry Pierce, surgeon, for 4. The five south side ratepayers in 1734 were 5, Esqre Brace; 6 Samuel Webb; 7 and 8, John Burch; and 9, John Wood. There were no ratepayers in 1734 for the west side and only two for the north, 22, Stephen Collins, and 23, William Greenway.

In 1736 all twenty-seven houses in Queen Square were rated. Mr. Wiltshire now paid for No. 7 on the south side, but 5, 6, 8 and 9 had the same ratepayers as in 1734. The new houses were 10 and 11, John Burch; 12, John George; and 13, Mr. Cary. The west side was comprised of three separate buildings, the south one formed by 14, Mdm Long, and 15, Esqre Greville. The central mansion within the forecourt was Sir John Buckworth's, and the north building contained 18a, John George; 19 and 20, Mr. Westbury. The north side was completed with 21, Samuel Emes; 22 and 23 as in 1734, 24, Mary Pearce; 25 and 26, Samuel Emes; and 27, Mrs. Chisly. The east side was also completed with 1a and 1, John Burch. From 1737 to 1740 the only change was the acquisition by 'Mr. Tibballs' of John Burch's houses in 1737. 'Mr. Tibballs' was the wealthy timber merchant of Lambeth, James Theobald.

Chapel Row contained twelve houses, the five rated in 1734 being 1 to 3, Mr. Parker; 7, Charles Gay; and 8, Mr. Leason. In 1736 they were joined by 4 and 5, Mr. Wiltshire; 6, Joshua Williams; and 9 and 12, William Sainsbury. In 1736 rates were also paid for the three single-fronted houses at the east end of Wood Street, 4 and 5, Mr. Dixon; and 6, Mr. Robins of Abbey Green.

On December 20th, 1733, John Wood signed an agreement with eleven other parties to 'erect build and finish a Chappel in Queen Square', each contributing £60 to Wood on execution of the articles, and a further £60 when the chapel was finished, all then becoming joint proprietors. The participants were Richard, Earl Tylney of Castlemain; Mary Pearce, of Bath; Thomas Harrison, gentleman, of Bath; Samuel Emes, mason, of Bath; James Theobald, timber merchant, of Lambeth; John Burch, carpenter, of Walcot; John George, innholder, of Walcot; William Sainsbury, carpenter, of Walcot; Stephen Collins, mason, of Walcot; Richard Strange, Limeburner, of Wick, Glos; and John Still, of Daynton, Glos. When St. Mary's Chapel was finished, except for the intended galleries, Wood and his wife Jenny agreed, on June 3/4th, 1743, to sell their share of one-twelfth part to John Still for the sum of £132. It will be observed that except for Harrison, Strange and Still, the proprietors of the Chapel were ratepayers in Queen Square and Chapel Row. It can also be assumed that Collins, Sainsbury and Burch collaborated as building tradesmen with Samuel Emes, whom Wood describes in his *Essay* as 'an old experienced Master Builder' who 'performed all the Rough Masons Work of Queen Square, as well as of the Houses round about it.'

It was the west end house, No. 21, on the north side, built by and belonging to Emes, that was gutted by fire on May 7th, 1747. This fire, which began in No. 22 and spread also to No. 23, then Dr. Harington's house, is described by Wood on page 335 of his *Essay*. There is also an account in Boddeley's Bath Journal for May 11th, which tells how Beau Nash opened a subscription for Emes, whose loss was calculated at £1,000. The ruin was purchased and fully restored by William Bumpstead, Esqre, who appears as ratepayer for No. 21 in 1749, having moved from No. 18a, for which he paid rates in 1746.

Having, presumably, the King's Circus already in his mind, Wood continued building northwards from Queen Square, leasing two plots of ground on which to build the north end of Berton Street, now part of Gay Street. The first lease, granted on August 6th, 1733, at a rental of £8, was for a plot fronting 80 ft. west and 219 ft. north, on which were built houses to form the south side of George Street and part of Berton Street. Eight underleases were granted by Wood from March 13th, 1733/4 to October 15th, 1741. The second lease, granted on October 14th, 1734, at a rental of £15, was for an adjoining plot 80 ft. deep and fronting 152 ft. to Berton Street. Underleases for six houses on this site were granted between October 21st, 1734 and December 15th, 1738.

The eleven houses in Berton Street are now numbered 31 to 41 Gay Street. Rates were first paid for 41, the handsome house overlooking Queen Square, by Richard Marchant in 1736. Marchant, a wealthy Quaker, was still the ratepayer in 1756. Other houses rated in 1736 were 40, Mr. Strong; 34, Mr. Bussell; and John Wood paid rates for a tennis court which

is shown on his 1736 Plan of Bath. The terrace, from George Street to Queen Square, was complete by 1740, when rates were paid by the following: 41, Mr. Marchant; 40, Mr. Sparrow (rector of Walcot); 39, Mr. Bowerbank (curate); 38, Mr. Bartrand; 37 and 36, Gratious Stride (carpenter); 35, Mr. Stevenson; 34, Mr. Bussell (joiner); 33 and 32, Mr. John Wood; and 31, Mr. Onslow.

With Queen Square completed, the elder John Wood had succeeded in erecting a monument to his architectural skills, and in creating two sets of rents, one amounting to £137 per annum being paid to Robert Gay and his heirs, the other amounting to £305 1s. per annum accruing to the Woods. In addition he had secured for himself and his family a fine house in the Square. This, as the ratebooks prove, was No. 9, the centre house on the south side, and not, as has often been stated, No. 24 on the north side. A more complete account of the relative evidence is given at the end of Appendix VI.

The Parades

When the elder Wood embarked on his second great building project, the Parades, he could feel assured of ready support from intending builders, while the very nature of the Abbey Orchard ground necessitated his taking a single lease of all that he required. As recounted on page 135 the ground was conveyed to Wood and his trustee, James Leake, by Evelyn, Duke of Kingston, under an Indenture of July 3rd, 1739, enrolled on September 22nd, 1739.

Assignments for building plots in the Grand (North) Parade were granted by Wood and Leake between October 1st and 30th, 1739, with releases generally dated May 30th, 1740. Thirteen plots, varying in frontage width, were assigned to the following—From the Town Wall to Pierrepont Street, Thomas Goulding, jeweller, (1) 12 ft. 0 in. (2) 40 ft. 0 in.; James Bevan, gent., 40 ft. 0 in.; Robert Carey, merchant of London, 24 ft. 0 in.; Samuel Hemmings, mercer, 17 ft. 0 in.; William Ralfs, colourman, 23 ft. 0 in. with return front of 38 ft. 5 in. From Pierrepont Street to Duke Street, John Taylor, watchmaker, (1) 17 ft. 0 in. with return front of 35 ft. 6 in. (2) 41 ft. 8 in.; George Lookup, gent, (1) 24 ft. 6 in. (2) 42 ft. 0 in.; Ralph Allen, Esq., (1) 24 ft. 6 in. (2) 59 ft. 6 in. with return front of 35 ft. 6 in. From Duke Street, eastwards, Francis Fauquier, gent, 73 ft. 0 in. with return front of 36 ft. 0 in. to Duke Street.

The Pierrepont Street plots were assigned between May 30th, 1740 and September 3rd, 1742. Five plots completing the east side were granted to the following—William Sainsbury, carpenter, (1) 24 ft. 0 in. (2) 24 ft. 6 in.; Charles Stone, vintner, 42 ft. 0 in.; Samuel Purlewent, gent., 24 ft. 6 in.; Gratious Stride, carpenter, 23 ft. 6 in. Ten narrow plots on the west side were assigned to the following—John Taylor, 18 ft. 0 in.; John Ford, mason, 18 ft. 0 in.; Joseph Shewring, mason, 18 ft. 0 in.; Edward Lluellin, joiner, 18 ft. 0 in. (Shewring and Lluellin each having the right to share in building above St. James's Portico); Stephen Ford, mason, 18 ft. 0 in.; John Ford, 18 ft. 0 in.; Edward Bussell, joiner, 10 ft. 0 in.; John Ford, 20 ft. 0 in.; Edward Bussell, 20 ft. 0$\frac{3}{4}$ in.; William Hoare, limner, 21 ft. 0$\frac{3}{4}$ in. (these last two plots fronted the intended Royal Forum).

The plots fronting to the South Parade, or Royal Forum, were assigned between June 14th, 1743, and October 10th, 1749, with building beginning at the west end. From Pierrepont Street to Duke Street, nine plots of varying frontage were granted to the following—Samuel Emes, rough mason, 21 ft. 0 in. with return front of 36 ft. 8 in.; Edward Lluellin, 20 ft. 0 in.; William Robinson, gent., 21 ft. 0 in.; William Sainsbury, carpenter, (1) 21 ft. 0 in. (2) 42 ft. 0 in.; Samuel Emes, 21 ft. 0 in.; John Mullins, sadler, 21 ft. 0 in.; Samuel Emes, 21 ft. 0 in. with return front of 36 ft. 8 in. From Duke Street eastwards—Samuel Emes, (1) 39 ft. 5 in. (2) 21 ft. 0 in.; John Taylor, 21 ft. 0 in.; William Hawkins, plasterer, (1) 22 ft. 0 in. (2) 22 ft. 0 in.

The Duke Street plots were assigned between June 15th, 1743 and December 9th 1748, the east side sites being taken by Ralph Allen, Esq., (1) 24 ft. 9 in. (2) 24 ft. 0 in. (3) 40 ft. 0 in.; Henry Fisher, mason, 24 ft. 0 in.; John Ford, 24 ft. 6 in. The west side sites were taken by Henry Fisher, 24 ft. 0 in.; John Hutchins, plasterer, 24 ft. 6 in.; George Hatherell, joiner, 21 ft. 0 in.; John Mullins (1) 21 ft. 0 in. (2) 24 ft. 6 in. (3) 23 ft. 6 in.

From September 23rd, 1742 to June 18th, 1751, assignments were made by Wood for house plots in his extension of Orchard Street. Plots forming the south and south-east side, beginning from St. James's Portico, were taken by John Hutchins, 24 ft. 0 in.; Edward Lluellin, (1) 20 ft. 0 in. (2) 17 ft. 0 in. (3) 11 ft. 0 in. (4) 21 ft. 0 in.; Roger Watts, gent., 41 ft. 0 in. Plots in the north-west and north side, from the south end, were taken by John Palmer, tallow chandler, (1) 23 ft. 0 in. (2) 21 ft. 0 ins.; William Blatchley, baker, 21 ft. 0 in.; Samuel Dancy, carpenter, 21 ft. 0 in.; Thomas Goulding, gent., (1) 16 ft. 0 in. (2) 20 ft. 0 in.; Katharine Goulding, widow, 40 ft. 0 in.

It will be seen from the foregoing that several plots were taken by the building tradesmen who evidently co-operated in building most of the houses. John and Stephen Ford, masons took five plots; Samuel Emes, rough mason, four plots; William Sainsbury, carpenter, four plots, Edward Lluellin, joiner, six plots; and John Hutchins, plasterer, two plots. Five plots, including two of the largest, were taken by Ralph Allen, from whose Combe Down quarries the building stone was brought.

Wood's annual income from the rents charged on the houses, and on the use of the garden in St. James's Triangle, amounted to the following—The Grand Parade, after the Duke of Kingston's reserved rent of £100 was deducted, yielded £49 10s. 0d. plus £7 16s. 0d.; the South Parade yielded £139 10s. 4d. plus £4 7s. 6d.; Pierrepont Street yielded £118 0s. 6d. plus £7 19s. 4d.; Duke Street yielded

£100 6s. 0d. plus £7 6s. 0d. Orchard Street yielded £76 5s. 2d.

On May 13th, 1755, in executing the elder Wood's will, his widow and son were obliged to mortgage the fee farm rents accruing from the Parades development to Dr. William Oliver for payment of £6,000. This sum was required to pay the marriage settlement of £5,000 on Jane Maria Coulthurst, nee Wood, and the legacy of £800 to Thayer Allen Wood which had already been advanced by Edward Harrington. This appears to have been the first of a sequence of mortgages which were to bedevil the younger Wood's finances.

The elder Wood had only a few months to live when he finally embarked on his third great building project, the King's Circus. As related on page 141, he had agreed to purchase the required nine acres of ground by a contract dated December 18th, 1753, and it is quite possible that he was able, in spite of illness, to supervise in person the setting out for the Circus. That this was fixed in a position further north than that originally intended appears from a letter now in the Braikenridge Collection, Bristol Central Library. This letter, dated March 23rd, 1754, was written by the elder Wood to an unstated addressee, probably Thomas Garrard or his agent, and it reads

'In adjusting the Levels of the Circus, since my last to you, we thought it necessary to carry our Center as far North as the Ground of the Middle Acre would admit of, by which the Building will have above six Feet Elevation more than was intended when I wrote for Liberty to lay our superfluous Earth on your Ground. This will be attended with a great Expence in Stone Work, but I think it will render the Circus compleat without exception.'

Much of the following information about the disposal of the sub-leases in Gay Street and the Circus has been derived from an inventory of the fee farm rents accruing to John Wood the younger (John Jefferys Papers, Guildhall, Bath).

Gay Street

The houses on the west side of Gay Street, numbered 2 to 17 from south to north, were all built under leases dated January 3rd, 1755, granted to the following—1 (demolished) Thomas Jelly; 2 & 3, John Ford; 4 & 5, William Sainsbury; 6, Thomas Browne; 7, William Edwards; 8, Prince Hoare; 9, J. Ford and T. Jelly; 10, Samuel Dancy; 11, Joseph Granger; 12, William Ralphs; 13, J. Ditcher and J. Coleman; 14, Benjamin Chilton; 15, Thomas Shipway; 16, Daniel Danvers; 17, Dr. William Oliver.

The east side houses above George Street are numbered 18 to 30 from north to south. The leases were granted on the following dates—January 3rd, 1755 for Nos. 26 to 30; July 20th, 1757 for Nos. 20 to 25; and December 14th, 1759 for Nos. 18 & 19. The grants were made as follows—18 & 19, William Sainsbury; 20 & 21, John Mullins; 22, Stephen Ford; 23, John Ford; 24, Mary Masters; 25, Thomas Jelly; 26 & 27, J. Ford and T. Jelly; 28 to 30, Samuel Emes.

The Circus

Building began in the south-west segment, under leases dating from January 3rd, 1755 to July 20th, 1767. The houses are now numbered 1 to 10, the eleventh house being No. 1, Brock Street. Leases were granted as follows—1 & 2, J. Ford and T. Jelly; 3, William Colbourne; 4, James Coleman; 5, Grace Trevor; 6, Lucy Stanhope; 7 & 8, The Rt. Hon. William Pitt; 9, William Ainslie; 10, Edward Fisher; 1, Brock Street, Benjamin Colbourne.

The twelve houses forming the south-east segment are numbers 19 to 30, from Bennett Street to Gay Street. They were built under leases dating from October 2nd, 1762 (No. 14) to August 9th, 1766 (No. 19), which were granted as follows—19, John Latty; 20, Richard Upton; 21, Markes Davis; 22, John

Brabant; 23, William Bolwell; 24, Henry Coulthurst; 25, William Street; 26, Thos. and Daniel Brown; 27, James Coleman; 28, Samuel Dancy; 29, Richard Maddocks; 30, William Sainsbury.

The north segment was the last to be built, under leases granted between June 19th, 1764 (No. 14) and July 29th, 1766 (the east end house). The present numbering begins at the west end but the first house is No. 36, Brock Street, built together with 11 to 14 by Andrew Sproule. Charles Rodborne built 15, George Clarke 16, Hugh Penny 17, and John Davis built 18 and the east end house.

The east end of Brock Street forms part of the 'nine acres' site, the five houses on the south side being built under leases granted between October 4th, 1763 (Nos. 5 & 6) and January 4th, 1766 (Nos. 2 &3). The leaseholders were—2 & 3, Benjamin Colbourne; 4, Miss Thresher; 5, John Ford; 6, Stephen Ford. Nos. 31 to 35 on the north side were built by Andrew Sproule under leases dated 2nd May to 26th June, 1767.

The fee farm rents payable annually to Wood and his heirs in respect of Gay Street and the Circus, with the contiguous houses in Brock Street and Bennett Street, amounted to £311 8s. 4d.

The Assembly Rooms and Queen's Parade

On November 17th, 1764, *Boddeley's Bath Journal* informed its readers that

'This Day is open'd a Subscription for erecting a large Building at the North-East Corner of Queen Square in this City; to consist of a Tavern, a Coffee Room, and a Compleat Set of Assembly Rooms. The Articles of Subscription and Plans of the intended Building are to be seen at Mr. Wood's in Queen Square. 120 shares to make up £12,600.'

This was followed on November 26th by the announcement that

'The Marquis of Carnarvon has begun

the Subscription for erecting the Assembly-Room in Queen-Square, by subscribing for two Shares: and we hear that there are upwards of fifty shares already engaged for.'

As the subscribers failed to agree on the proposal to include a tavern in the building, the scheme was allowed to lapse until 1768 when a new subscription was opened for 'a New Set of Assembly Rooms to be built on the Lands of Andrew Sproule and John Wood Esqre, on the East side of the Circus'.

Meanwhile, Wood and Thomas Brock leased the Queen Square site of one and a half acres from Sir Benet Garrard, by an indenture dated December 19/20th, 1766, at a yearly rent charge of £35. Wood and Brock then granted underleases for building the twelve houses of Queen's Parade to the following—William and Edward Yescombe, George and William Clark, John Latty and John Brabant, William and Samuel Sainsbury, Daniel Brown, Nicholas Tucker, John and Stephen Ford, Richard Singers, and James Lancashire.

The Royal Crescent

As already stated on page 148, the ground required for building the Royal Crescent was leased from Sir Benet Garrard by the younger John Wood and his trustee, Thomas Brock, on December 20th, 1766. For two years, dating from March 25th, 1766, Wood and Brock undertook to pay Sir Benet Garrard, or his heirs and assigns, an annual rent of £30. Thereafter the annual rent charge was to be £220, payment of which was to be 'reserved and effectually secured' on the fee farm rents to be charged on some of the houses about to be built in Brock Street and the Royal Crescent, the sites for which were to be let at an annual rent charge of not less than four shillings per foot frontage. In 1767 the Walcot Estate passed into the possession of Sir Peter Rivers Gay, and in the building lease dated February 3rd, 1770, granted by Wood and Brock to Samuel Parmer, the latter undertook to pay 'yearly and every year for ever unto the said Sir Peter Rivers Gay and his assigns for and during the term of his natural life and from and after his decease to all and every person . . . entitled to the same by and under the sd codicil to the sd will of the sd Sir Benet Garrard the perpetual yearly sum or annual rent charge of £10 10s. . . . in the Guildhall of the sd City of Bath.' This probably accounts for the fact that the inventory of Wood's own fee farm rents lists only eight houses in the Royal Crescent, underleases for these being granted between February 4th, 1770 and July 30th, 1771. The grantees were Samuel Stephens, 9; John Cannings, 10; Thomas Linley, 11; Hannah Reed, 12; John Fielder, 17; Simon Crook in trust for Mr. Jefferys, 19; James Bishop, 20; and Richard Upton, 21. Wood's rents amounted to £108 6s. 8d. per annum.

The lease, already referred to, granted on February 3rd, 1770, to Samuel Parmer, carpenter, and his trustee, George Clarke, carpenter, relates to a plot in the west arm fronting 24 ft. 9 in. to the Crescent, 114 ft. 0 in. in depth, and 49 ft. 4 in. in breadth east to Church Street, lying between plots granted to Thomas Clement on the south-west and Charles Davis on the north. The second plot from the east end (No. 2) was taken on February 21st, 1770, by Joseph Williams, carpenter, and that for the east end house (No. 30), was taken on December 4th, 1770, by George Clarke, carpenter, John Fielder, tiler and plumber, and Daniel Tanner, mason. Fielder and Tanner also took a plot 'fronting south, extending north to a new building by Fielder and bounded west by the house of Charles Coles and east by the house of Henry Mullins. The lease relating to the third house from the west corner (No. 28) was taken on December 28th, 1771, by Fielder and Clarke. John Ford, mason and statuary, and Charles Coles, plasterer, combined with Sampson Parsons and Robert Cummings to build No. 25.

Parmer's lease is typical of others granted to builders of houses in the Royal Crescent, in stipulating that

'he shall and will erect and build one substantial stone and timber messuage or tenement . . . which house shall in front cover the whole breadth of the ground conveyed, and shall set out and build the front wall thereof in and upon such line as shall be marked out by the sd John Wood or some other person whom he shall appoint for that purpose, so as such line shall cause the front of such messuage to range and be in an uniform line with the whole pile of building intended to be called the Royal Crescent.' He 'shall and will cover the roof of the sd messuage with blue stone tile and finish and make the same messuage of the same height and with the like ornaments in front only as the west front of the messuage or tenement lately built by the sd Thos Brock at the east end of the sd Crescent.' Parmer was to 'make an area 16 ft. wide' before the front, put a proper stone plinth on the pavement next the area, finished with a 'near iron rail and palisadoes', make a terras or footway 16 ft. wide finished with the best sort of Pennant stone, pitch a coach road 24 ft. wide, and pay a proportionable share of the cost of providing a 'proper iron rail or palisadoes as shall be fixed to bound in the open area of the said Royal Crescent.'

To safeguard the amenities of the Royal Crescent, Sir Benet Garrard covenanted that he and his heirs or assigns would not at any time permit any houses to be built on the Kingsmead Furlong, part of the Hayes Lower Furlong, and part of the Hayes, nor would they set or plant any part of the said land which should grow so as to exceed eight feet high. Should this undertaking be breached, Wood and his representatives were empowered to enter and 'throw down and wholly reduce to the ground all and every such house . . . built contrary to the tenures of that covenant and agreement.' Nevertheless, it was agreed that Sir Benet should be at liberty to build a farmhouse and offices (still existing) on the south-east corner of the Kingsmead Furlong, and plant around. On behalf of the Bath Water Works, Wood had permission to construct a reservoir 'not less than a semicircle of 300 ft. diameter' in the centre of the open ground before the Royal Crescent. Wood, his heirs and assigns were also granted free use of a footway or passage for chairs and passengers only, 40 ft. wide, to lead from Queen Square, behind Gay Street and the west wide of the Circus, up to Brock Street and the Royal Crescent, for the use and convenience of the inhabitants who should live and reside in the Crescent, Brock Street, and the Circus. This way, the Gravel Walk, Wood and his assigns undertook to fence in with a handsome wall or iron pales, and to make a handsome and convenient terras for a footpath into and through the same.

The surviving ratebooks show that twenty-six houses in the Royal Crescent were occupied in May, 1775, Nos. 1, 17, 18 and 30 being empty, but in April, 1778, only No. 18 was still void. All the houses were occupied in September, 1778, the rates being paid by or for the following—1, Mr. Henry Sanford; 2, Mrs. Elesha Macartney; 3, Mr. George Burgis; 4, Mr. Christopher Anstey; 5, Mr. John Bathoe; 6, Mr. Winthrop Baldwin; 7, Mrs. Elizabeth Tyndale; 8, Mr. John Bennett; 9, Rev. Mr. Whalley; 10, Mr. John Riddle; 11, Capt. John Martin; 12, Dr. Edward Cooper; 13, Mr. John Charnock; 14, Hon. Charles Hamilton; 15, Mr. McGillchrist; 16, Dr. Claud Champion de Crespigny; 17, Mrs. Victory Kynaston; 18, Mr. Edward Hoare; 19, Mr. John Jefferys; 20, Lady Hester Malpas; 21, Lady Stepney; 22, Dean of Ossory; 23, Dr. William Watson; 24, Lady Isabella Stanley; 25, Col. John Stibbert; 26, Mrs. Mary Cunliffe; 27, Lady Mary Stanley; 28, Philip Thickness, Esqre; 29, Col. Champion; 30, Hon. Henry Grenville. Most of the aforenamed were ratepayers in May, 1775, April, 1778, and April 1781, the exceptions being that in 1775 Ann Roscoe paid for 2, Mr. Hare for 5, Samuel Stephens for 9, John Burdett for 21, Dr. Anthony Rethan for 24, Mrs. Ince for 27, and the Rev. Frederick Hamilton for 29. Lord Ailesbury paid for 28 in April, 1788, and Mr. S. Oliver for 16 in 1780.

Catharine Place, Rivers Street, Russell Street and Bennett Street

Around 1770–72 the younger Wood leased from Sir Peter Rivers Gay the ground on which were built the houses of Catharine Place, Rivers Street, Russel Street and the western part of Bennett Street. By 1779 Wood had disposed of twenty-three plots in Rivers Street where four of the houses were built by Daniel Fowles, three by Richard Hewlett, two by John Fielder, two by Charles Coles, two by William Kingston, one by George Clarke, and one by James Broom. All of these names recur in the building history of Bath. Kingston had served Wood as clerk of works during the building of the Assembly Rooms, while Fielder, Clarke and Coles had participated in building houses in the Royal Crescent. In 1790 Hewlett and Broom leased from Sir Peter Rivers Gay the ground on which St. James's Square was built, and both were major participants in other large projects, Hewlett in Grosvenor Place (page 80) and Broom in Norfolk Crescent (page 180).

Appendix VI
SOME FURTHER BIOGRAPHICAL DETAILS OF THE WOODS

The elder John Wood's birth in 1704, in or near Bath, is now an accepted fact. The name Wood appears frequently in local church registers of the 17th and 18th centuries, and John Wood's attachment to Swainswick, where he, his wife, children and grandchildren were buried, suggests that a John Wood buried there on September 26th, 1697, might well be a forbear. Bath's Charity or Blue Coat School provided his basic education 'in the English Tongue, in Writing and in Accounts', but it was apparently Robert Benson, Lord Bingley, who gave him the opportunity to master the practices of architecture and surveying. Bingley was an amateur of the arts, especially architecture, whose advice was sought and valued by his friends. In his 'Essay' Wood records his being in the north of England during the summers of 1725 and 1727, no doubt working for Bingley at Bramham Park, near Leeds. There, one may fairly assume, Wood had access to a well stocked library where he could study the works of Vitruvius and Palladio, and especially Vitruvius Britannicus by Colen Campbell, whose designs were a most potent influence on Wood's own work. Later, Wood was bold enough to challenge Campbell's authority by designing for Ralph Allen at Prior Park, a portico 'with Columns of a larger size . . . three Feet one Inch and a half Diameter', by making the 'Intercolumnations of that Kind which Vitruvius calls Systylos', and by giving it 'two Compleat Intercolumnations to the Flank, instead of the compleat Interval and small Portion of another at Wanstead'.

While at Bramham, Wood made a survey of the great park, assisted in constructing the water works, and almost certainly designed part of the stables. In the Bath collection of Wood's drawings there is one which possibly relates to the Bramham stables, and another for an aqueduct. Wood was also working in London from 1725 to 1727, living in Oxford Street and building houses on the Cavendish-Harley Estate. While there he worked on Bingley's great house in Cavendish Square and, on Bingley's recommendation, was considered by the Duke of Chandos for some work on another large house in the Square.

Wood must have married his wife Jane, or Jenney, soon after he returned to Bath in 1727, for his son and namesake was baptised in Bath Abbey on February 25th, 1727/8. Jane Wood's identity seems to be established by the evidence of a letter dated October 9th, 1729, wherein the Duke of Chandos instructed the architect-builder Edward Shepherd to bargain with Wood's mother-in-law, Mrs. Chivers, for her garden adjacent to St. John's Hospital. Incidently, Chandos failed to obtain this coveted site and in 1740 Wood himself built a large house there.

John and Jane Wood had three sons and at least three daughters. The sons were christened John, Thayer Allen, and William Lewis, and the daughters Jane Maria, Elizabeth, and Anna. Only John followed his father's profession, Thayer Allen being apprenticed to John Dowling, a Trowbridge clothier, while William Lewis died young and was buried at Swainswick on December 18th, 1750. Having the assurance of handsome dowries, two daughters married well, Jane Maria to Henry Coulthurst, Esquire, and Elizabeth to William Street. Both husbands took underleases for building houses in the Circus.

The elder Wood designed at least four houses in the vicinity of Bath, Francis Yerbury's Belcombe Brook Villa, near Bradford-on-Avon, in 1734; Ralph Allen's Prior Park, Widcombe, in 1735; Jerry Pierce's Lilliput Castle, Lansdown, in 1738; and Southwell Pigott's Titanbarrow Logia, Bathford, in 1748. He probably designed Tyberton Court, Herefordshire, built in *c.* 1728 for William Brydges, a cousin of the Duke of Chandos, and the apsidal chancel of Tyberton Church is evidently Wood's work. He also designed the Palladian church built in 1734–36 within the ruins of Llandaff Cathedral. However, Wood's finest buildings outside of Bath are the Exchange at Bristol, built 1741–43, and the Exchange, now Town Hall, at Liverpool, built 1749–54 under the younger Wood's direction. It was to recommend Wood's employment that Mrs. Sarah Clayton wrote from Bath to an influential friend in Liverpool. Declaring that all who knew Wood regarded him as a 'great genius', she quoted the opinion of Mr. Jerry Pierce, an eminent Bath surgeon, who had told her that 'except Lord Burlington, there was no person in England that had a juster and better taste in architecture'. She also praised Wood's abilities as a country house architect, mentioning that he had 'planned Mr. Ward's house at Capestone'. This has been correctly identified by Mr. Stanley Harris as Capesthorne, near Macclesfield, a property then belonging to John Ward, an eminent lawyer of the Inner Temple. Wood certainly knew Ward, who subscribed to some Bath charities and in 1732 acted for Wood and his fellow subscribers over the building of St. Mary's Chapel in Queen Square. Capesthorne Hall has been twice rebuilt and the Hall referred to by Mrs. Clayton was erected between 1720 and 1735. The Smiths of Warwick were first employed and John Wood possibly later in 1733. The adjacent chapel has been attributed to Wood, but was built in 1722 and is more likely to be the work of Francis Smith.

The elder Wood was justly proud of all that he had achieved in Bath, and is easily forgiven if he was, as seems probable, personally responsible for writing the 'letter from Bath' from which an extract was published in the *Whitehall Evening Post* and quoted in the *Bath Journal* of February 18th, 1754. This panegyric was occasioned by Wood's laying the foundation stone of the King's Circus.

'A general Joy diffuses itself through every Rank of Inhabitants here, on the Prospect of the Advantage that will arise to the Trade of this City from the New Buildings going to be erected on the North Side of the Town, after the Designs, and under the Directions, of that celebrated and eminent Architect and Antiquarian, John Wood, Esq., who this Day laid the first Stone towards the Execution of them, with great Solemnity, amidst the Acclamations and unanimous Applause of Thousands. His Buildings, already erected in this City, have been of so great a Benefit to this Place in particular, and to the Country in general, that while they remain standing Monuments to the World of his Taste in Architecture, they will with grateful Hearts be looked on by our latest Posterity, as the Works of that great Benefactor, and the Name of WOOD, the Restorer of Bath, will always be sacred here.'

According to Sarah Clayton, Wood was 'not one that chooses to be put much out of his way. He appears to be in a bad state of health, but they tell me he has been much the same way for many years.' He died in his fiftieth year on May 23rd, 1754, and his will, dated December 10th, 1753, was proved in London on June 20th, 1754, by his widow to whom administration was granted. The contents of the will are here summarised: Wood expressed his desire to be buried 'wrapt up in the cloathes then about him' in Swainswick Church, and that no more than £20 should be expended on his funeral. He left to his son John Wood, during the joint lives of the said son and testator's wife Jenney, an annuity of £150. To his daughter Jane Maria Wood he left an annuity of £100 until her marriage, when she was to receive a dowry of £5,000. To his son Thayer Allen Wood he left an annuity of £20 to be paid during his apprenticeship, £800 to begin his trade, and a further sum of £700 in five years from the time he set up in trade or business. He also left in the care of trustees acting for his daughter Elizabeth, the sum of £1,000 for investment to pay interest to her for life and after her death to her children.

Wood left to his wife, and after her death to

his son John Wood, all his leasehold estates, chief rents and hereditaments in Walcot, and all the residue of his personal estate. All his lands, tenements, &c in the City of Bath were left to his wife, and after her death to his son Thayer Allen Wood and his heirs. In default of such issue that part of his estate was to revert to his daughter Elizabeth and her heirs.

Jane Wood died on April 1st, 1766, 'after a long and painful Illness. . . . By her death a considerable Fortune devolved to her Son, John Wood, Esq.' Her burial in Swainswick Church is thus recorded in the register '1766, Jessie Wood, Widow (of John) buried 4th April'.

It was, presumably, through his father's work for Ward of Capesthorne that the younger John Wood met his future wife Elizabeth, the daughter of Richard and Mary Brock, of Bostock Hall, Davenham, Cheshire. The marriage probably took place in 1752 or early in 1753, for on December 7th, 1753, their daughter Jenny was baptised in Walcot Church. There also Mary, their fourth daughter, was baptised on December 17th, 1758, as was Sarah on June 22nd, 1766, Catharine on April 17th, 1768, and Dionysia on December 12th, 1769. Four more daughters, Elizabeth, Anna, Barbara, and Dorothy, were privately baptised, although the last three were recorded in the Bitton register on October 18th, 1765, by Wood who was then living in Bitton Rectory. There were two sons, John Brock, baptised in Walcot Church on March 5th, 1771, and Richard, baptised in Batheaston Church on September 6th, 1773. Nothing appears to be known of the sons, although one John Wood was buried in Swainswick on May 26th, 1781, and another on October 20th, 1811. Two of the daughters married well, Mary to James Tomkinson, Esquire, of Dorfold, Cheshire, and Elizabeth to Thomas Clutton, Esquire, of Kinnersley Castle, Herefordshire. Their son Thomas, in pursuance of the will of his maternal great-uncle, Thomas Brock, assumed in 1809, the surname of Brock in addition to his patronymic Clutton. Thomas Brock, John Wood's brother-in-law and par-

ticipant in building the Royal Crescent, etc., was Town Clerk of Chester.

Besides continuing his father's development of Bath's Upper Town with the Circus, the Royal Crescent, the Assembly Rooms, etc., and building the Hot Bath for the Corporation, the younger Wood designed a fine Palladian country house, Buckland, near Faringdon, Berkshire, built in 1755–57 for Sir Robert Throckmorton, and he added the wings to Standlynch, now Trafalgar House, Wiltshire, for Henry Dawkins, in 1766. Both houses were illustrated in volumes IV and V of Vitruvius Britannicus, for which Wood subscribed. He also designed the gothick Tregenna Castle, St. Ives, Cornwall, built in 1773 for Samuel Stephens, the original lessee of No. 9, Royal Crescent. Hardenhuish Church, near Chippenham, built in 1779, was designed by the younger Wood for Benjamin Colbourne, the underlessee of houses in the Circus and Brock Street. Woolley Church, near Swainswick, a small eclectic building of 1761, has been reasonably attributed to Wood.

The younger Wood was an unsuccessful competitor for two important commissions. Between 1758 and 1760 he submitted three designs for rebuilding Bristol Bridge, accompanied by explanatory letters but lacking detailed estimates. His designs were not accepted but he was paid £150 for his trouble. In 1766 he was invited, along with Thomas Lightoler and Richard Jones, to submit designs for Bath's new Market and Town Hall. His plans failed to find approval although he was paid 30 guineas for his second plan.

When the younger Wood died on June 16th, 1781, he was deeply in debt, although nominally receiving the fee farm rents on some 250 houses. Having had to provide substantial dowries for his sisters, and a legacy for his brother, under the terms of his father's will, the younger Wood and his mother had been obliged to raise the necessary funds by mortgaging some of their fee farm rents. Needing to pay the interest on these loans, and having a large family to support, Wood was compelled to resort to further borrowings. One of his chief creditors was his attorney, John Jefferys, and as he and the other creditors had received no interest for some time, they acted together and by resorting to law ensured that the rents were paid directly to them. No copy of Wood's will seems to have survived, but it seems obvious that shortage of money compelled his executors to advertise, during August 1781, their willingness to let for four and a half years the family's home, Eagle House, Batheaston, then described as 'A HOUSE fit for the reception of a genteel family, late in the possession of John Wood, esq; with convenient offices, stables, and coach-house thereto belonging, a very good pleasure and kitchen garden, hothouse, green-house, &c. And Also a Farm-House adjoining, with barns and stables, and about 70 acres land'. There followed on November 1st, a sale of Wood's farming stock, comprising six horses, eight cows, two heifers, poultry, etc.

On January 18th, 1787, Wood's fee farm rents and other properties were sold by auction in seven lots by Mr. Winstanley, at Garraway's Coffee House, Exchange Alley, Cornhill, London. From a priced catalogue it appears that the rents offered as Lot 1 fetched £8,520, Lot 2 £1,100, Lot 3 £14,000, Lot 4 unstated, Lot 5 £3,150. Lot 6, the Woods' house on the south side of Queen Square, a leasehold property with 41 years to run, fetched £1,100, and Lot 7, a freehold site lying west of the Royal Crescent, sold for £1,970. This was the site on which most of Marlborough Buildings was eventually built.

In 1807, Wood's widow was living in Richmond, Surrey, in such poverty that she appealed for help to the Bath Corporation. Their favourable response is recorded in the Minute Book No. 12—'6th April 1807. £20 per annum to be allowed Mrs. Eliz. Wood of Richmond, widow of John Wood, formerly architect of Bath, she being 80 years of age and in a very distressed condition'. Two of the Wood daughters were elected, on June 28th, 1810, as renters of the Pump-rooms.

Appendix VII

The elder John Wood published the following—

c. 1736 A Plan of the City of Bath, Copied from the Original Survey of Mr. John Wood, Architect, A.D. 1735, and Engraved by Mr. John Pine. The plan is framed in an oval surrounded by descriptive matter ending with this advertisement—'For the Convenience of Builders, Mr. Wood intends, very soon, to set up a Deal Yard in Bath, in which Persons may be supply'd with the best of Norway Goods for ready Money at the most reasonable Rates; and for their Encouragement, shall be directed in the Use and Choice of their Materials, from whence great Advantages will arise (at least 10 Pounds in every hundred) to the Buyer.'

1741 The origin of Building: Or, the Plagiarism of the Heathens Detected. Illustrated with 25 copper plates. This curious work appears to derive from a study of G. B. Villalpando's 'In Ezechielem Explanationes', and seeks to prove that the harmonic proportions of the classical orders, and therefore of classical architecture, were divinely revealed to Solomon when commanded by God to build the Temple.

1742 An Essay towards a Description of Bath (parts 1 and 2)

Appendix VIII

SOME POSSIBLE INFLUENCES ON THE WOODS' ARCHITECTURAL CONCEPTIONS

The sources, real and imagined, that might have provided the material inspiration for the elder Wood have long been a subject for architectural theses. This is because Wood's professed intention to re-create the Forum, Circus, and Gymnasium of a hypothetical Romano-British city cannot be seriously reconciled with what he actually set out to build in the houses of Queen Square, the Parades, and the Circus. So far, the most illuminating analysis of Wood's probable sources is the chapter titled 'John Wood and the English Town Planning Tradition' in Sir John Summerson's *Heavenly Mansions*. The fact that this admirable essay was published in 1948 will serve as the excuse for the following observations.

Before Wood began building Queen Square two architects, at least, had published designs for grouping several houses into a formal composition, John Price in 1720 and Colen Campbell in 1725. Price's design for the The Lawne at Headley, near Epsom, is a monstrously monumental composition with a grandiose assembly-house standing between long wings, each of nine houses, some accented to form intermediate and terminal pavilions.

Campbell's far more sophisticated design was for a terrace of seven houses in the Palladian style, intended for the whole east side of Grosvenor Square, London. This last design might have been made for John Simmons, who began building this east side in 1725. His seven houses were much simpler in style than Campbell's, and formed a composition having a pedimented centre, plain wings of two houses, and end pavilions crowned with attics. This was, in fact, the same basic composition used by Wood for the seven-house north front of Queen Square. Wood, however, achieved so much more by seeing his sunlit north front as a noble Palladian palace, and giving it subservient wings in the houses forming the east and west sides of the Square. One can only regret that he was obliged to change the west side by redesigning it as a composition of three separate buildings, an idea probably derived as much from the Monmouth House side of Soho Square as from the west and north sides of Cavendish Square.

Wood's grandiose conception of the Royal Forum had no obvious precedent, and one must regret that only the Parades were built. There, Wood intended to repeat on the single plane of the Grand Parade his idea of a splendid Palladian palace with subservient wings.

The elder Wood's most remarkable achievement was, of course, the King's Circus, certainly conceived by him although carried out by his son. The plan adopted for the Circus appears first in the garden layout Wood designed about 1740 for St. James's Triangle in front of the Grand Parade, actually the site originally intended for a Circus. It is, however, worth noting that in 1736, before the Parades were begun, Wood published his Plan of Bath 'made after the Manner of the celebrated Plan of Paris'. This suggests that he knew at least the circular plan of J. H. Mansart's Place des Victoires, the more so as the King's Circus was to have at its centre an equestrian statue of George II. So the basic idea of a circle of houses was not original, though Wood's treatment of it certainly had no precedent. By designing the uniform elevations in a 'theatrical' style highly suggestive of the Colosseum, and by dividing the circle into three equal segments, he created for the spectator entering the arena the illusion of a Roman amphitheatre, even though it was 'turned outside in'.

Sir John Summerson suggests that the plan adopted for the younger Wood's Royal Crescent probably represents one-half of the ellipse of the Colosseum. While this may be so, there is a closer source to be found in Palladio's Teatro Olimpico, where the semi-elliptical auditorium is backed by an impressive colonnade of the same form. In this connection it is worth observing that the younger Wood employed for the Crescent's colonnade the engaged Ionic order that his father had used for the engaged portico on the south front of Prior Park.

Appendix IX

THE WOODS' RESIDENCES IN BATH

When writing the first edition of this book, the author had no reason to question the veracity of some commemorative plaques placed on certain Queen Square houses, the more so since confirmation seemed to be offered by all that had, till then, been written about the Woods and Bath in general. It was only after 1948, when conducting further research towards a second edition, that it became evident that the wrong houses had been singled out for identification with the two John Woods. A letter pointing out this case of 'mistaken identity' was written by the author to *The Times*, and published during the Wood Bicentenary celebrations in May 1954. The following evidence sets out to prove that the Woods' house in Queen Square was not No. 24 on the north side, but No. 9 on the south side.

From 1734 until 1754 Queen Square was not listed as an entity in the Walcot ratebooks, but as forming part of the entering streets. The south side appears as part of Wood Street, with five houses in 1734 and nine in 1736. The rates for the fifth house, now No. 9, were paid by John Wood in 1734, and he continued to pay rates for this house until 1754, when he appears as Esqre Wood. In this year of his death it is probable that the Woods lived for much of the time at Swainswick, for during February 1754 Boddeley's *Bath Journal* contained an advertisement offering to let 'The Centre House on the South Side of Queen Square, in Bath, containing three Rooms on a Floor, with proper Offices behind it; a Stable for six Horses, and Ground for a Coach-House. Enquire of Mr. Samuel Purlewent.

Attorney at Law, in Green Street, Bath.' Purlewent was Wood's lawyer and continued to
act for his widow and son.

The elder Wood's deliberate choice of house
in this exact situation is made clear by what he
wrote in his 'Essay' regarding his original
conception of Queen Square. 'From the
Square, we now come to the Buildings fronting it, which were so contrived, that those
facing the North, East, and West Sides should
have the Appearance of a Palace of five
hundred Feet in Extent, when view'd from the
Center of the Building fronting the South
Side.' One can easily imagine the pride with
which he would have conducted visitors to
view the prospect from his first floor windows.

Queen Square was listed as such for the first
time in 1756, with the rates for the fifth house
on the south side still paid by 'Mr. Wood'.
Although the younger Wood moved to Brock
Street in the 1760s, and his real home was at
Swainswick, the Queen Square house
remained nominally in the Wood family until
1787.

The north side of Queen Square appears in
the early ratebooks as part of Queen Street,
but the seven houses are easily identified.
From 1736 until 1746 the rates for No. 24 were
paid by Mrs. Mary Pearce, entered as the late
Mrs. Pearce in 1749. In 1754 the rates were
paid by 'Mr. Barnston' and in 1756 by the
executors of 'Mr. Barnston'. Barnston is probably a mistake for Bannister, for in February
1756, his house was advertised to be let in the
Bath Journal, and described as 'The Centre
House, North Side of Queen Square, lately in
possession of Mr. Bannister. Five rooms on a
Floor, three Parlours, and a Commodious
Dining-room, with other Conveniences, and a
large Garden adjoining.'

Although it bears no plaque, No. 15 Queen
Square has been singled out as an earlier
residence of the elder Wood. It was, as Wood
himself indicated in his 'Essay' designed by
him for a Mr. Greville, who paid rates for it
from 1736 until 1740. The rates were paid by
Colonel Fleming in 1742, and by Captain
Hardy from 1743 until 1749. In 1754 the house
was occupied by Sir Robert Throckmorton,
who must have admired the handsome house
of Sir John Buckworth next door, and, as a
probable consequence, commissioned the
younger Wood to design his new seat of Buckland House, Berkshire.

There is no evidence at all to suggest that
the younger Wood ever lived, even for a brief
period, in No. 41 Gay Street. The ratebook
show that this handsome house, first rated for
1736 in Berton Street, was built for Richard
Marchant, a wealthy and influential Quaker,
who continued in occupation until at least
1756, although there is an indication that in
1746 it was let to Francis Fauquier, Esqre, the
future Governer of Virginia, and the builder of
the easternmost group of houses in the Grand
Parade.

Another misleading plaque purports to
record the residence of Dr. William Oliver in
the large house that originally formed the
recessed centre of Queen Square's west side.
This house was designed and built by the elder
Wood for Sir John Buckworth, who paid rates
for it from 1736 until 1754. However, Dr.
Oliver did pay rates in 1742, for the house now
numbered 19, and by 1754 he was rated for the
three houses now numbered 18a, 19 and 20. In
1755 he leased the site for a new house, No. 17
Gay Street.

BIBLIOGRAPHY

BACON, Edmund N., Design of cities (Eighteenth and Nineteenth-Century European Design). 1967

COARD, Peter, Vanishing Bath. 1972

EGAN, Pierce, Walks through Bath. 1819

FERGUSSON, Adam, The Sack of Bath. 1973

GADD, David, Georgian Summer (Bath in the Eighteenth Century). 1971

GREEN, Mowbray A., The Eighteenth Century Architecture of Bath. 1904

LITTLE, Bryan, The Building of Bath, 1947

MARKS, Stephen, Architectural Review (Bath Analysed etc.) May, 1973

PEVSNER, Sir N., North Somerset and Bristol (The Buildings of England). 1958

ROBERTSON, Charles, Bath, An Architectural Guide (introduction by Jan Morris). 1975

SMITHSON, Peter, Bath, Walks within the Walls. 1971

SUMMERSON, Sir John, Heavenly Mansions (John Wood and the English Town Planning Tradition). 1949

SUTTON, Denys, (editor) APOLLO (Special Issue on 'Bath in the Eighteenth Century) November, 1973

WOOD, John, An Essay Towards a Description of Bath, 1742, 1749 (Reprinted by Kingsmead Press)

UNPUBLISHED MATERIAL SOURCES

City of Bath Collections.
Corporation Minute Books.
Hunt Collection.
John Jefferys' Papers
Parish Registers.
Parish Rate Books.

INDEX